1983

WOMAN-BATTERING

Volume 129, Sage Library of Social Research

RECENT VOLUMES IN
SAGE LIBRARY OF SOCIAL RESEARCH

WOMAN-BATTERING

Victims and Their Experiences

MILDRED DALEY PAGELOW

Foreword by **DEL MARTIN**

Volume 129
**SAGE LIBRARY OF
SOCIAL RESEARCH**

 SAGE PUBLICATIONS   Beverly Hills   London

For information address:

SAGE Publications, Inc.
275 South Beverly Drive
Beverly Hills, California 90212

SAGE Publications Ltd
28 Banner Street
London ECIY 8QE, England

Printed in the United States of America

Library of Congress Cataloging in Publication Data

Pagelow, Mildred Daley.
   Woman-battering.

   (Sage library of social research; 129)
   Bibliography: p.
   I. Abused wives—United States. 2. Wife abuse—United States. I. Title. II. Series.
HV6626.P33   362.8'3   81-9233
ISBN 0-8039-1681-7
ISBN 0-8039-1682-5 (pbk.)

SECOND PRINTING, 1982

CONTENTS

To Lloyd W. Pagelow, a gentle and loving man

FOREWORD

When I was researching my own book, *Battered Wives,* in 1975-1976, I found that most sociological studies of violence in the home concentrated on non-gender-identified references to "family" or "marital" or "spousal" abuse. There was a very apparent reluctance to deal directly and specifically with wife beating or the battering of women involved in intimate relationships with men.

Why? I soon learned that there is a tacit acceptance of woman-battering and that its roots are in historical attitudes toward women, the institution of marriage, the economy, criminal and civil law, and the delivery system of social service agencies. I found that people tend to ignore the assailant's responsibility for his violent acts and instead blame the victim. Why does she stay?

Implicit in this question is the assumption that the victim is responsible, that she has some deep-seated masochistic need to be abused. But sheer numbers—the millions of women who are battered and the millions of men who batter them—indicate that the question might better be phrased: What is it about our society that keeps a woman captive in a violent home?

Mildred Pagelow, in Chapter 2, builds a strong theoretical framework for her hypothesis that the fewer resources, the more negative the institutional response, and the more intense the traditional ideology of the battered woman, the more likely she is to remain in a violent relationship and the less likely she is to try to alter her situation. Pagelow makes a distinction between primary (first, and sometimes only, attack) and secondary (repeated) battering. Her study

7

focuses on secondary battering, which tends to increase in frequency and severity as time goes on and sometimes leads to murder.

Pagelow's scholarship is impeccable. Her review and critique of the literature and research on battered women to date is exhaustive. Her analysis of the depth and breadth of the problem is thorough. She examines every myth, every belief system or model, every conclusion that others have drawn and tests her data against them. Keenly aware that researchers too often ask the wrong questions and thus come to the wrong conclusions, she takes every question that has been raised about battered women and turns it inside out and outside in, examining it from every imaginable angle. She applies all the tests and techniques of her sociological discipline and is hypercritical of her own survey instrument.

The result is a sound piece of work, a highly welcome and most valuable contribution to our ever-increasing knowledge and understanding of battered women.

Del Martin

ACKNOWLEDGMENTS

Their story *had* to be told, finally! They shared their experiences, they opened up to a stranger and exposed lives of physical and psychological abuse filled with terror and pain—those hundreds of courageous and strong people we call battered women. They are truly survivors, especially the one who died after a few weeks in a shelter. She lived long enough to show her daughters that there are some people in this world who care about victims and want to help. Perhaps if there had been shelters when her husband first started beating her, or even ten years ago, she might still be alive today.

Many of the women beaten by spouses had never before disclosed their secret lives of recurring violence, but when they learned that the purpose of the study was to gain understanding of woman-battering and to help other women beaten by their spouses, their words flowed like a torrent, from pain dammed up too long. They mentally returned to their childhoods, then the beginning of their relationships, the courtships, the first instances of violence, and all the traumatic experiences up to the interviews. They relived all this because they hoped that perhaps others could benefit from knowledge of their private hells. Telling could not change the past but might bring some good out of bad.

This book is a special tribute to all those fine women who earned my sincerest respect, admiration, and thanks. I hope they gained from giving so much.

There are also hundreds of others in the shelter movement, mostly women but also a few very exceptional men, who worked so long and hard as victims' advocates in various ways and struggled to provide safe places for them and their children. Without shelters, a study like this would have been impossible because the security and support system they provide allowed victims to leave the violence behind and finally be able to tell their experiences. Service providers in the shelter movement are the ones who obtained the settings and opened the doors so that researcher and respondents could make contact.

During the course of this study, countless people assisted in many ways. Even though all of them cannot be mentioned by name, I hope they understand that I am deeply grateful and thank each of them. Some must be singled out because their contributions were very special. These include fellow sociologists Marilynne Brandon Hampton, Fred Samuels, and Parvin Abyneh who provided a support system as well as opportunities for rich and rewarding exchange of ideas.

The design and implementation of the study benefited greatly from the skillful guidance of Maurice Jackson, who not only shared his professional expertise but was always supportive and available when needed for advice. Dr. Jackson never controlled or directed; he asked provocative questions, listened carefully, introduced new ideas for discussion and exploration, and allowed me to find my way in this uncharted area. His inspiration to good scholarship is a debt that can never be repaid. He tirelessly read the manuscript through many revisions with an eagle eye for errors or ambiguity in expression, as did distinguished scholars E. Gartly Jaco and Edna Bonacich.

Other professionals who labored in similar research vineyards are Drs. Lee Bowker, John Johnson, and Kathleen Ferraro, who all offered valuable critiques of the manuscript in earlier stages. Other experts who exchanged ideas and progress reports are Drs. R. Emerson and Russell Dobash and Irene Frieze.

During the course of the study and the writing of this book, many people at two universities assisted in a variety of ways: secretarial staff, librarians, and computer room staff such as Ed Hall, the "guru" at California State University, Fullerton, and Buz Dreyer and John Archibald, gurus at the University of California, Riverside.

Finally, in these times when the American family seems to be endangered and fragmented, my family has been a constant source of strength and inspiration to me. Daniel Hoxie, my youngest son, was still a resident member of the family when the study began and his pride in his mother's work made an especially important contribution in a crucial period. There was never a generation gap; we share mutual love, respect, friendship, and pride. Dan's brothers Robert, Kenton, and Jack helped in other ways from a greater distance; during this study it was reassuring to be reminded that there are strong and nonviolent men. My mother, Frances J. Carse, helped in countless ways and sacrificed personal pleasure so her daughter's labors could progress without interruption. My sister, Bea Lucci, always strong and ready, helped in any way possible. Last but by no means least is Lloyd W. Pagelow, a marrige partner who cheerfully shouldered the major burden of household responsibilities during the long research and writing process and helped in countless other ways, such as by coding, filing, and donating his excellent typing skills. Perhaps the greatest gift of all was his unswerving loyalty and belief that this work was important and deserving of any assistance he could give.

This book represents the combined contributions of a loving, extended family and all the others mentioned earlier. Like a beautiful stained-glass window, each person donated unique pieces that fit together into the final product.

M.D.P.

INTRODUCTION

How could he beat me the way he did? Why did he become so violent all of a sudden? I've known him for years and never saw him act like that—like a crazy person—like he wanted to kill me! He hit me so hard and I didn't do anything to deserve it. What am I going to do now?

This statement could have come from any of hundreds of women interviewed in shelters for battered women in the United States or abroad. The attractive 21-year-old woman who said these words at the beginning of an interview echoed the puzzlement, pain, and concern expressed by many others. She was talking about the death of a dream—the dream of living "happily ever after."

Nan's story was like those of many other women beaten by the men they loved.[1] The mother of a 16-month-old son, she was beaten the first time after two years of marriage when she was about five months pregnant. Her batterer had been her high school sweetheart; their families knew and liked each other. They began married life like thousands of other couples, after a lovely church wedding. The first beating occurred when Roy was drunk; he reacted violently to Nan's complaints about his coming home late and his intoxication. His first blow knocked her against the wall. He lunged at her, grabbing her by the throat and pinning her to the wall. Hysterical, Nan managed to get loose and ran for the telephone, but Roy yanked it off the wall. However, in doing so, he lost his balance and fell to the floor. Crying from pain but afraid that Roy was hurt, Nan bent over him. Suddenly, he grabbed her and pinned her to the floor, pounding her belly with

13

his fists—he ended his beating with kicks. As soon as she could do so, Nan got to the bathroom and locked herself inside. She does not remember how long she stayed there, but it was long enough for her to believe that Roy had finally gone to sleep. Afraid to enter the bedroom for fear of awakening her sleeping husband, she spent the rest of the night in fitful sleep on the living room couch.

The following morning Nan went to her parents' home and told them what had happened. They were incredulous and wanted to know what she had done to cause such terrible behavior. They permitted her to stay with them, but by the end of the week Roy had convinced everyone that he was truly sorry, that he had been drunk and did not know what happened, and that he would never do such a thing again—ever. Nan forgave him; it was the first time she had ever seen him cry. She felt he really did not remember his assault, it must have been temporary insanity due to alcohol. And after all, she remarked, he was her husband and the father of her unborn child, so she returned home to a loving and contrite husband. The second time he beat her, six months later, he was again drunk, but the third time occurred on a Saturday night when he had been home all day and had not been drinking. By that time, the baby was three months old. The day Nan left home for the shelter was after Roy had struck her when she had the baby in her arms.

The topic of woman-battering began receiving widespread attention from the American media early in 1976. A search of the literature revealed that, with few exceptions (Goode, 1971; Straus, 1973), sociologists had largely ignored or overlooked the possibility that relationships that begin with vows to "love, honor, and cherish" sometimes include physical violence that occasionally results in death for one of the spouses (Boudouris, 1971; Wolfgang, 1958, 1967).

This study was initiated in March 1976 in response to the apparent need for empirical research on spousal violence. It began as an exploratory study in an attempt to fill the gap in our understanding of force and violence against women by the men with whom they live. This is the first sociological investigation to date that focuses on the victims themselves to learn their perceptions of the violence, their attempts to prevent or avoid the violence, and responses to their efforts to obtain outside intervention or assistance. Some further data were obtained from social agents to whom victims are most likely to turn for assistance, to serve as a backdrop against which to place victims' reports.

An attempt was made to find some answers to the puzzle of why some women remain in conjugal relationships with their spouses after violence begins. One of the most frequently asked questions is, "Abused wives: why do they stay?" (Gelles, 1976: 659). According to Gelles (p. 660), "The question itself derives from the elementary assumption that any reasonable individual, having been beaten and battered by another person, would avoid being victimized again (or at least avoid the attacker)."

It is an important question, and finding answers to why many women remain with spouses who continue to batter them, sometimes for many years, may be a first step toward suggesting solutions to the problem. The family is a primary institution where individuals are introduced at birth and in subsequent years to norms, values, regulations, and roles they are expected to perform both within the home and in the larger society. The socialization process begins in the home; Goode explains that the lessons children learn in the home about force and violence are not lost to them but are "extended to other social roles as well" (1971: 634). Children born and raised in a violent home learn modes of adult behavior as well as child behavior from their role models (Owens and Straus, 1975).

There are other important reasons besides the impact on children for attempting to discover why women stay in violent relationships. The price to our society as well as to individuals is extremely high, directly in costs in medical, legal, criminal justice, and social services, and—in the case of homicide—lives lost. There are also indirect costs in lost working hours, emotional and physical incapacities, and extended costs for children's behavior problems at school and in the community. These social expenses were described in detail in testimony before congressional subcommittee hearings on pending domestic violence legislation (Pagelow, 1978a). This testimony suggested that much of what children learn in their homes of orientation is carried over into adulthood, which is then transmitted to the next generation, and so on. If the home is warm, loving, and secure, then the potential is good that adults who emerge from it will pass on these benefits to persons in their own social environment. But if there is violence, terror, and insecurity, the home becomes a breeding ground for dangerous and destructive behavior. If we could trace over generations the effects of unhappy and violent homes upon citizens in this country today, we would undoubtedly find that many current remedial social programs were instituted to treat the effects of domestic violence. This country spends billions of tax dollars each year on crime prevention programs, mental hospitals, alcohol and drug abuse programs, and juvenile delinquency; it is possible that the roots of many of these social problems may be found in the violent family.

The issue of woman-battering was approached from a social learning perspective, which led to the development of a major hypothesis that is the only one to be tested in this study. It states:

> The fewer the resources, the more negative the institutional response; and the more intense the traditional ideology of women who have been battered, the more likely they are to remain in relationships with the batterers and the less likely they are to perform acts that significantly alter the situation in a positive direction.

Independent variables are resources, institutional response, and traditional ideology. Resources are the positive and negative, present and/or obtainable material goods, capabilities, physical features, and the type and quality of human support systems in a woman's life sphere. Institutional response is defined as the amount and type of support and assistance, or its lack, available to or received by battered women from social institutions and their agents. Traditional ideology encompasses a broad range of internalized beliefs favoring acceptance of the rightness of the patriarchial-hierarchical order of the social structure. It is a set of beliefs and attitudes that is a fundamental part of the way persons evaluate life and circumstances and serves to guide and motivate behavior. Traditional ideology is the configuration of all the conservative wisdom passed down through the ages as the inherent "natural" order of things. The dependent variable is the length of time women remain in relationships after violence begins until they terminate the violence either by leaving the relationships or by other means.

This investigation proposes to overcome the major shortcomings of some other studies. It has a much larger data base, it focuses specifically on abused women, and it follows a preset design and theoretical assumptions. The study is unlike other studie< as well for these reasons: (1) It is broader than some which have mainly focused on battered wives, wherein the marital contract is considered to be a major contributing factor (Dobash and Dobash, 1978, 1979; Eisenberg and Micklow, 1974; Kirchner, 1977a, 1977b, 1978). (2) It is narrower in focus than some which study the family unit as a whole, using intact couples as respondents (Gelles, 1974; Steinmetz, 1977a; Straus, 1978). (3) It studies women respondents as the best available sources of information which may lead to an understanding of the sociocultural environment in which they live and why they stayed with violent men. It investigates their constraints and perceived lack of alternatives rather than using them as subjects in psychological and personality tests (see Star, 1979). In brief, this is a sociological examination of the lives and events in the lives of women who were battered by their spouses that is significantly unlike other studies.

Chapter 1

THE INDIVIDUALS, THE SOCIETY, OR BOTH?

Most cases of woman-battering that have come to the attention of professionals were long-standing relationships involving repeated assaults and physical abuse. In almost all cases the violence had increased in frequency and intensity over time. Most researchers and theorists puzzled over why these destructive relationships endured and, in particular, why the victims remained with their batterers.

The Individuals

The topic of woman-battering and the broader topic of domestic violence that had earlier been almost entirely ignored have recently been addressed from a number of perspectives. The first professionals to discuss this widespread social problem were from the fields of psychiatry, psychology, and social work. Not unexpectedly, most of the early writers saw the problem in terms of individual psychopathology, defining the victim, her abuser, or both, as neurotic or "mentally ill" (Dewsbury, 1975; Faulk, 1974; Gayford, 1975a, 1975b, 1975c, 1976; Lion, 1977; Marsden and Owens, 1975; Saul,

1972; Schultz, 1960; Scott, 1974; Shainess, 1977; Snell et al., 1964). Some of these reports were generated from a few case histories, while only two focus specifically on the batterers (Faulk, 1974; Schultz, 1960); Schultz presents an analysis of ten prisoners convicted of wife assault.

Many studies concentrated on personality factors of the victims— not the aggressors—which "discover" personality defects in one form or another. Probably the best known of these is the Snell et al. (1964) report, "The Wifebeaters Wife." This article was written by three psychiatrists who were assigned 37 accused wife-beaters for court-ordered analysis. Couples were called in for interviews, but the writers report: "The men were usually resistive to psychiatric contact, tending to deny that problems existed in their marriages which required outside help" (1964:108). As a result, the conclusions contained in this report are based on a sample of only 12 of the men who did not resist treatment, and their wives. They were interviewed at the clinic three or more times by this team of psychiatrists. The 12 women were ultimately diagnosed in contradictory terms as passive, aggressive, indecisive, masculine, domineering, masochistic, frigid, overprotective of their sons, and emotionally deprived people who needed periodic punishment "for her castrating activity" (Snell et al., 1964:111).

A British psychiatrist's evaluation of 100 women who obtained refuge at Chiswick, a London shelter for battered women, was published in four articles: The first three give a descriptive psychoanalytic account, but in the last article Gayford classified victims into derogatory stereotypes, such as "Tortured Tina," "Violent Violet," "Fanny the Flirt," and "Go-Go Gloria" (1975a, 1975b, 1975c, 1976).

In light of professionals' concentration on individual characteristics and frequent conclusions that the women were the cause of their own victimization, it is no wonder that victims who turned to these persons in the mental health field in the past were likely to receive negative institutional response—that is, little or no help or real understanding.

Some of the more recent research reports from a psychoanalytic perspective are much less pejorative about the female victims. Hilberman and Munson (1978) write that 60 women had been patients of male psychiatrists for an extended period of time, a few for as long as five years. These analysts discovered that their colleagues had been treating 60 patients for a variety of physical symptoms, including severe depression and insomnia, but never uncovered the actual cause of these symptoms: severe and repeated physical abuse at the hands of their spouses (Hilberman and Munson, 1978). From a feminist attribution theoretical perspective, Frieze (1978, 1979) compares women who had been beaten by their husbands with a control sample of nonbeaten wives. Walker (1978, 1979) utilizes a behavioral paradigm of "learned helplessness" in her study of battered women, and describes the dyadic interaction as a cycle theory of violence. She elaborates on a three-stage process which she labels "The Tension Building Stage"; the violence eruption, called "The Acute Battering Incident"; and "Kindness and Contrite Loving Behavior," the making-up period (1979:55-70).

Enough evidence exists now to show that woman-battering occurs to such a large extent in this and other industrialized countries that it cannot be viewed as a relatively rare problem of individual neuroticism or psychopathology. A substantial number of writers have recently addressed the issue of woman-battering and contributed much to our understanding (Fojtik, 1976; Gingold, 1976; Martin, 1976a, 1976b; Pizzey, 1977; Pogrebin, 1974; Warrior, 1977). The Pizzey book (1977) was an important stimulus in arousing public awareness of previously hidden crimes of woman-battering. Andersen (1977) similarly describes the process of establishing and maintaining a shelter since 1974 in Amsterdam called "Blijf m'n van lijf," which roughly translates to "keep your hands off my body." Martin (1976a) documented the need for shelters for battering victims and their children in the United States. Gathering statistics and other evidence, Martin provided one of the most comprehensive documentaries possible at the time. Warrior (1977) put together a directory that lists shelters, their mailing addresses, and contact persons around the United States and most foreign countries, as well as publications, papers, and other educational materials.

The Society

Violence is undeniably endemic to American culture on a national scale, and woman-battering crosses all racial, ethnic, religious, age, and socioeconomic strata. Some sociologists addressed the issue of spouse abuse or family violence either theoretically or through empirical research (Dobash and Dobash, 1976, 1978, 1979; Gelles, 1974, 1975, 1976; Gillespie, 1971; Goode, 1969, 1971; O'Brien, 1971; Russell, 1976; Russell and Van de Ven, 1976; Stark and McEvoy, 1970; Steinmetz, 1977a, 1977b; Steinmetz and Straus, 1974; Straus, 1976, 1977, 1978; Straus et al., 1980; Vanfossen, 1977; Young, 1976).

Family sociologist Goode (1969, 1971) addressed the issue of spousal violence from an exchange theoretical perspective at a time when most of his colleagues appeared to have been unaware of force and violence in the family and were still largely concentrating on premarital dating patterns and sexuality both within and outside of marriage (Reiss, 1976). In his articles, Goode presents a theoretical argument for legitimate authority and the use of force, when necessary, to uphold family authority. He also shows that the social system is set up to enforce maintenance of authority that is usually vested in the adult male in the family. In his discussion of force (and the threat of force) and violence in the family, Goode (1971) deplores excessive exertion of power in the family but nevertheless sees the need for force, bolstered by social supports, to maintain the family structure. He calls on the reader to "imagine away" the supports of force, giving a list of examples of husbands without force who cannot "press" children's obedience, "threaten, press, or persuade" their wives into various wifely duties; he concludes that "it is easy to see that a substantial part of the structural strength of the family would be undermined" (1971:627). Goode further states:

> Thus, force plays a role even when no deviant act is actually committed. The rebellious child or wife knows that the father or husband is stronger, and can call upon outsiders who will support that force with more force. . . . Within the family itself, the harsh fact must be faced that the member with the greater strength and willingness to use it commands more force than others do. This is usually the father. . . . Women, children, slaves, Colonials, lower castes, and other disadvantaged segments of any society are constrained more than others by force—although all are to some extent—or they are enjoined to refrain from its use, simply because the existing structures would change without these buttresses [1971:625, 628, 635].

An early study on attitudes and use of violent behavior by Stark and McEvoy (1970) made an important contribution to our understanding of the frequency of violence between spouses. Their representative sample showed that there was a high rate of approval of slapping one's spouse, yet men were more likely to approve of this behavior than women. One of the most unexpected findings of their research was that middle-class people are more likely than people of the lower classes to approve and use violence. The Stark and McEvoy study showed that as socioeconomic status increases, so does the likelihood that couples approve of slapping one's spouse and either experience, or are willing to engage in, violence (1970:52-54).

A proliferation of sociological approaches to studying the problem began developing in the past decade. There are not only vastly different research designs with assorted theoretical perspectives but also differing units of analysis and definitions. In capsule form, there seem to be two major divisions categorized by focus: one group studies the family as a whole in a violent culture framework where spouse abuse is only one of many forms of violence (Gelles, 1974; Steinmetz, 1977a; Straus, 1978; Straus et al., 1980); the others focus on the marital relationship within the patriarchal family (Dobash and Dobash, 1976, 1978, 1979) as discussed below.[1]

Studies in the violent culture framework include Gelles's early doctoral dissertation research which selected 40 intact families identified as violent by either police or social agencies. He interviewed a member of each of these violent families and one family in the same neighborhood; thus, his sample included a total of 80 families. These interviews yielded data on husband-wife and sibling violence as well as adult violence toward children.

In her doctoral research project, Steinmetz (1977a) interviewed at least one member of 49 intact two-children families in New Castle County, Delaware. Like Gelles, she also was interested in all forms of intrafamily violent behavior that her respondents were willing to report. Among findings indicating a relatively high rate of violence within these middle-class families, Steinmetz discovered four wives (but no husbands) who were victims of serious assault (1977b).

Both Gelles and Steinmetz utilized a violent culture structural theoretical approach as did Straus, with whom they worked. Straus was the principal investigator in the only large-scale sociological study to date on intrafamily violence (Straus et al., 1979). This nationally representative sample of 2143 intact couples was administered the Conflict Resolution Techniques (CRT) Scale by interviewers who inquired mainly about violent acts performed in 1975, the year prior to the interviews. The CRT scale categorized violent acts on a continuum that ranged from a slap to using a knife or gun. Five of the eight items, one of which was "beat up," were combined into a "severe violence index." The complete report only recently became available, but earlier papers and articles about the study revealed that there were some limitations and as yet unanswered questions (Straus, 1978:447). In that study, all forms of intrafamily violence reported to interviewers were recorded, including husband to wife, wife to husband, "mutual combat" (a self-explanatory term discussed below), parents to children, between siblings, and children to parents.

Straus et al. obtained a numerical count of the frequency of violent acts in one year; and although there was some measure of events preceding violent episodes, there were no measures of event following each act, the intensity of the blows, the severity of injuries (if any) sustained, and the meanings attached to these acts by both the aggressors and victims (Pagelow, 1977a; Safilios-Rothschild, 1978). As pointed out in an earlier paper, there is an important difference between hitting and trying to hit, yet these acts receive the same count (and weight) in the CRT scale (Pagelow, 1977a). Also, a kick with an open-toed sandal administered under a bridge table and an angry kick from a pointed western boot are vastly different in both the aggressor's intent to cause injury (the social meaning behind the act) and possible injury sustained.[2]

The above-mentioned factors were not measured by the CRT scale. Thus, according to Safilios-Rothschild, Straus et al. accumulated numbers of acts with no clear understanding of what the acts represent. Another limitation to the Straus et al. study was its primary focus on acts committed only in the previous year. Straus admits that violence occurring at any time previous to that year received very slight attention in his study, yet prior acts may have great significance for the duration of a couple's relationship. Straus says:

Unfortunately, our data for events before the year of the survey do not distinguish between who was the assailant and who was the victim. . . . In some cases it was a single slap or a single beating. However, there are several reasons why even a single beating is important. . . . It often takes only one such event to fix the balance of power in a family for many years—perhaps for a lifetime [1978:446].

In sum, while the Straus et al. study has served an important purpose in showing conclusively that the home is frequently the arena of intrafamily violence, its broad focus is vastly different from the focus of this study. The Straus et al. investigation included all forms of intrafamily violence: child, parent, sibling, and spouse abuse. Woman-battering was only one form of several types of violence inquired about. No attempt was made to determine if the victims of spouse abuse had made any efforts to stop the abuse or to terminate the relationships by leaving. Ferraro notes that when the topic of "wife-beating" or battering arises, general recognition is given to Straus, Gelles, or Steinmetz as the leading sociological experts on this form of violence. Ferraro claims that "their work has set the standards for conducting research on battering" (1979:2). Since the study by Straus et al. addresses phenomena other than those addressed in this study, it cannot serve as a model here. Some of the limitations in the Straus et al. research are overcome in this study, which, while it is disadvantaged by lack of funding precluding large sample size, compensates for lack of breadth by greater depth and a narrower, more concisely defined focus on a precise target sample. This study asks specific questions: Were these women beaten more than once? If so, what did they do about it, and why did they stay?

Some of the most outspoken critics of studying the family unit to gain an understanding of spouse abuse have been Dobash and Dobash (1976:35). Bandura (1973:11) lends support to the position that different types of violence, although sharing some common ingredients, cannot be assumed to have the same determinants. The Dobashes state their position thus:

To conceive of violence in the family as "marital violence," "family violence," or even "spousal violence" ignores the obvious fact that several types of violence occur in the family. . . . Even this degree of delimination may not be enough since violence may mean anything from a slap to severe beatings resulting in death. The point is, we must be more concrete about our conceptions of violence, partialling out various types and forms of violence, not assuming a necessary inter-relatedness between these forms and types and seeking explanations and understanding of these concrete forms in the wider society, as well as within family interaction [1978:435].

The Dobash and Dobash study initiated several years ago was recently completed (1979). These researchers examined police and court records in two cities in Scotland; their investigation also in-cluded in-depth interviews with 109 women who had been battered by their spouses. They show that in spousal assaults wives are far more frequently the victims than are husbands. Out of 1044 cases of assaults occurring between family members, 791 wives were victims compared to 12 husbands; of the total assaults, 75.8 percent were directed against wives while only 1.1 percent were directed against husbands (Dobash and Dobash, 1978:436-437). It seems obvious that official records reveal only the "tip of the iceberg" (Martin, 1976a), because the Dobashes found through their interview sample that only 2 out of every 98 wife assaults were reported to the police (1978:437).

This research team draws conclusions that the hierarchical struc-ture of the patriarchal family historically has legitimized wife-beating for subordination, domination, and control of women and that women are victims of men's brutality to a far greater extent within marriage than outside marriage. They say:

Females, whether they be sisters, mothers, wives or daughters, are more likely to be subject to control through the use of physical force than are their male counterparts—and it is in their capacity as wives that the risk is the highest and the danger the greatest. . . . Women were very rarely assaulted by strangers on the streets; only 15 percent of the cases involving female victims occurred outside the family setting [Dobash and Dobash, 1978:437].

The Dobashes' conceptualization and analysis are valuable contri-butions to our knowledge of wife abuse; they searched for explana-tion and understanding of the problem based on the social and cultural

contexts in which it exists (1976, 1979). They made great strides over
the popular, narrow focus on problems within the victims themselves,
a topic discussed above and in some earlier papers (Pagelow, 1977b,
1981a). By itemizing all types of family violence, they produced
statistics to show that the most common type is wife-beating (Dobash
and Dobash, 1978:436-437). In addition, they provide extensive
documentation that shows victims' lack of resources, negative institutional response to victims in their help-seeking efforts, and victims'
traditional ideology fostered by the patriarchy (1979).

Violent Individuals in a Violent Society

While it seems that the marital situation may contribute to woman-
battering, and although Straus has noted that the "marriage license [is
made] a hitting license" (1976:543), battering of women who cohabit
with but are not legally married to their assailants also occurs with
great frequency. As Martin (1976a:18) suggests, it may be that the
shared living situation contributes more to interpersonal violence
than do the legal documents.

The focus of this investigation is narrower than intrafamily violence as studied by Straus, Gelles, and Steinmetz (1979) and somewhat broader than those studies that concentrate mainly on marital
violence (Dobash and Dobash, 1979). This study more properly may
be included with the remaining group of research efforts that address
male-female violence in conjugal settings, whether or not the relationships include legal marriage. This research addresses the problem
from the perspective of the victim as "expert" within her personal and
cultural environment (Fields and Kirchner, 1978; Kirchner, 1978;
Martin, 1976a, 1976b; Vanfossen, 1977; Visser, 1978; Walker, 1978,
1979). If we truly want to discover why some women remain in
violent relationships, then it seems likely that an investigation of the
victims, their social environment, their efforts to deter or avoid the
violence, and the reasons they present for maintaining their relationships will provide clues toward answers to this question. The next
chapter presents the underlying theoretical assumptions guiding this
approach.

Chapter 2

WHY IS THERE BATTERING?

The underlying theoretical assumptions of this study are based on social learning theory because its basic propositions provide the clearest explanation of the important questions raised in this study. Social learning theory suggests reasons why some men use force and violence against their spouses, violent behavior is unlikely to cease once initiated and rewarded, and some victims have great difficulty in either stopping the violence or terminating the relationships. Social learning theory's propositions concerning reinforcement and punishment, intermittent reinforcement, modeling, socialization, and other basic concepts and their relevance to the study of spouse abuse are detailed below.

After a pilot study and preliminary analysis of data obtained during an exploratory phase, some new ideas suggested a tripartite model. This model separates out the cultural and historical development of woman-battering (Pagelow, 1981b); the initial instance of violence in contemporary relationships—*primary battering* (Pagelow, 1977c); and the phenomenon of repeated violence—*secondary battering* (Pagelow, 1977a).

The concepts primary and secondary applied to battering may be suggestive of Lemert's important theoretical contribution to the study of deviance (1951, 1972); he clearly distinguished between primary and secondary deviation. There are complementary features of the terms as used here, but there are also important differences. The similarities are that Lemert views deviant behavior as a process, as violent behavior is viewed here, and primary deviance is separated out from later performance of similar (or same) deviant acts. "Primary deviance, as contrasted with secondary, is polygenetic, arising out of a variety of social, cultural, psychological, and physiological factors, either in adventitious or recurring combinations" (Lemert, 1972:62). According to Lemert, primary deviance is dealt with through either normalization or management and nominal controls, which may easily apply to primary battering.

But the differences are significant because Lemert's secondary deviance requires a process of societal reaction, stigmatization of the actor through degradation rituals, social control, actors' acceptance of the deviant status, and change in self-identity to fit the new role (1972:62-85). Secondary battering usually involves no such public reaction and actors' response. In cases of woman-battering, the acts may continue for extended periods without any of these processes following primary battering. In fact, it is questionable if many batterers even define themselves or their behavior as deviant, and many of their victims do not either—at least in the beginning. The differences are apparent; yet, when Lemert expands on secondary deviance, he makes statements that are supportive of the transition from primary to secondary battering developed herein:

> If nothing else, common sense dictates that some variant of the law of effect be made part of the explanation of secondary deviance. This is true even in the face of the formidable task of specifying what is rewarding or punishing to human beings. . . . Restated and applied to deviance, the law of effect is a simple idea that people beset with problems posed for them by society will choose lines of action they expect to be satisfactory solutions to the problems. If the consequences are those expected, the likelihood that the action or generically similar action will be repeated is increased. If the consequences are unsatisfactory, unpleasant, or make more problems than they

solve, then the pattern of action will be avoided. The fact that anticipation of satisfactions or expectation of punishments is a cognitive process based upon symbolic learning as well as experience does not vitiate the principle of effect [Lemert, 1972:84].

These same principles apply to the viewpoint that suggests that when a male spouse first acts violently against a female spouse and that act provides satisfactory solutions and the consequences are not unpleasant (at least for the batterer), those acts are likely to be repeated. Studying the dynamics of the interactive process suggests that the female spouse rewards the violent male spouse by renewed effort to meet all his demands and to adjust whatever he claims caused his violence. Following the principle of effect, the probability of repetition of violence (secondary battering) is substantial.

The major focus of this study is a test of the secondary battering model, but all three models are introduced because they propose a distinct temporal ordering with underlying commonalities that connect one model to the other. They suggest that male violence directed against females is learned in a society where men are trained into competition, aggressiveness, dichotomized sex-specific role behavior, physical force, and a need to dominate and control women in the hierarchical structure of the patriarchal family. Suggestions regarding the responses of female victims to spousal violence and the reasons they maintain their relationships despite violence are also detailed. Viewed from the framework of learning theory, the interaction before and after the occurrence of violence suggests explanations for why these women seem unable to prevent or avoid the violence. Social institutions promote rather than discourage male violence against women and tend to keep women in conjugal relationships to preserve the "sanctity of the home" (Kremen, 1976) despite the damage being done to all family members.

Some researchers have proposed other theoretical explanations, but the most publicized of these is the "violent culture theory" or "social-structural theory of violence" (Gelles, 1974; Goode, 1969, 1971; Straus, 1978; Straus et al., 1976, 1980). The violent culture theory, briefly summarized, identifies woman-battering as one of many manifestations of violence learned in the family which is legitimated by a violent society. This viewpoint is compatible with the theoretical framework of this study to a certain point. What is largely overlooked by proponents of the violent culture theory is that not all men are physically violent with their spouses and that women are victims, not perpetrators, of the violence to a far greater extent than are men.[1] The violent culture theory cannot explain spouse-battering any more than the subculture theory of violence can adequately explain rape as Amir (1971) attempted to explain it. The subculture theory of violence fails to explain lower-class female victims' disapproval of rape, whereas Straus fails to point out that "cultural norms legitimizing intrafamily violence" (1976:545-555) legitimate male violence but not female violence. The fact that many women continue to cohabit with their spouses after being battered cannot be considered conclusive evidence that these women approve or condone the violence. While ours is a violent culture, only half of the population (males) is encouraged in violence while the other half (females) is encouraged to avoid and fear violence and perhaps initially to accept it. As Weis and Borges (1976) point out, a theory that can only "explain" the violent behavior of one segment of the population but that ignores the nonparticipation of other segments of the same population (nonviolent men and most women) is not an explanation at all.

Conceptual boundaries are narrower than in the violent culture theory proposed by Straus and some others but extended beyond the marital relationship, as suggested by Dobash and Dobash (1979). These parameters include crimes of physical violence perpetrated by men against women both within and outside marriage. This framework eliminates many other far-ranging forms of interpersonal violence. Russell and Van de Ven (1976:127) explain the interrelationship:

> Assault of women, or "woman battering," as it is now commonly called, both within marriage and outside of it, has much in common with rape. The fear of men that both rape and battering instill in women has similar political consequences. Both are often accompanied by an agonizing fear of death, and both sometimes result in womanslaughter—or femicide.

These are the reasons conceptual boundaries were set where they are: because the investigator sees a closer theoretical relationship between woman-battering and other violent crimes against women such as rape than between woman-battering and other intrafamily violent crimes. Following this reasoning, these new ideas are presented here.

Definitions and Scope

In this investigation, *battered women* refers to adult women who were intentionally physically abused in ways that caused pain or injury, or who were forced into involuntary action or restrained by force from voluntary action by adult men with whom they have or had established relationships, usually involving sexual intimacy, whether or not within a legally married state.

Battering is generally one-way violence (Gelles, 1974:80-82; Steinmetz and Straus, 1974:11) that may or may not be accompanied by victims' attempts to defend themselves. Steinmetz and Straus theorized about "one-sided aggressive acts" (1974:13), although the survey instrument used later was incapable of screening out violent acts which some respondents may not define as violent behavior. Thus, their categorization of some women (and some men) in their sample as "battered spouses" was ultimately based on decisions reflecting the value judgments of the researchers (Ferraro, 1979). Battering is here defined as physical assault which ranges from painful slaps at one end and homicide at the other end of a continuum.[2] Physical abuse has been somewhat expanded to include force into involuntary or from voluntary action, so that being tied to a chair, locked in a room, closet, or house, or being locked out of one's home (in the middle of the night, for example)—which are clearly abusive actions—may be included. This sample of battered women reveal d accounts of each of these types of abuse.

The term "adult" arbitrarily designates from age 13 upward because it is felt that any female younger than 13 abused by an adult male should be considered the victim of child abuse or incest. The use of the term "established relationship" indicates that short-term, employer-employee, social acquaintance relationships and the like are excluded from this investigation. However, scope conditions are expanded from conjugal relationships to encompass as well sexual

relationships not involving cohabitation, marital relationships terminated by separation or divorce, and kinship relationships which include females residing in the same household with a father, brother,
stepfather, stepbrother, or foster father.[3]

Enlarging scope conditions to include nonmarital, nonsexual, or
noncohabitational relationships places this study somewhere beyond
the marital-familial setting alluded to by Dobash and Dobash (1978)
and makes it narrower than the more general intrafamily violence in
the home researched by Gelles (1974) and Straus et al. (1979).
Woman-battering may be better understood when it is lifted out of the
frame of reference that ties it so strongly to sexually intimate relationships; yet other types of familial violence, such as sibling violence,
are beyond these boundaries. Although the vast majority of battered
women appear to receive abuse from men with whom they share
intimate sexual relationships prior to or at the time of the assaults, it is
clear that many women are battered by men other than husbands or
lovers (Brownmiller, 1976; Martin, 1976a; Russell and Van de Ven,
1976).

For simplicity and consistency, references to male-female interpersonal relationships are categorized as "conjugal," and the interacting persons are designated as "spouses." Beyond the scope of interest
are two phenomena frequently confused with issues concerning
woman-battering: sadomasochistic practices[4] and "mutual combat."[5]

In contrast to other research, there is a conceptual distinction between woman-battering, the focus of this study, and mutual combat
and/or sadomasochistic practices. Gelles (1974:78-80) attempts to
distinguish between the meanings attached to violence and his term
for when spouses strike back, "Protective-Reaction Violence," which
comes closest to mutual combat discussed here. Gelles also distinguishes "One-Way Violence," which most closely resembles woman-
battering, the focus of this study. Steinmetz apparently does not
differentiate between the two, for she refers to "reciprocal physical
violence" (1977a:86, 1977b:67); yet she includes these cases with
other evidence of "battering." In addition, the Conflict Resolution
Techniques (CRT) scale employed in the Straus et al. study of intrafamily violence (Straus, 1978) is unable to distinguish between mutual combat or sadomasochistic practices because the CRT scale was

designed to measure the types and frequencies and—in a theoretical sense—the seriousness of violent acts that a member of an intact couple was willing to admit happened in the previous year. The CRT scale was insensitive to the interactive environment within which the acts occurred, the personal meanings attached to these acts by both the respondent and his or her spouse, and the amount of damage inflicted by these acts. The severity distinction is a theoretical one— not an empirical one—since there were no measures of meanings attached by either actor or object or of physical damages, if any, sustained.

The present study attempts to overcome some of the deficiencies in previous studies by taking into account the perceptions of victims of violent acts regarding what happened before, during, and after the violence and the meanings they attached to these acts. With greater knowledge of the ancillary features of victims' lives, it may be possible to explain why these women remained with violent men after the first instance of spouse abuse. Although they may interact in privacy, victims and abusers do not exist in a vacuum; both of them are part of a larger cultural system that helped design the roles they play and to which they were socialized. Social learning theory appears most appropriate for this investigation, as explained below.

Social Learning Theory and Woman-Battering

A number of researchers of woman-battering utilize social learning theory to greater or lesser degrees (Walker, 1979). Social learning theory has been defined as

> an extension of differential-association and reinforcement theories, holding that social sources, or people with whom one interacts, are the reinforcers that result in the learning of nondeviant and deviant behavior. The type of behavior that is most frequently and consistently reinforced by people will be the one most often exhibited [Stark, 1975:506].

Social learning theory is a fundamental part of the substructure of the tripartite theoretical framework of this study; it provides a useful explanation for the learning and transmission of traditional ideology, a construct integral to all three phases. This theory contributes to our understanding of spousal violence and helps explain sex role social-ization and perceived appropriate and inappropriate gender roles. Social learning theory provides the most reasonable and testable explanation for violence between intimates such as spouses if we are willing to reject the innate aggression models of Lorenz (1966) and Ardrey (1966) and Freud's "instinctual inclination" (Bandura, 1973:13). Anthropologists Mead (1973) and Montagu (1973, 1976) provide strong evidence that culture has a more important role in developing personalities and behavior than do innate characteristics of aggression. Instinctual inclination and innate aggression are popu-lar theories competing with learning theory, but they cannot be veri-fied empirically (Bandura, 1973:14). There is dwindling support for a clear-cut dichotomy between hereditary and environmental influ-ences, as Bandura explains:

> Both sets of factors interact in subtle ways in determining behavior. Where certain biological equipment is needed to perform manual aggressive acts, structural factors, which have a genetic basis, may partly determine whether initial aggressiveness proves successful and is further developed, or whether it fails and is discarded. Possession of a brawny physique . . . increases the probability that physically ag-gressive modes of behavior will prove effective [1973:26].

Relatively few men may possess a "brawny physique" compared to other men; yet, on the average, men are taller, heavier, and physically stronger than women (Pagelow, 1978a:8; Straus, 1978:447, 449).

One of the basic propositions of social learning theory is that reinforcement following behavior increases the probability that the behavior will be repeated and another is that intermittently reinforced behavior is the most difficult to extinguish (Hilgard and Bower, 1966). Akers points out that two major parts of the learning process are reinforcement and punishment (1977:49). Emphasis is placed on reinforcement rather than punishment, because punishment has been shown to have relatively short-term effects on extinguishing behav-ior, and immediate reinforcement outweighs effects of delayed pun-ishment in controlling behavior (Bandura, 1973:13; Hill, 1971).

In addition to reinforcement, another important factor for learning is modeling (Wrightsman, 1977:226-228). In a variety of social-psychological tests, children observing aggressive behavior not only showed they remembered aggressive acts (although girls somewhat less than boys) but they closely imitated them, particularly when the acts were performed by a male adult model. And while initially the boys exceeded girls in imitation, when rewarded for imitation, both boys and girls increased imitative performance approaching an almost equal level (Bandura, 1973:72-85; Ulbrich and Huber, 1979:1). Bandura stresses that "people learn more than they usually perform, unless given positive incentives to do so," and the girls demonstrated that reward for displaying aggression was even more important for them than for the boys (Bandura, 1973:80).

Earliest socialization occurs in the home; thus, children receive reinforcement and/or punishment from their adult models. While they learn appropriate behavior from many other social sources, studies have shown that "children were much more inclined to imitate a familiar aggressive model than an unfamiliar one. This was especially true of boys, who performed approximately three times as many matching responses as the girls," yet a nurturing relationship with the model had no effect on either sex (Bandura, 1973:80). This indicates that familiarity with a model is more important than a warm relationship with a model for behavior to be imitated, which means that children may be equally likely to imitate a feared or hated parent as a loved parent. These findings are relevant for understanding why the home is the cradle for future adult violence-nonviolence and sex role behavior. As Bandura explains,

> If the model's behavior appears to have functional value, as it often does, observers have strong incentives to practice the modeled patterns and to overlearn them. Conditions of observational learning combining repeated exposure with opportunities for overt practice and symbolic rehearsal ensure more or less permanent retention of modeled activities [1973:78].

In summary, important elements of social learning theory are functional value, repeated exposure, opportunities for practice and symbolic rehearsal, plus the findings that (1) boys are more inclined to remember and to imitate more aggression without rewards, (2) familiarity not necessarily involving nurturance has a greater influence on boys, and (3) a male adult model is most likely to be imitated by both boys and girls. Modeling, both within the home and outside it, is achieved by observing individuals, written words, and audiovisual modes; individuals can learn from each of these modes provided they are capable of processing information received and paying attention to it (Bandura, 1973:73). Attention is also an important factor in learning; the first formulation of appropriate and inappropriate behavior patterns is established within the parental home while a young child is in a relatively closed social system with fewer distractions (which impede learning) so that reinforcement and models receive a major share of the child's attention. Bandura states:

> The people with whom a person regularly associates delimit the types of behavior that he will repeatedly observe and hence learn most thoroughly. . . . The behavior of models who possess high status and prestige, power, and competence hierarchies is more likely to be successful and therefore to command greater attention from others than the behavior of models who are socially, occupationally, and intellectually inept [1973:69, 70].

In the hierarchical structure of the patriarchal family, the husband-father position carries highest status in prestige and power (Dobash and Dobash, 1976, 1978), which may help explain why girls as well as boys are most likely to imitate an adult male model. Goode also contributes to our understanding of early socialization and the impact that use of force has on the very young:

> In this process by which we transform infants into people, inculcating in them the values, norms, and role habits of the family and society, or more specifically by which children come to accept as right and desirable the family patterns we approve, not only do we use force and threat in order to socialize our children, we also teach them thereby that force is useful, and we do in fact train them in the use of force and violence. . . . We are all trained for violence. . . . The child experiences it directly and watches it in others—the fright of his mother when his father is furious, arguments and threats among neighbors, the battles with his own siblings, and so on [1971:627, 630].

It should be clear that social learning theory has great explanatory value for the problem of woman-battering and why some women remain with their assaulters.

Next, the tripartite model based on learning theory is outlined. Each major component addresses distinct aspects of woman-battering, particularly those that occur at different points in time; but there are underlying commonalities and connecting links. These components are Model I, Development; Model II, Primary Battering; and Model III, Secondary (or second-stage) Battering.

Model I: Development

It would be a major error to try to draw causal inferences from the contemporary setting when studying woman-battering, other forms of crimes against women, or violence in the family. Instead, it is necessary to analyze the sociohistorical foundations of the family if we want to understand why modern men in industrial societies still demand positions of "head of household" and domination and control of women and children in the home, and why many women appear to accept the status of "perpetual infantilism" (Richette, 1978), continuing to reside with men who beat them. Concepts of male superiority/female inferiority, subordination of women and children, the caste/class system of male power (Gillespie, 1971), and inequality in social institutions have been fostered for centuries and are evident today. They are the symptoms of power long ago assumed, and since maintained, by men over women. Some social scientists have made great contributions in sociohistorical analyses of woman-battering (Davidson, 1977a; Dobash and Dobash, 1976, 1978, 1979; Hanmer, 1977; Martin, 1976b; Pleck, 1979; Sutton, 1978; Young, 1976). These writers have generally singled out as the starting point for a theory of wife abuse the patriarchal foundations of the family itself and the hierarchical power structure that provides the framework of modern social systems.

These ideas are suggested as the most fruitful areas of study for the development of a causal explanation of woman-battering. They are starting points toward better understanding of a contemporary problem. Careful sociohistorical research is essential to explain why some men today believe they not only have the right to own, control, and dominate women and children but sometimes even see such behavior as their duty. Today's women and men perform according to culturally transmitted ideologies from many centuries ago which were transferred through generations via social institutions such as mythology, law, history, textbooks and other literature, religion, psychotherapy, and the media (Pagelow, 1981b). Gender role socialization which defines women as perpetual children and property of men had its basis in earliest civilization.

Borrowing the two most important concepts from socio-historical analysis—patriarchy and the hierarchical social structure—a new theoretical construct (see Willer and Webster, 1970—"traditional ideology"—was created for this new perspective. It designates a sense of traditionalism encompassing patriarchy, of which the family is one of its most important institutions, and hierarchy, which demands an ordering of power positions. Traditional ideology is more than patriarchal family ideology: It is a ranking of human beings based on male superiority and female inferiority, and designates greater status and power for males than females, regardless of other attributes, skills, knowledge, or accomplishments. Traditional ideology is an important construct, central to the development of a perspective on battered women. It is the common thread that binds the components of this tripartite perspective together and is a major variable in determining social response, both individual and institutional.

Traditional ideology is defined here as encompassing a broad range of internalized beliefs in acceptance of the "rightness" of the patriarchal-hierarchical order of the social structure. It includes internal attitudes and motivating forces that guide, shape, and determine behavior, that are not limited to behavior within families but extend beyond to influence relationships in other areas as well. In the family these can take the form of obedience to directives (servitude to a husband) or rejection of the forbidden (no divorce). Outside the family they can take the form of men's patronizing attitudes or low expectations toward women as well as women's similar attitudes toward women. Societies provide institutions (law and religion) that support and legitimate traditional ideology and other institutions (education and family) that socialize the masses by transmission of traditional norms for sex-appropriate behavior.

Socialization, acceptance, and internalization of traditional ideology occur in greater or lesser degrees, which accounts for variability among countries, communities, families, and individuals. Traditional ideology is ascribed to by both women and men: the maximum expression for women is through excessive femininity, such as in the "feminine mystique" (Friedan, 1974). The "masculine mystique" (Komisar, 1976) of traditional ideology for men is the macho gender role of tough, hard, unsentimental, aggressive behavior. Whereas passivity and dependence are key elements of femininity, aggressiveness and independence are key elements of masculinity. David and Brannon note that one of two definitions for the word "aggressive" is *"Tending to aggress, making the first attack,"* and they deduce: "Our society has a deeply ambivalent attitude toward aggression and its less savory first cousin, violence" (1976:28).

In sum, traditional ideology is the configuration of all the "conservative wisdom" passed down through the ages as the inherent "natural" order of things (it's right because it is, and it is because it's right). And traditional ideology is learned. One of the major failings of theories of deviance offered in the past has been that the paradigms were limited to understanding of socially defined undesirable behavior (Lemert, 1972; Merton, 1957; Sutherland and Cressey, 1974), but they largely failed to explain conformity. Social learning theory appears equally capable of explaining conforming as well as deviant behavior. Akers (1977) integrated Sutherland's "differential association" theory with "reinforcement" theory as Akers and Burgess proposed, into a new and broader paradigm. Social learning theory helps explain why some persons or even groups of persons accept or reject traditional ideology when the types and degrees of reinforcement and punishment are examined.

Model II: Primary Battering

It is important to differentiate between the first single incidence of battering and associated variables, which is the focus of Model II, and the phenomenon of systematic, repeated batterings involving a different set of explanatory variables, which is the major focus of Model III and this study. This distinction should be made in order to avoid much of the confusion and conflict among current theoretical viewpoints. Almost all theoretical and empirical attention has focused thus far on victims and perpetrators of secondary battering, although no distinction has been drawn between the first (and sometimes only) occurrence of battering and those batterings that occur on a continuing basis. It is no wonder that there are conflicting answers to the problem of woman-battering—it appears that sometimes we are asking the wrong questions. This model has been described in detail elsewhere (Pagelow, 1977a), and only its relevance to the tripartite schema and Model III is presented here.

When writers speculate on the extent and severity of the problem of woman-battering, estimates range from 15-25 percent (Flynn et al., 1975:8) to 50 percent (Dussich, 1976:17; Walker, 1979), but it is not clear if these percentages refer to regular and frequent conjugal violence or to one physical assault in half of all marriages. Whatever the extent of woman-battering in this society, we must first recognize that not all batterers continue this behavior; nor can we assume that all women who maintain conjugal relationships have never been battered. Nevertheless, there seems to be a popular assumption that (a) all battered women stay in a battering situation until the battering becomes, for one reason or another, intolerable—at which point they leave or seek help, or (b) that all women involved in "stable" conjugal relationships have never experienced battering. At this point in time, we have no idea how many relationships are terminated after one incident of physical abuse. Nor do we know how many long-term relationships continue despite repeated violence that never becomes a matter of public record. The important question to ask is: What are the characteristics (social and personal) that distinguish among women who are never battered, never battered a second time, or battered repeatedly? Conversely, are all men potential batterers? And if a man batters a woman once, does he always repeat this behavior?

Although it was not tested in this study, this model suggests some tentative answers to questions like these; it begins with the single instance of battering with no prior occurrence and postulates the conditions that must exist for battering to occur in the first place and that determine the probable response of the victim. On the part of male spouses, this model proposes (1) learned acceptance of the use of violence in conjugal relationships and (2) strong commitment to traditional ideology. Childhood battering experiences alone do not account for all batterers because all men do not necessarily grow up to pass on this behavior. Men will use force or even violence to the extent that they are convinced of their right or duty to dominate and control women and children. Traditional ideology calls for men to have and maintain power over subordinates in the family. If a man, believing that to be a man he must have control over his life and the lives of weaker others, finds himself losing control, then he will attempt to regain control by the best resource at his disposal. If he has learned that men gain control of others by force and violence, he will use that method.

On the part of female spouses, the predicting variables are (1) willingness to invest in their relationships and (2) strong commitment to traditional ideology. It is hypothesized that if a woman has great willingness to invest in maintaining a conjugal relationship—if she is strongly committed to it for a variety of reasons, and if she firmly accepts traditional ideology—then she will neither retaliate nor terminate a conjugal relationship if she is battered.

Despite the apparent frequency of battering, it seems safe to assume that not all men with the described characteristics batter women. It also seems reasonable to speculate that not all women with these characteristics always end up with a battering spouse, nor do all primary batterings continue to the next stage. There are relationships in which (a) there is never physical violence, (b) battering occurs once and never again, and (c) primary battering moves to secondary battering.

The strongest predictive variable is the construct "traditional ideology." If women are strongly committed to patriarchy and the hierarchical order of power statuses, it is extremely likely that their spouses are aware of these attitudes and behave accordingly. Within the context of intimate relationships, people usually relax many external defenses and reveal innermost attitudes and beliefs. Men may be expected to know if the women they live with are most likely to blame themselves, rather than their spouses, for almost all disruption of domestic tranquility. The type of ideology that insists "a man's home is his castle," along with a strong commitment to maintain conjugal ties, provides the strongest predictor that the victim will take no overt action that will successfully deter secondary battering. In sum, if the man has strong traditional ideology and accepts violence as proper behavior in conjugal relationships, and if the woman has strong traditional ideology and willingness to invest, this combination is postulated to be sufficient to predict that the relationship will continue. And if it does, secondary battering will occur.

The responsibility for taking decisive action at the first occurrence of battering appears to fall almost entirely on the woman. If a man responds to frustration, anger, or stress in a manner he has learned to believe is appropriate and this behavior appears to be accepted by his spouse because of lack of negative feedback, he is most likely to continue it. According to Akers, learning is accomplished by negative and positive stimuli: if behavior is not followed by punishment or is rewarded, the behavior will continue to be elicited. Akers explains: "The basic process is this: *Stimuli following or contingent upon an operant determine the probability of its future occurrence.* The two major parts of this process are *reinforcement* and *punishment*" (1977:45: italics in original). Both positive and negative reinforcement strengthen behavior, while positive and negative punishment have the effect of weakening or changing behavior. Positive punishment takes the form of a "punisher received," while negative punishment is "reward removed or lost" (Akers, 1977:46).

The first time a man batters a woman is probably the most difficult for him; conflicting norms tell men to be "protectors" of women and also to maintain power and control over them. Battered women told of the contrition, tears of repentance, and swearing never to do such things again following battering (the phase Walker describes as "Kindness and Contrite Loving Behavior," 1979). It seems reasonable to expect that very few men (except possibly sadists) actually enjoy beating women, particularly those with whom they interact frequently, usually within the framework of sexual intimacy. Beating requires an expenditure of time and energy as well. On the other hand, there must be some satisfaction derived from the act or the rewards the act brings or most likely it would not recur (Lemert, 1972:84). The act not only becomes easier with each succeeding occurrence, but rationalizations are organized to resolve cognitive dissonance. If there is no retaliation or termination of a conjugal relationship following battering, the batterer is very likely to continue battering. The longer battering continues, the more frequently the battering occurs and the greater the intensity of the battering.

Social learning theory provides the best explanation of why battering is likely to continue. There are usually no (or insufficient) punishments received and there may be (and from evidence gathered usually are) reinforcements. For example, some men may experience feelings of increased control and power, and the women may try harder to placate them or to remove all sources of irritation and stress, such as keeping the house cleaner, keeping the children quiet in their presence, and so forth—anything the men claimed led to the beating in the first place.

One of the few things about which almost all researchers agree is that batterings escalate in frequency and intensity over time (Gayford, 1975a: 1976; Scott, 1974:436; Nichols, 1975:31). Sometimes the violence culminates in homicide. Accidental or purposeful, the results are the same: death of one or the other spouse (Field and Field, 1973; Eisenbert and Micklow, 1974; Martin, 1976a; Truninger, 1971; Wolfgang, 1967). Fortunately, most of these destructive relationships seem eventually to disintegrate by less terrible methods before they reach this level of intensity. The continuation of violence is addressed in detail in the next section, and this study serves as a test of the secondary battering major hypothesis.

Model III: Secondary Battering

This theoretical model addresses conjugal violence that persists beyond primary battering: Model III offers a tentative explanation for the continuation of destructive relationships. It seeks to provide answers to questions like "Why do they stay?" It is the component of this tripartite perspective which will most easily yield to testing by researchers because almost all the current studies involve drawing samples from populations that have been subjected to extensive and repeated batterings. Whereas testing of Model II requires a reliable random sample of women and men from the general population, Model III seeks to explain why some women seem to be "locked into" battering situations. Since there is an unknown population of battered women who continue to reside with their spouses, a test of the model at the present time must rely on a sample of either volunteers or women who identify themselves as battered women by seeking assistance outside their homes. Most women who go to residential shelters have been battered more than once; thus, they may be considered victims of secondary battering.

The sample for this study and test of the secondary battering model was obtained from such shelters and non-sheltered volunteers, and findings are restricted to Model III. The length of the relationships after primary battering showed the length of time they had experienced secondary battering. The questions this model seeks answers to are: Why do some women remain in and why do some leave conjugal relationships in which they are battered by spouses? Second, what has changed when a woman leaves after the second or third beating or after regular abuse over a period of years?

The three key variables suggested to provide answers to these and similar questions are labeled (A) *Resources,* (B) *Institutional Response,* and—the construct common to all three models—(C) *Traditional Ideology.* The major proposition of Model III is:

> The fewer the resources, the more negative the institutional response; and the more intense the traditional ideology of women who have been battered, the more likely they are to remain in relationships with the batterers and the less likely they are to perform acts that significantly alter the situation in a positive direction.

This was the only hypothesis tested in this study. Each of these three theoretical constructs are variable, measurable, and operationally defined in Appendix A.

The inclusion of some elements of behaviorism such as stimulus-response inherent in learning theory might encourage some critics to accuse this conceptionalization of being reductionist. It is, on the contrary, a sociological viewpoint of a major social problem which recognizes that social institutions as well as individuals store, de-

velop, and transmit cultural values and norms of behavior to succeeding generations. However, there appears to be no complete consensus
on norms and values; they are interpreted ambiguously and are differ-
entially responded to by actors. There are vast differences in behavior
in the general population and among interacting individuals, and the
differences must ultimately be explained by the learning processes
whereby people develop the rules, codes, and sets of belief that guide
most of their behavior. This conceptualization attempts to suggest
why some women remain in violent conjugal relationships and why
others take action in ways to break the cycle of violence. This paradigm suggests:

> If a woman lacks necessary resources, receives negative institutional
> response, and is strongly traditional in her beliefs, she is highly un-
> likely to take any action that will significantly alter her situation in a
> positive direction. In these circumstances, women perceive no option
> for change, and only the most severe trauma will compel them to seek
> relief—either by escape, homicide, or by other means. If the balance
> shifts in a positive direction and the victim perceives options that were
> not available to her before, she may take action favorable to her own
> situation.

People who find themselves in a violent domestic situation cannot,
totally and by themselves, either create or alter the situation in a
vacuum. Much of their response depends on the social and cultural
environment within which they live. If we wish to address alternatives, we should also examine forces that tend to prevent, block, or
obscure alternatives. If it is true (as suggested in an earlier paper—
Pagelow, 1981a) that female victims of domestic violence, far more
than the aggressors, are culturally defined as rule-breakers ("deviants"), then they will be the objects of social pressure to enforce
conformity and will meet resistance when they seek alternatives.
Empirical evidence shows that victims do find resistance or obstruc-
tions to alternatives (Gelles, 1976; Hilberman and Munson, 1978;
Kremen, 1976; Martin, 1976a; Pizzey, 1977; Straus, 1976).

Alternatives have been systematically obstructed, obscured, or
blocked in many ways, including the following: traditional social
agencies remained deaf and unresponsive to the needs of battered

women while taxpayers poured billions of dollars into these agencies
to address community needs. Psychiatrists treated patients' symptoms for years without discovering that some patients were victims of
spouse abuse (Hilberman and Munson, 1978). Medical doctors prescribed tranquilizers (Gayford, 1975a), and medical personnel healed
wounds and sent victims back home without giving the kind of help
that was needed (Waterbury et al., 1976). Police insisted crime in the
home was a "private matter" (Bannon, 1975); clergymen advised
prayer; counselors advised communication; and parents advised
daughters "You made your bed, now you lie in it." Victims are
"locked up" in shelters while the perpetrators of this crime remain
free; "victims' rights are constantly abrogated and defendants' rights
constantly applauded and approved" (Fields, 1978). Only a tiny segment of the world's population has come to recognize that women and
their children for centuries have been coerced, beaten, tortured, and
killed by their male "protectors" (Brownmiller, 1976).

Although at first it may seem to be an oversimplification, ultimately there are two major alternatives for battered women: one is to
stay and attempt changes while remaining in the relationship and the
second is to leave the relationship. A process model (see Figure 2.1)
illustrates some of the complexity of decision-making for victims of
secondary battering. The diagram does not take into account the
constellation of negative and positive resources of victims, both personal and material, or the interlocking consideration of victims after
leaving, such as economic, social, and religious penalties. If there are
dependent children, these considerations are even more serious.

Included in the model's alternative "to stay" is to have the man
leave, but the prospects of this happening are slim unless he decides
to leave voluntarily. In most cases, if the couple has shared a residence, the only way a woman can evict a man is through court process
and the requirements are frequently so overwhelming for the average
woman that it is easier for her to leave, even if there are children. In
the event she has the man evicted, the woman may be in even greater
danger of attack, regardless of restraining orders or orders of protection, which are merely pieces of paper to the dispossessed man. In
nonmarital relationships it may be easier to evict a man, but not
necessarily.[6]

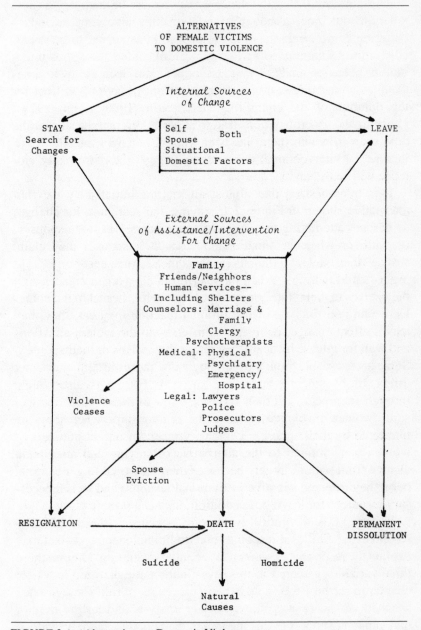

FIGURE 2.1   Alternatives to Domestic Violence

The possibility that "violence ceases" must be included as one potential outcome, although in relationships involving secondary battering being discussed here the probabilities appear to be decidedly slim. As mentioned earlier, almost all studies have shown that violent behavior tends to increase rather than decrease over time. Couples-counseling seems to repress violent behavior—at least for the duration of the counseling (Blackburn, 1980; Lynn, 1977). Learning theory propositions lead to expectations that the shorter the time span in which there has been violent behavior and the more intense the interventional pressures to change, the more likely violence will cease, and vice versa.

It is hypothesized that almost all victims initially try the first alternative shown in Figure 2.1: staying and searching for change, sometimes attempting for years to change themselves, their spouses, or both, or whatever situational factors their spouses may claim "cause" their violent outbursts (such as meals, finances, housekeeping, or child rearing). When those efforts fail, women either resign themselves to their "fate" or attempt to get help external to the home. Depending on the type of institutional reaction they get, they may leave, effect change, or resign themselves to the violent situations and wait for release by death—of either themselves or their spouses. Some try to escape through psychological withdrawal, liquor or other drugs, or by suicide; and some succeed. Escape is also sought through attempts to kill their spouses; a few of these succeed. Also, some women involuntarily leave the relationships when they are murdered by their spouses. Until very recently, untold numbers of women were limited to the alternative of staying and attempting change from within, largely because when they tried to get external help, they received negative institutional response and lacked necessary resources for leaving. In addition, they had no safe place to go.

In sum, this theoretical viewpoint designates the variables—resources, institutional response, and traditional ideology—that may explain the responses of women to secondary battering. Data on these three variables gathered in this investigation are analyzed in a later chapter to see how they help explain the length of time these women spent in violent relationships. Further analysis and testing may or may not lend support to this theoretical perspective, but it provides a new way of examining the issues in this ancient, but newly "discovered," social problem.

Appendix A provides the research design and methods employed in this investigation into battered women's perceptions of their violent relationships and the search for reasons they stayed after primary battering.

Chapter 3

COMMON MYTHS AND STEREOTYPES

This chapter focuses on some popular myths and stereotypes about victims, batterers, and the crime of assault and battery of women who cohabit with the perpetrators. It serves to provide a broader look at the issues that surround the question of why women remain with their batterers and allows for the introduction of qualitative data from the study. The employment of a variety of research techniques provided a rich data base of both "hard" and "soft" data (Bernard, 1974:23) so that they complement each other by filling in the gaps in understanding. The problem for victims, their children, and their abusers is very complicated and will yield to no simple solution. Many professionals and paraprofessionals in community helping agencies complain "why do they stay?" but fail to understand these complexities and that there is no easy answer. It is a fact that many people in positions most likely to come in contact with victims, and the ones who have the resources to be of assistance to them, are also persons most likely to have heard and may subscribe to these beliefs. In effect, these popular ideas may serve to create more difficulties for women who wish to improve or sever their relationships with men who physically abuse them.

Because so little was known about the phenomenon of woman-battering, the study in the spring and summer of 1976 was basically exploratory. At the very onset, and despite the lack of scientific research, the investigator quickly discovered that everyone seems to be an "expert" on the subject. People from all walks of life know some woman or women who are or were victims of spouse assault, and they usually volunteer very firm opinions on the causation and the cure. As a result, the researcher in the field soon becomes acquainted with common myths and stereotypes subscribed to by many in the general population, the helping agencies, and the criminal justice system. Since a substantial number of the persons who advance these myths are the same persons to whom female victims turn for help, it may well be that the stereotypes serve to victimize the victims further if untrue. Therefore, it seems appropriate to address these myths and examine them in light of the data gathered in the pilot study and beyond. These myths and stereotypes are outlined below and then explored in turn, comparing them to the data.

(1) "These are pathological individuals"
   (A) Masochistic women
   (B) Weak women
   (C) Batterer is "sick"
   (D) Recidivists—the women "seek out" the batterers
(2) "But what did she do to provoke him?"
   (A) Justified force: He is a victim of nagging
   (B) Battered women must somehow be at fault
(3) "Why did she stay?"
   (A) Why complain now? (revenge-seeking)
   (B) What did she "get out of" the relationship?
   (C) Trade-off for "meal ticket"
(4) "But they never press charges"
   (A) Frustrations of the criminal justice system
   (B) Weak-willed women do not follow through
(5) "The problem is restricted to the lower classes"

(1) Pathological Individuals

Basic assumptions underlying this idea are that the problem is an individual one rather than social, that it is a rare occurrence, and that one (usually the victim) or both in the dyad are "sick" people ("mentally ill"). Foremost among the diagnoses of pathology is that the victim is masochistic and that she and her attacker receive satisfaction of certain personal needs from her beatings. Also, these women are said to be particularly weak, dependent individuals. Offered as proof for the "sick individuals" claim is the comment that these women frequently work their way out of one battering situation into another. A common assumption is that they choose to be victimized by selecting men who will batter them.

(A) MASOCHISTIC WOMEN

Not only do syndicated advice columnists with extremely wide readership advance the idea that females tend to be masochistic (Landers, 1976a, 1976b), but the constellation of beliefs that view women as "willing sufferers" has been handed down for generations through the Bible and later "explained" by Freud and others. These preconceived notions are accepted as scientific knowledge by many professionals in the mental health field and indirectly serve as a basic set of assumptions many professionals use to evaluate patients and render judgment. Szasz explains how these basic assumptions affect diagnoses as he attacks judgmental aspects of psychiatry:

> The psychiatrist does not stand *apart* from what he observes, but is, in Harry Stack Sullivan's apt words, a "participant observer." This means that he is *committed* to some picture of what he considers reality—and to what he thinks society considers reality—and he observes and judges the patient's behavior in the light of these considerations [1960:116].

The Broverman et al. (1970) study illustrates the "reality" by which some mental health experts judge women's behavior. Their study revealed that practicing clinicians assigned traits to females that were considered pathological for males or adults. That is, traits that were *least* valued for "normal healthy adults" were *highly* valued for "normal healthy females." These traits included items such as dependent, emotional, submissive, passive and illogical.

It should not be surprising if women, psychosocialized to these stereotypes, have difficulty rejecting them for themselves. As one young woman stated:

I knew right along that marriage wasn't going to be any bed of roses, but this was a lot worse than even I expected. Even the marriage vows say "for better or for worse," so I was prepared a little to go through hard times, but this was *really worse!* Anybody who likes getting slugged in the mouth is *sick*—man, that really hurts!

Another woman said, "My psychologist kept hinting that I got some kind of 'kinky kicks' out of being beaten, but that just wasn't true!"

Fifty-one questionnaires, 15 in-depth interviews, and numerous group observations analyzed after the pilot study failed to reveal one adult woman who believed herself in any way a "willing victim." Even though some in this sample had lived relatively isolated lives, they all seemed aware of the stereotype of masochism or neurosis, had compared their own reactions to it; their usual response to such suggestions was anger, resentment, or denial. Only one person, a juvenile, said that at first she mistook beatings at the hands of her lover as being proof of his "love." Describing his attack and subsequent rape when she was 13 years old, this girl said that although she was hurt, she was also flattered by the attention of an older man. When she had the opportunity to move into her lover's home a few months later, she willingly agreed. Once there, she vied for his attention with his legal wife and another young woman who lived with him, until one beating was so severe she had to be taken to a hospital. Although hospitalized for two weeks because of internal injuries, she lied to the doctors about the cause of her wounds because she feared retaliation from her "foster father." A few months later, this girl and the man's wife made their escape with a neighbor's help while the man was away from home. Neither one knew how to drive a car, nor did they have access to money. Separate interviews with both young women revealed identical tales of fear, brutality, and virtual captivity.

(B) WEAK WOMEN

Many persons likely to be contacted by victims for assistance flatly claim that any woman who allows a man to beat her more than once is a particularly weak woman. One Pennsylvania attorney said, "Any man can make a mistake once and let her have it. But if she lets him do it a second time, she has given him her permission and she has nobody but herself to blame." A California attorney willingly expressed his opinion of battered women:

> Perhaps as many as half of the women I see mention some kind of slapping, hitting, or shoving but of these, about ten percent involve repeated or serious battering. . . . These women could get out of the situation if they really wanted to, but they don't want the responsibility of setting out on their own. They just don't have the courage to make the decision until something finally happens to them that makes the marriage intolerable, or else he decides to get rid of her.

The women themselves express opposite opinions. One shelteree was aware of the common perceptions of battered women as "mentally ill" or weak individuals and denied that she or the other refugees fit the stereotype:

> The amazing thing about these women here is the way they have their heads on straight, in spite of all they've been through. These are extremely courageous and strong women here—we all *had* to be strong, or we couldn't have survived what we went through.

A week after the interview, this woman died of a degenerative disease which had gradually rendered her incapable of walking without the aid of crutches. She and her three adolescent daughters (also abused) had escaped her spouse with the assistance of a stepson. In their fear and rush for safety, the four females left their home with nothing but the clothes they wore.

During one of several interviews this shelteree, Doris,[1] stated that the first time her husband became violent was two years after their marriage. It was the second marriage for both Doris and her husband; she was a widow with a year-old baby and he was a divorced father of three. Doris subsequently raised her own son, the stepchildren, and the three daughters that were products of this union. When the first attack occurred, Doris said she was able to defend herself with a kitchen breadboard. There were only a few minor attempts at violence for the next few years and Doris fought back each time until after the onset of her disease, when the beatings increased in frequency and severity. When the children tried to interfere in their mother's behalf, they also became objects of attack. The major child abuse centered on the youngest child after she became chronically ill. The little girl's older sister wrote:

> When my little sister got sick [diabetes] and kept needing water and needing to use the "necessary" room, he kept hitting her and make her wet her pants even worse. . . . When I first noticed the "conflict" between my parents, I just thought, "They're at it again!," later it was, "There he goes." . . . Before my mom got sick, he tried a few things on her, but he didn't get far. . . . And when my mom got sick, that's when everything went to hell. She can barely hobble around and he knows she can't defend herself. Her hips are really sore and he would drive her around in the car slamming on the brakes—which is agony for her. . . . He was always telling me how my mother was brainwashing me and how she was breaking up the family, but all I could think of was that I want the family broken up (or him broken off) and that if my mother was brainwashing us, she was doing the best job of it I had ever seen. . . . The worst thing about him is that he's so smart. We went to family counseling once and he drove the poor psychiatrist up the wall by sending the conversations around in circles as well as scaring him to death.

The child's mother wrote on the questionnaire: "This man is a walking time bomb. If he does not receive help he will eventually kill himself or someone else. He does not want help—he says."

(C) BATTERER IS "SICK"

The popular stereotype describes not just the woman as pathological; frequently her batterer is included. Sometimes the women agree; Doris was one who felt that her spouse was dangerously mentally ill. Other women insist that their mates are ill by saying, "He can't always help himself. He's an alcoholic and you know that's a sickness." (Also see Straus, 1973:120, for examples.)

Outsiders frequently insist that men who batter women must be mentally ill; they contend that only a deranged man would hit his spouse. For example, during a televised talk show, the host persisted in attempting to draw out an admission from a guest that her spouse was sick. He finally asked pointedly, "What do you think? Wouldn't you say your husband is mentally ill or something like that?" With obvious reservation, the woman reluctantly agreed: "Well, I know the way he acts isn't right and all that, but I can't really say if he's ill or not. Probably he is, but I don't know—I'm not an expert on things like that. That's up to psychiatrists to say." Later the host turned to the same woman and said, "You said before that your husband is an alcoholic. Maybe that's why he beat you." With far more conviction this time, her response was: "Sure he's an alcoholic but I don't think that's why he beat me. It's true he beat me when he was drunk, but there were other times he beat me when he was cold sober, too!"

In group discussions among battered women, the opinions seem to be about evenly divided between accepting and rejecting the sickness label. About half of them maintain that their spouses were perfect gentlemen in public, functioned well in their public social spheres, and never behaved violently outside the home. Many insist they would never be believed if they confided their awful secret to mutual friends because of their husbands' unblemished respectability. One example seemed to confirm these suspicions. Shortly before she died, Doris received a telephone call from a woman friend of many years. This "friend" berated her for the shameful way Doris was treating her poor husband, running away from him, worrying him to death, and so on. The investigator was nearby when the conversation occurred; Doris did not try to defend or explain her actions but later expressed depression and futility. Ganley and Harris (1978:5) report about male batterers: "The men are not always violent. They can also be charming and quite lovable both with their victims as well as with others outside the family."

(D) RECIDIVISTS—THE WOMEN "SEEK OUT" THE BATTERERS

Added as proof of the "sick individual" claim is the idea that these women deliberately seek out men who satisfy their need to be battered because many of them are repeaters. Questionnaire responses indicated that 17 percent (N = 60) reported at least one earlier romantic relationship (husband or boyfriend) in which battering occurred; of the 127 women who had been married before, 33 percent (N = 42) were beaten by a prior husband. During a group discussion, the women themselves pondered the question of why so many of them had more than one relationship with a battering man. They all described the attributes that first attracted them to the men; with few exceptions, these men had initial appeal because they were charming, gentle, considerate, and kind. Many women said they could not recall any display of violence until long after the relationships were established—sometimes after years of cohabitation. In response to a question about why some women seem to go from one battering spouse to another, the consensus of opinion was that women want to be married and that nonviolent men are scarce. One woman in the group volunteered:

Most of us here were brought up to believe that a woman's most important job in life is to be a wife and mother. I can tell you for myself that when I couldn't stick it out any longer with my first husband, I figured my whole life was ruined. And do you know what it's like being a single mother with a couple of kids? I didn't want to be single the rest of my life. . . . I guess we have a hard time finding a gentle man, a man who won't belt a woman, because there are so few of them in this world to begin with.

Another "recidivist" said:

You know, I really thought he was too good to be true—and I was right, as it turned out! Actually, when you get right down to it, what man in his right mind would have anything to do with someone with three teenaged kids? What's available out there to a woman like me? I'll tell you—all that is left is what some other woman couldn't stand.

The women revealed that they not only felt less desirable to other men because they brought into their new relationships the burden of children by other men but that their previous marriages restricted their field of choice for new husbands. There were also expressions of guilt about having dissolved their first marriages, which they had entered believing would last their lifetimes. In the short duration of the pilot study, the descriptive data yielded a dual image of female victims of spousal assault that was borne out as the study progressed. The women appear to fall into two distinct categories. On the one side are women who came from predominantly conservative childhood homes, usually religious, where divorce never or rarely occurred, and where physical punishment was absent or, at the most, very mild. These were either loving homes or very controlled, traditional, paternalistic-authoritarian homes; but in either case, they report a lack of physical violence. These women reacted to violence with shock, did not know how to cope with it from past socialization, and were unable to reveal personal shame to parents and relatives. Because of religiosity, they apparently entered marriage with the sincere goal of marriage for life—for better or for worse.

The other profile is of women who grew up in homes where violence was common, with beatings by one or both parents; homes which seem to have served as springboards from domination by fathers to domination by husbands. These women appear to enter the relationships with some expectations of physical assault and with the belief that they have the endurance or wits to overcome these problems. An example is a young woman named Peggy who told of her father's threats on her life if she refused to marry the man who was courting her. She married him and began a career as a battered wife, has had two children in three years, and is still trying to make her marriage "work." (This woman related that her two-and-a-half-year-old son is already beginning to copy his father's behavior: When he gets angry or frustrated, he punches her and abuses his year-old brother.)

There emerge two different childhood environments of polar opposites, producing women who are either inexperienced or very experienced in household violence. Analysis of these dual images reveals some commonality: Women reared in homes either devoid of overt conflict or full of conflict both may be handicapped by an inability to have developed a realistic perspective on violence. Most important, both types of background reveal parental emphasis on traditional sex-role socialization. These women generally appear to be persons most likely to expect to make extreme personal investments in their relationships with mates. In addition, the first-mentioned conservative category from nonviolent homes appears to include women who, in the event of dissolution of their first marriages, are likely to invest even more in subsequent relationships.

It seems premature to conclude that women seek out men to batter them simply on the basis of repetitive experiences. In fact, it may be well to consider at least the possibility that batterers seek out women who are most likely to stick by them "through thick and thin," regardless of personal pain and suffering. Many interviewed women evidenced firm determination to maintain conjugal relationships; they were ready and/or willing to make great personal investments in sustaining their relationships. It is probable that batterers (or potential batterers) can also perceive these qualities in the women.

On the other side of the coin, it may be that some male spouses are likely to be violent with any women with whom they cohabit. Data from questionnaire item II-2 (see Appendix B) regarding their spouses' earlier marriages show that 44 percent (N = 153) of the men had been married before at least once (nine percent of these had more than one prior marriage). According to the survey respondents, 57 percent (N = 86) of their spouses were known to be violent toward another wife. Eighty-six percent of these earlier marriages were terminated by divorce. There is further evidence that batterers are likely to be violent with any women with whom they establish intimate relationships. Ganley and Harris state:

> The men we have interviewed or seen in treatment have been violent in more than one relationship. . . . It is our assumption that battering men will continue to be violent even if they change partners, unless a major change occurs within the individual men. It is not a matter of his finding the right partner who will solve his problem of assaulting others. Our experience has led us to believe that violence is not a function of the intimate relationship but a function of how he expresses and resolves stress [1978:6].

The Ganley and Harris sample of batterers seeking rehabilitation from violent behavior revealed that 86 percent of their previous long-term relationships had included violence against other wives or lovers (1978:6).

(2) "But What Did She Do To Provoke Him?"

The assumptions underlying this oft-repeated question stem from experience with the patriarchal foundations of the nuclear family in the United States. The hierarchical structure of the patriarchal family established men (whether they are husbands, fathers, brothers, or lovers) as heads of household, with women and children in subservient positions. The idea that domination and control of subordinates in the home properly belongs to men is compatible with the notion of women as property requiring varying degrees of control, much like children, domesticated animals, and pets. Only in the last few years has the traditional wedding oath of "love, honor, and obey" been altered (in some ceremonies but not all) to delete the word "obey" from the brides' vow to confirm with the grooms' traditional vow of "love, honor, and cherish."[2]

Nevertheless, Dobash and Dobash refer to such changes, when they occur, as a "superficial, cosmetic patch" (1976:4). They remind us that many ceremonies are still being performed in which the bride swears obedience to her husband, the significance of which cannot be overlooked. If the wife disobeys her husband, what are his rights and duties? If a child disobeys parental authority or even challenges it, the socially approved response is the use of force, which may include physical force when necessary. It requires no leap of the imagination to see that if the wife and children are to obey the husband and father—if they are both subservient to him—then he is "justified" when he uses physical force for control. The idea prevails that women should be dominated, and if they are recalcitrant, authority must be maintained even if it requires a degree of physical force. The question in the minds of many is not *if* the use of force is justified, but rather centers on the question of *how much* is justified. There is a thin line between necessary and excessive measures to control which slides up and down the continuum, depending on the individuals who judge. The tendency then becomes one of looking for what offense the woman committed and measuring the "punishment" against it to see if it was merely justified or if perhaps it was excessive.

(A) JUSTIFIED FORCE: HE IS THE VICTIM OF NAGGING

There is an interest in looking for the "reasons" a woman was beaten that is similar to asking why a woman was raped, unlike in other crimes—for example, few people ask why a person was robbed (Hafer, 1976). It is true that in the intimacy and isolation of the home, many persons are in forced interaction that creates friction. Undoubt-edly, many women are unreasonable, infuriating, or castrating; but, by the same token it is safe to assume that many men are equally offensive. How can the predominance of wife-battering compared with the almost undocumented husband-battering be explained? Fe-males are involved in far fewer crimes of violence than men (and when they are, they are more likely to play the assistant role); are much less often assaulters of men than men are of women; are more frequently murdered by husbands and lovers; and when they are the murderers they are much more often involved in victim-precipitated homicide than men (Bowker, 1978; California State Department of Justice, 1975; Dobash and Dobash, 1978; Martin, 1976a; Rasko, 1976; Ward et al., 1969; Wolfgang, 1967).

(B) BATTERED WOMEN MUST SOMEHOW BE AT FAULT

Even if there is no evidence that the victims are guilty of nagging, there seems to be a propensity to search for "reasons" women cause men to be violent (Pogrebin, 1974). Some writers have shown that "the cause is sought in the battered woman herself" (Kremen, 1976). Metzger addresses the question, "What Did You Do to Provoke Him?" (1976), and provides evidence showing that organized reli-gions, social service agencies, and many counseling centers concen-trate on preserving the home, bending every effort to maintain the bonds of matrimony by advocating corrective measures instituted by the women. Since it is women who make contact with these institu-tions, it is assumed that the women, not the men, are the ones who need help. When the men are called to participate in counseling they either refuse, denying there is a problem, or, if they do participate, they continually tend to minimize their own contribution or violent behavior (Ganley and Harris, 1978:5). Other writers infer that batter-ing occurs not only because females nag their spouses but because they have better verbal skills than males and their mates resort to violence to overcome this disadvantage. Gayford concludes an article on battered women with a statement that includes both the assump-tion about recidivism discussed above and the assumption of female provocation:

Though they flinch from violence like other people they have the ability to seek violent men or by their behaviour to provoke attack from the opposite sex [1975b:197].

Some sociologists are more specific about why battered women may be at fault because of their assumed superior verbal abilities in provoking attacks. Straus et al. write:

Victims often precipitate their fate through the use of verbal aggression. Gelles concluded that wives often are acutely aware of their husbands' points of vulnerability and also tend to possess superior verbal skills compared to their husbands. This combination of factors can lead to the physical victimization of the wife [1976:23].

Family sociologist Goode states:

In the immediate situation of conflict, the emotions aroused are often high enough, even among those who are pacifically inclined, to call for a strong resolution. The conflict . . . in the war of words is so sharp, the feeling of betrayal and loss so great, that redress must be physical and destructive. This impulse is the stronger because the person who wins the war of words—*often the woman* since she is perhaps ordinarily more facile verbally—is not necessarily the person with the greatest sense of outrage or even with the better case to present. The *person who is least fair may be most competent in verbal attacks* [Goode, 1971:632, italics added].

Interviewed women did not agree with these ideas; they stated repeatedly that there was no apparent reason for the attacks, that there was no pattern, nor did all batterings have identifiable precipitating factors. A number of women reported having been asleep when some attacks began by spouses just arriving home. During a televised interview in which the investigator participated, a woman named Beth explained to the host that provocation was unnecessary for attacks to begin:

It didn't matter what I did. When he wanted to hit me, he'd do it for *no* reason or *any* reason at all! If I talked, I was hit, if I didn't talk, I was hit. It could start over *anything*—you name it. Maybe he didn't like the way I fried his eggs, or the way I made a bed; say the sheets weren't tucked in right. It didn't matter, he'd start yelling at me, and between punches he'd ask me questions. If I tried to answer he'd hit me, and if I didn't understand his question and couldn't think of what he wanted me to say, he'd hit me again. It was a case of damned if you do and damned if you don't; you can't win. I used to think maybe it was something about me that was wrong; maybe I was doing things to make him mad like that. But after 16 years I finally came to the conclusion that it wasn't me—that the problem was him!

Another woman on the same televised program responded to the host's query, "What did you do?" with statements that attacks could start as soon as her military officer spouse came home, or after a verbal argument, or as soon as the door was shut on departing guests. She said:

There was no "pattern"; there didn't have to be a reason. He could be as nice as pie at a party, smiling and all, and as soon as the last guest left the house he might lay in to me for something I said or did.

In this study, 51 percent of the questionnaire respondents gave a negative answer to the item, "Did you say or do anything to trigger the attacks?" The ones who denied provocation frequently added comments such as "I always tried to calm him down when I saw what was happening to him," or "He thought so, although I was just stating the facts." The others who felt they did provoke attacks wrote such

TABLE 3.1   Survey Women's Responses to Prevent Spousal Abuse

Response Category	Percent	N
Did not know was coming	8.0	22
Tried talking him out of it	24.3	67
No use—too scared	5.1	14
Stood up for own ideas	6.5	18
Tried to pacify him	29.0	80
Tried to prevent—begged him to stop	10.9	30
Got out of his way	16.3	45
Total	100.0*	276

*In this and all following tables, percentages may not add to 100 because of rounding errors.

comments as "I wouldn't agree with him," "I talked back," or "I saw it coming but did nothing to stop him."

Table 3.1 shows the responses to questionnaire item III-13 on actions taken or not taken to prevent the attack(s). Of the 321 women responding to the first part of this item (no or yes), 78 percent (N = 251) said they tried to prevent the attacks; 22 percent (N = 70) said they did not. The table combines categories from the open-ended explanations following both the yes and no responses.

One third of the survey respondents said they did not even try to defend themselves once an attack began, but of those who said they attempted self-defense, many added a statement similar to the following: "I tried to once and he really flipped out and beat me worse than ever. He told me if I ever tried that again he'd kill me. I never tried again. I believe he would."

The open-ended responses to item III-12 pertaining to retaliatory or defensive acts after an attack began are listed in Table 3.2. It should be noted that there is a similarity between responses to preventive measures before an assault occurred, as shown in Table 3.1, and after an attack began, as shown in Table 3.2.

Many group discussions, even among social scientists, suggest that victims feel they "deserved" to be beaten because many of the women initially blame themselves for the deterioration of relationships into violence and because some believe they provoked attacks by things they said (or did not say). These assumptions are not supported by this survey sample. The difference is probably because many people confuse the concepts of provocation and justification. Scale item III-14 asked directly if respondents felt they deserved the beating(s); 99.4 percent answered "no" and many added strong state-

TABLE 3.2   Survey Women's Responses to Physical Attacks

Response Category	Percent	N
Fought back	25.5	68
Tried (at least once) but it got worse	16.5	44
Self-defense only	29.2	78
Scared of being killed	22.8	61
Used avoidance techniques	6.0	16
Total	100.0	267

ments to give further emphasis to deny any justification for this kind of violent behavior. (Two women answered "Yes, sometimes.") In all the many direct encounters in this country and abroad with women who had been battered, not one ever said to the investigator that she believed she deserved any of the physical abuse she experienced.

(3) "Why Did She Stay?"

When this question is introduced, it frequently is with a hint of amusement, seemingly denying the realities of pain and terror described by many victims. Nonprofessionals frequently ask, "If she was *really* abused, why did she stay?" But psychologists and sociologists ask the latter half of the question and find different answers, depending on their focus. Gelles's article, "Abused Wives: Why Do They Stay?" (1976), finds a complex relationship of factors that are discussed fully in the following chapter. Straus (1976) expands slightly on his earlier violent culture theory to include sexism as a component of the culture that keeps women tied to their abusers. These two sociologists look for answers in the social structure of the family and social institutions, whereas many psychologists, social psychologists, and others in these disciplines appear to concentrate on dependency, negative self-image, hostility, locus of control, attribution, and the like (Frieze, 1978; Star, 1979; Walker, 1979).

(A) WHY COMPLAIN NOW?

Sometimes suggestions are made that there may be underlying reasons other than the battering for the women's complaints—for example, revenge. Implications are that prior to complaints of battering some needs were fulfilled which are no longer being met. For example, a judge is likely to discount a woman's complaints about battering if she continued to live with the man a number of years after violence began; a police officer is likely to suspect that a woman's complaint is stimulated by jealousy over a rival for her spouse's affections. Attention then focuses not on their complaints, but rather on their reasons for complaining now, which probably is an important area for investigation but digresses from the major issues.

(B) WHAT DID SHE "GET OUT OF" THE RELATIONSHIP?

Seldom do the assumptions underlying the question "Why do they stay?" become as obvious as when one psychoanalyst said, "What I wonder is, *what* do these women get out of the relationships?" Conversely, many of the women encountered in field research who are still living in a battering relationship seem to ask the question, "*How* do I get out of the relationship?" Many persons in the "helping" professions reflect the same assumptions voiced by this psychoanalyst (who is a marriage and family counselor), but they are not always as obvious. Spousal violence almost always occurs in privacy; when long-standing relationships are publicly revealed as unhappy, outsiders tend to focus on the benefits of continuity. The longer the relationship lasted, the more likely social agents are to believe that the violence served some purpose in the couple's life.

Almost all social institutions, agents, and agencies traditionally have been most likely to endeavor actively to reconcile couples, stress "talking things over," and "patch things up." Symbolic of the pressures to preserve the family structure is the inscription over the doors of the New York Family Court: "The Sanctity of the Home and the Integrity of the Family," which is the focus of Kremen's paper (1976:4). No agencies actively encourage a wife and mother to dissolve a relationship with a man, but many of them seek to keep her in her situation, even if he batters her. Popular assumptions are that intact marriages represent stability, thus "success," and dissolution represents failure and breakdown in the family system (Crosby, 1980).

Until the last few years, when the media and scientific educational campaign occurred, the most favorable response victims could usually expect was neutrality and courtesy from social agents. But frequently, professional courtesy merely masked underlying contempt. For example, a medical doctor interviewed in 1976 in his plush office located in an affluent area described himself as neutral, and then stated in a semiamused manner:

Many of my middle class patients who come to me with suspicious wounds make up some cock-and-bull story of how they got hurt. But yes, I've seen women who come in for treatment of injuries they claimed were given to them by their husbands. A lot of them are repeaters; they come back time and again. I ask them why they put up with it, and they can't give any good answers. It may be a matter of money, maybe they figure they'd lose out by leaving. I don't understand it—they just don't make sense. There's nothing you can do for them.

An obstetrician/gynecologist whose office is located in a working-class area claimed that women come to him for his specializations and during examination he observes suspicious bruises and lacerations. He estimated that half the battered women he sees are pregnant. He also expressed puzzlement over why they "put up with" this treatment:

I guess some women will put up with a lot of hell just to get a little loving . . . it sounds like "you only beat the one you love." . . . They start out loving a man and they'll put up with a lot until they finally lose respect for him. When that's gone, then they leave.

This doctor reported that he treats his patients' wounds and prescribes "relaxants" for the victims. Prescribing tranquilizers for victims appears to be a common practice of physicians and psychiatrists, judging from the fact that the majority of women arriving at shelters bring prescribed drugs with them. Psychologists Hilberman and Munson (1978) and Walker (1978) claim that being tranquilized is the worst possible condition for any woman living with a violent spouse. Their reasoning is that women living with violent men must be alert and sensitive to changes in moods or other signs that may help them avoid or deter the escalation of violence. The phenomenon of medically tranquilizing battered women is not restricted to the United States; van Crevel (1978) estimates that over 90 percent of victims arriving at the Amsterdam shelter bring along prescription tranquilizers.

Even when medical service providers do not give evidence of contempt for victims, they still are not likely to show any real concern. An emergency room head nurse who admitted she had seen many women who probably had been battered by spouses told interviewers Waterbury et al.:

We don't try to question them—it's their own business. It's not like a battered child that you have to report to the police, or like an animal bite report [1976:67].

The Waterbury et al. research team was comprised of three nurses who were shocked at the apparent lack of concern or even disdain for victims they encountered among medical professionals.

(C) TRADE-OFF FOR A "MEAL TICKET"

The first community agents to make contact with battered women frequently are the police. One veteran officer of many years' service expressed disgust with the women he encounters in domestic disturbance calls, claiming "they're all alike." Urged by the interviewer to describe the "typical" woman he sees on these calls, he said:

Well, we go in there, and there's this old broad who's in her 40's, who's yelling and screaming and three or four kids hollering, too. She's usually a gal that's never worked a day in her life. . . . The kids look OK, except they're all upset and things are about average clean except sometimes the house is torn up from the fight. But she's the kind of . . . that couldn't get out there and earn her own living if her life depended on it! That's why she doesn't want him arrested, just wants us to make him stop hitting her, 'cause she knows she needs him for a meal ticket.

Perhaps the most obvious of negative assumptions underlying agents' response to victims is the casual unconcern revealed in an interview with a police department officer reported by Waterbury et al.:

As a liaison officer who is available to the community, [he] teaches a class on self defense for rape victims. He describes battered women as a "victimless" crime like rape and prostitution. He feels the predominant attitude is that women are used to that type of life style. "The husband 'thumps' them once a week. It's a way of life. They must like it or they wouldn't stay" [1976:77].

These myths and stereotypes are neither rare not exaggerated, as the researcher in the field quickly discovers. Battered women obviously encounter many of the same attitudes when their "private crime" becomes public or when they seek assistance outside the home. Actually, most of the interviewed women revealed that they were well aware of popular ideas about them and their relationships. When they were asked directly, "Why did you stay?" they usually stated that they felt they had few or undesirable or no alternatives. Their reasons for staying included sympathy or need for their spouses, fear, no safe place to go, or as follows:

> I feel my husband is a sick man. I loved him and felt I could help him. At one time I really believed he would never hit me again. Then I was afraid he would hurt someone else if I left.

> Loneliness and I thought my child should have a father.

> I was afraid he would kill me if I left. Also I had no place to go. My husband is extremely anxious to find me and will go to any extreme to do so. I'm going to have to be very careful.

> Fear, mostly, of him and his threats. Doubt as to being able to care for my children as my health was very poor at that time, physically and mentally. Surgery was required, which he refused to let me have and my health became progressively worse. After four hearings and finally a trial, a dissolution or divorce, as it was then called, was finally granted. My private physician wrote to the judge, which had a great influence on the case and finally ended it.

> I did not know where to go or who to turn to. I was too afraid to tell him I was leaving him. I tried once. I'm afraid he'll find me now. But it would be a lot worse for me and my kids if I went back.

> For three years I've been trying to get away but there was nowhere to go—until now.

TABLE 3.3   Survey Women's Prior Attempts to Leave Batterers

Response Category	Percent	N
Once	24.6	59
Two-three times	33.7	81
Four-six times	25.4	61
Seven-ten times	7.1	17
Over ten; many times	9.2	22
Total	100.0	240

Mostly because of stupidity, I guess. I have no money, no car—but I can't drive anyway—and no friends left. My parents kicked me out before. They sure as hell don't want me now. What chance is there for me, with two kids under three? I ran away once to . . . and he found me, came after me and took me back. I could never get far enough away from him.

The last quotation came from a young woman who had received admittance to a shelter, but at the end of the allotted 30-day stay she had not been able to find a job, a place to live, or child care for her two small sons. She did not feel that there was any way she could live independently of her husband, so she returned home. The interview occurred during one of her return visits to a shelter discussion group on an evening when her spouse was out of town.

From the point of view of battered women, options may be few or nonexistent, and without the assistance of others to give social support and to introduce alternatives, they may well be locked into their situations. Almost 80 percent of the survey sample indicated they had made at least one earlier attempt to leave their spouses—attempts that failed—for one reason or another. As shown in Table 3.3, 240 women told of the number of previous attempts they had made.

Only 21 percent reported they stayed separated from their batterers for over six months and a mere 7 percent stayed away more than a year. It might appear that these separations were more symbolic than actual attempts to sever the relationships, yet a considerable number of these women report they established a new home during their time away, as shown in Table 3.4. The table shows responses to questionnaire item I-8(c), which asks: "Where did you go?"

TABLE 3.4   Where Survey Women Went When They Left Batterers

Response Category	Percent	N
Parents/relatives	40.9	103
Established own home	22.6	57
Stayed at motel, in car, or wandering	24.6	62
Went to shelter for battered women	11.9	30
Total	100.0	252

TABLE 3.5   Why Survey Women Returned Home

Response Category	Percent	N
Spouse found her/threatened more violence	11.7	26
He repented/believed he would change	72.5	161
No cash/nowhere to go	7.2	16
No resources to live independently	5.9	13
Found was pregnant	2.7	6
Total	100.0	222

Perhaps most informative of all were the responses to the following item, I-8(d): "Why did you return?" The categorized responses in Table 3.5 indicate that the majority were persuaded to reconcile because they believed their spouses' repentance and promises to reform.

While the major influence to return appears to be faith that the violence would cease, there is no way to determine how much influence lack of other alternatives had on the decisions to reconcile. Seventy-one women indicated they did not willingly choose to return.

Distance from social, psychological, and/or economic support from close family members may be expected to contribute to perceptions of lack of alternatives, but geographic distance alone does not necessarily explain the sense of isolation expressed so frequently. Less than half the survey respondents resided within 20 miles of their nearest relatives and 44 percent lived more than 100 miles from relatives. Many women explained during interviews that even though their families were aware of the violence, they refused to "get involved." Others said that their families were unable to offer more than sympathy. Less than half (40 percent) of the survey respondents said they had relatives able to give them (and their children, if they had any) a place to stay, but 60 percent indicated they believed their relatives would be unwilling to give them (and their children) a place to stay.

Survey respondents numbering 261 said they turned to relatives or close friends for help, about evenly divided between friends or relatives. Some of them received advice which fell into the categories shown in Table 3.6; almost 60 percent were told they should leave their spouses. When the women were asked if they were offered any

TABLE 3.6   Advice Given to Survey Women by Relatives and Friends

Response Category	Percent	N
Leave him	59.5	144
Stay with him	21.9	53
Call police	5.0	12
Seek marriage counseling	4.1	10
Did not believe	2.9	7
Gave no advice	6.6	16
Total	100.0	242

help, their responses indicate that slightly over half (58 percent) received some form of assistance, 13 percent received advice only, and 29 percent report that no help was either given or offered.

Discussion groups frequently centered on the topic of assistance from family, friends, and neighbors. Almost all the women had sought help from outsiders at least once, but they generally concluded that assistance either was not offered, was limited, or was short-lived. This was especially true of friends or neighbors who soon recognized that sheltering or in other ways befriending women with violent spouses could easily endanger them and their families, whereupon they withdrew their involvement.

(4) "But They Never Press Charges"

This statement is made most frequently by law enforcement officers and persons in the judicial system and repeated by sympathetic others. It is introduced as a disclaimer to accusations by victims and some service providers that the police do not adequately protect women physically abused by spouses. "But they never press charges" is usually preceded by reference to the high price police officers pay for their response to "domestic disturbance" calls, a fact that is beyond question. Statistics reveal that the majority of calls for police assistance are in the domestic disturbance category and that many officers are killed and injured each year while answering these calls (Goode, 1969; Martin, 1976a). In 1974, 22 percent and in 1975, 16 percent of all police officers killed were responding to "disturbance calls (family quarrels, man with gun, etc.)." In 1974, 27.5 percent of all assaults on law enforcement officers occurred in this category of calls, higher than any other type of activity (FBI Uniform Crime Reports, 1974, 1975).

(A) FRUSTRATIONS OF THE CRIMINAL JUSTICE SYSTEM

The investigator has been a panelist or been in the audience at 14 public meetings that focused on domestic violence or woman-battering since 1976 (for example, meetings at Cypress College, 1976; Stanford University, 1977; California State Polytechnic University, Pomona, 1978; and an Orange County seminar sponsored by the League of Women Voters, 1979). Whenever one of the panelists was a member of a law enforcement agency, inevitably a statement was made to the effect that police officers are frustrated in their efforts to keep the peace because of the victims more than the offenders. These officers repeatedly insist that female victims expect assistance they are not prepared to or cannot give: to protect the women without making an arrest or to arrest without having witnessed a crime. Yet the traditional approach to "noncrime" calls of domestic disturbance has been an official policy of "adjustment without arrest" (Parnas, 1967). Parnas investigated police response to these calls because

> the social context of the domestic disturbance and the policy of nonarrest, with the resulting use of discretionary methods of adjustment by the patrolman, provide a look at the police officer's role in giving assistance to an alleged offender as well as to the complainant [1967:915].

Parnas's extensive research of the Chicago Police Department was one of the first of several studies that effected gradual change in police training methods and establishment of some family crisis intervention units (1967; see also Bard, 1969, 1970 and Bard and Zacker, 1971, 1974, 1976). Despite recent reeducation and sensitization of administrative personnel to the dangers and inconsistencies inherent in some statutes and official policies, changes are slow to filter down to many officers who must answer these calls. Added to their cognition of the dangerousness of the situation is an admixture of the officers' own perceptions of women's "proper" position in relationship to spouses, reluctance to interfere in "family squabbles," and distaste for what they perceive as social work rather than law enforcement. Responding officers frequently see themselves as victims: entering into extreme personal danger in situations where their actions and decisions are based on sometimes ambiguous codes, and where their sense of professionalism is reduced. In addition, officers know by experience and reputation that women who claim they were battered are highly unlikely to press charges.

Commander James Bannon (1975), a veteran of the Detroit Police Department, points out the effect of compatibility of perceptions of male-female roles of the policeman and the male spouse offender, the likelihood of officers' traditional veneration of the sanctity of the home, and the paradox of sending persons to "arbitrate" who are themselves heavily socialized to masculine role images and the use of coercive physical force.

> This paradox suggests to me that traditionally trained and socialized policemen are the worst possible choice to attempt to intervene in domestic violence. . . . In my view the police attitude, which seems to say that what happens between man and wife in their own home is beyond the authority or ability of the police to control, is a "cop out." The real reason that police avoid domestic violence situations to the greatest extent possible is because we do not know how to cope with them. And besides we share [society's] view that domestic violence is an individual problem and not a public issue [1975:3].

The involvement of law enforcement seems to hinge on two factors: whether or not to make an arrest initially and whether or not the victim will make a dependable witness for subsequent prosecution. Officers have discretionary powers on whether to arrest or not, yet sometimes their decisions are based not so much on if a crime actually occurred as on whether they believe the case will ever reach court (Bates, 1980:30-32; Wellins, 1980).

(B) WEAK-WILLED WOMEN DO NOT FOLLOW THROUGH

During a televised interview, a Los Angeles police officer seemed to provide documentation for Bannon's complaints about police attitudes and response when he made the following statements about arresting abusive husbands:

> It depends on what the situation is when the officer arrives. It's the policy to protect life, of course. What our problem is that so often there is a wife who really does not want to prosecute. She wants the husband to be told not to do this again and the matter to be dropped at that point. . . . The officer is in the middle of a family matter, and of course he has to tread water as he makes the arrest or decides whether to arrest. It's a difficult decision to make; when the policeman arrives he is actually in social work at that time. He's trying to satisfy both parties.

On the other hand, a California attorney who specializes in family law stated: "A man has no right to beat up his own wife any more than he has a right to beat up the wife of a neighbor." She said that in California, wife-battering can be either a misdemeanor or a felony, depending on severity of injuries, presence of weapons, and so on. The officer must witness the crime if it is a misdemeanor, but the victim can make a citizen's arrest. The attorney warned against this procedure because of dangers of retaliatory suit, particularly if the assault occurred without witnesses. She also mentioned California Penal Code 142, which states that if an officer refused to arrest when a crime has been committed, that officer can be fined or imprisoned.

Even if an arrest is made, there is no assurance that the case will be prosecuted. A Los Angeles Superior Court judge described the unwillingness of prosecutors to process anything but the most "airtight" cases with reliable witnesses. Recalling his early law career in the district attorney's office, the judge described an office hearing of a wife beating complaint:

> I could see that the technique was to *really* put the pressure on the woman to make sure this was something she really wants to do. . . . To make sure that this is a case, that when we get to court, this woman's not going to change her mind like most of the others and back down. So he "put the screws" to her, she buckled under and decided no, it's better I shouldn't do it, and she didn't. Four months later that woman was a victim of a murder, and her husband was the murderer. Now that

got to me. . . . These women *have* to be willing, when they start the ball rolling, to keep pushing it with the rest of us, because if they stop, nobody else wants to push the ball, either.

The judge said that he did not know of any man in California who had ever received the maximum felony wife-beating sentence of 10 years in state prison. He added that there is no additional punishment for repeaters. As for protection for victims while the assailant is free on bail awaiting trial, the judge admitted there is very little the system can do for her:

It's a fact of life that if somebody says, "I'm going to kill you," you've got to be on your guard because the law can't do anything about it until he takes an overt step to try to accomplish it. Mere threats don't put people in jail. [There's nothing that can be done] until he takes that first step that goes beyond planning.

Yet the issue of protection and safety of the victim is seldom mentioned when the statement "But they never press charges" is introduced. Victims' fears of retaliation for prosecution is a significant problem when the perpetrator of a crime resides with his victim, a fact that was well documented at the June 1979 Washington, D.C. American Bar Association Hearings on Victim/Witness Intimidation (Hampton, 1979). Yet "fear of reprisal" is a reason commonly mentioned by victims of any crime for not reporting those crimes to police (Sourcebook, 1977:366-367). (Other reasons for nonreporting include: "nothing could be done," "victimization not important enough," "police wouldn't want to be bothered," and "it was a private matter.") These fears are compounded for spouse victims and they are frequently played upon by police or prosecutors, a fact seldom mentioned by people in the criminal justice system. The director of a shelter for battered women explained what happens:

I have repeatedly taken women who want to press charges down to the police station. When they walk in there they are determined to get justice for themselves, at last. They've made up their minds to go through it. But damn it! Every single one of them has been talked out of it by the time these people get through with them. They'll . . . play on their fears of the guy, remind them that he'll only be locked up for a couple hours at the most and then back out on the streets on bail, looking for them! They're reminded that the man knows where her relatives and friends live; maybe he'll go there looking for her and make all kinds of trouble. And if he beat her before, just think of what he'll do this time when he catches her. Maybe this time he'll kill her! One officer's favorite phrase is, "My best advice to you, lady, is to run and hide."

The director finished by reluctantly admitting that most of what the women are told is true; they recognize this and change their minds about prosecuting. She concluded: "But what good is the law if it can't protect half the citizens?"

Most states have some laws intended to protect victims and/or witnesses, such as orders of protection or restraining orders. But there are frequently problems in obtaining and enforcing these orders, and most women have little confidence in their efficacy. An experienced divorce attorney stated:

The only men who are actually restrained by these are the ones who have fear or awe of the legal process in the first place. Most of them see it as nothing more than a piece of paper and its protective value is just as strong as that—a piece of paper. If a man is determined to get to her, he will—if he can find her.

The women themselves largely expressed feelings ranging from dissatisfaction with police attitudes to hostility and disgust for the entire criminal justice system. Some representative comments are listed below.

They wouldn't come.

They said to cool down, to talk things over.

They didn't witness a crime, there's nothing they can do.

One said: "Shut up lady or I'll run *you* in."

They wouldn't let me sign anything.

I asked them what I should do and they said to come in on Monday morning.

I'm standing there bleeding; I didn't know what to do and they didn't tell me.

They wouldn't take a report.

More than half the survey sample (N = 200) reported that the police responded on at least one occasion of battering, and 56 percent of these women (N = 112) say they asked to have their spouse arrested. Instrument item IV-3(2) responses are categorized in Table 3.7, showing the responses of 86 women who answered the open-ended question, "What happened?" As may be noted, of the women who said they asked officers to arrest their assaulters, the majority was refused. About one-fourth of the batterers were arrested and released very quickly (usually on their own recognizance or by posting bond), and only 15 percent of the victims indicated that their spouses were subsequently tried in court. Twenty-two women replied to item IV-3(b) asking about disposition of the case after arrest; their responses are shown in Table 3.8. It is difficult to realize that, out of 350 survey respondents beaten by their spouses, not one claimed that her spouse was arrested, tried, found guilty, and sentenced to jail on a charge of assault and battery. But that is what these data show.

TABLE 3.7   Police Response to Survey Women's Request
             to Have Spouse Arrested

Response Category	Percent	N
Police refused to make arrest	60.5	52
Arrested and released shortly afterward	24.4	21
Arrested and brought to trial	15.1	13
Total	100.0	86

TABLE 3.8   Disposition of Arrests of Survey Women's Spouses

Response Category	Percent	N
Case still pending	50.0	11
Case dismissed	22.7	5
Tried on other charges	9.1	2
Received probation	9.1	2
Fined/suspended sentence	9.1	2
Total	100.0	22

While these data are provocative, their value is somewhat limited unless they are supplemented by qualitative data obtained by other techniques. For example, there was the situation explained by Doris, a respondent mentioned earlier, who could be one of the women police complained about because she dropped charges against her spouse. Doris had no trouble getting the police to arrest her writer-husband because when they arrived at her residence in an exclusive neighborhood, her husband became abusive toward the officers. There was a struggle to restrain him and he was arrested on charges of resisting arrest; Doris signed a complaint and moved out of the family home with her three daughters. Within two weeks, her husband "kidnapped" the girls on their way home from school and then telephoned Doris that if she ever wanted to see her daughters again, she would have to come home. She did and the charges were dropped; the police noted her action as a "reconciliation." Officers were called on two later occasions, but they were not interested in her signing a complaint and her attorney advised against it.

During interviews and group discussions, battered women were asked why they did not press charges against their spouses. Their responses revealed three fundamental reasons: (1) They are ignorant of their civil rights; they were seldom informed and almost never encouraged to demand them. (2) They are systematically persuaded not to demand equal justice under the law. For example, although both husband and wife have title to their home, police are more inclined to encourage a wife to take the children and go elsewhere than they are to attempt to get a husband to leave. (3) They have little or no protection under the law against retaliation, except for recently established shelters they may be able to utilize for usually no more than 30 days.

(5) "The Problem Is Restricted To The Lower Classes"

In the social sciences, most of the emphasis of those working in the areas of social problems, disorganization, or deviance has been turned toward the economically disadvantaged and prisoners and other confined populations (Liazos, 1975). The subject of battered women is nothing new to the police, welfare workers, and other social agents to whom women in the lower socioeconomic classes most frequently turn. The phenomenon has been credited to the lower classes both in popular myth and by some writers (see for example Field and Field, 1973; Goode, 1969, 1971) and by some researchers who have restricted their samples to only the lower class (Scheirell and Rinder, 1973). Although the accusing finger is still pointed at "those people," a gradual awareness has developed that there is no such class barrier. England publicly recognized the problem of woman-battering a few years ago, and Pizzey declared that money and privilege do not distinguish the nonviolent man from the woman-beater:

> Wife-beating has gone on for hundreds of years. . . . For ages wife-beating was thought to be a working-class activity, for the middle- and upper-class women never let on. As far as I can see the reason why "battered wives" are getting a hearing is that for the first time a middle-class woman has said, "It's happened to me." That makes it respectable and all the more shocking [1977:46].

It is possible that the American public would have remained only vaguely aware of the "skeleton in the closet" (Martin, 1976a: 15-17) and continued to ignore this distasteful topic as long as it was confined to the lower strata of society. However, the study conducted by a group of women in affluent Montgomery County, Maryland, revealed that a high percentage of these women reported frequent and serious physical abuse (Martin, 1976a). Washtenaw County in Michigan, described as the thirty-first richest in the country, has a high level of reported violence against women (Fojtik, 1976). Martin (1976a:19) reports that Bard conducted two separate studies in a ghetto community with a 98 percent nonwhite population and a white, upper-middle-class community, and came up with approximately the same level of reported wife-abuse cases. Perhaps the realization that this problem crosses class lines was the catalyst necessary to give it the "respectability" needed to become a serious social concern.

Although O'Brien (1971) included no member of the lower class in his sample for his study on intrafamily violence, other writers have come to the conclusion that woman-battering crosses age, ethnic, racial, and socioeconomic group lines. Steinmetz and Straus (1974:7-8) attack several myths associated with intrafamily violence, one of which is that it is primarily a working-class phenomenon. Metzger (1976) concurs, and Straus reports the story of a woman severely beaten by a man she lived with for 12 years—Greek shipping magnate Aristotle Onassis (1976:546). Truninger suggests: "In fact, the middle class is more oriented toward beating and slapping than the poor" (1971:259). Flynn et al. (1975:30) also report finding no identifiable class barriers in spousal violence. The Stark and McEvoy (1970) study of the approval of violence among middle-class couples and the Parcell and Kanin (1976) sudy of sexual aggression at a prestigious university both point to a positive relationship between socioeconomic status and approval and/or use of physical violence.

This investigation may be overrepresented by members of the working class, since 91 percent of the survey respondents are battered women who fled their homes to a house of refuge. It seems safe to assume that middle-class women have somewhat greater access to financial and other resources and, with more available options, may be able to leave a battering spouse without this action becoming a matter of public record or knowledge. The socioeconomic status of shelterees may vary from one shelter to another, but 31 percent (N = 107) of the survey respondents stayed at the Women's Transitional Living Center (WTLC), the only shelter for residents of affluent Orange County, California. The records at WTLC show that 40 percent of the women the center admits are identified as middle class, based on critera of education, income, residential property, and so on. Although lower than population averages, this is still a sizeable proportion. In addition, the 9 percent of the sample that volunteered to participate in the study were largely from the middle class, which may have served somewhat to counterbalance the lower-class bias.

Over one-fourth of the survey sample reported homeownership, and 35 percent of these estimated the value of their homes at or above $60,000. Almost 30 percent of their husbands had some college education, and 19 percent of the women reported their spouses' net income was above $15,000 per year. Thirty-five percent of the women had some college education, but only one-third of them were presently employed (32.3 percent), and of those who were employed

TABLE 3.9   Ethnic Group Identity of Survey Respondents

Response Category	Percent	N
White/Caucasian	77.9	271
Black/Negro	14.1	49
Mexican-American/Chicana	3.7	13
Asian-American	0.9	3
Other*	3.4	12
Total	100.0	348

*This category consisted of American Indian, Puerto Rican, biracial mixtures, and immigrants from Near Eastern countries.

at the time, only three percent reported net incomes over $15,000 per year. Educational attainment of this sample ranges from grammar school to Ph.D. for both the women and their spouses. The women's occupations range from housewife to teacher, therapist, nurse, and librarian. The occupations of their spouses range from unemployed laborer to doctor, psychiatrist, writer, engineer, and minister. Based on these data, it is difficult to determine exactly the social class proportions, but the investigator assumes that the middle and the working class are about evenly represented. Table 3.9 shows responses to survey item I-1(d) that asks women's ethnic group identification. Since almost half the respondents came from California shelters, where representation of Mexican-Americans in the population is relatively high, it seems obvious that Chicana shelterees are unfortunately underrepresented in the sample.

Woman-battering crosses socioeconomic class lines, yet there may be variations in the phenomenon due to class. From in-depth interviews and group discussions, there appear to be subtle differences in the style and type of abuse the women experienced. For instance, a middle-class batterer seems to be more inclined to use psychological battering and forms of "punishment" which neither destroy the home nor leave obvious marks on a woman's body. One example is the wife of a psychologist, who was locked outdoors on cold winter nights without keys or money.

> He'd twist my arms behind my back, pulling them up so hard I thought they'd come out of the shoulder socket. He knew better than to make marks on my body—and that doesn't make marks—but it's painful as hell. And there's no way to pull away; you can't do anything.

Another example was Doris, a college graduate mentioned earlier who lived in one of the most expensive areas in Southern California, whose husband raped her and caused her severe pain by driving his car erratically. Other women living in palatial homes with highly educated husbands in high income brackets also were living with men who kept tight control of all incomes and expenditures and watched their movements carefully. Some arrived at shelters with no money or credit cards, or access to a checking or savings account. One woman, the wife of a multinational corporation chief executive and member of the church board of directors, finally drove off one day in the family camper. She claimed that all her telephone calls were screened and the rooms of her home "bugged"; these statements were verified by her 20-year-old daughter.

Even in the "heat of passion," middle-class men seem more in-clined to strike their victims from the neck downward; several of the women report their spouses made comments to the effect that "no one will ever see what I did to you." Traditionally, middle-class women have tended to cover up visible bruises by neck scarves and clothing that covers arms and legs. A few middle-class women have more recently begun to disclose publicly what happened to them in the privacy of their homes. One of these is a dentist's former wife who testified before the Senate Finance Committee of the California legislature, who told of beatings to her belly while pregnant and attempts to get her to commit suicide by using drugs (Dales, 1977). Another spoke tearfully before a League of Women Voters confer-ence on domestic violence. She disclosed that beatings by her psychi-atrist husband, who had an income in excess of $200,000 per year, had caused spontaneous abortions twice. Because of his medical background, she said, her husband administered necessary care to her at home which avoided public records and incriminating evidence. She related to the audience that her husband inserted a hot hair curling iron into her vagina on the same day she was awarded the "Outstand-ing Woman of the Year" award by the regional YWCA.

On the other hand, working-class men seem less inclined to use covert forms of violence and frequently strike at the face, head, and neck of the women. Sixty-nine percent of the survey sample reported this was the usual target area of their bodies. When women from either class are employed, most report they tried to camouflage face and neck bruises by makeup and dark glasses; 67 percent of the survey sample said they attempted concealment.

Steinmetz and Straus suggest that reasons exist for the popular but erroneous notion that woman-battering is confined to the working classes. Some of the reasons they mention include interpretation of the data, greater visibility of intrafamily violence in low-income neighborhoods, and the greater tendency of the poor to rely on police intervention (1974:8). Other reasons may be that researchers have greater access to people from the lower classes (Kirchner, 1977a, 1978), and frequently their samples (such as Field and Field, 1973; Gelles, 1974; Hilberman and Munson, 1978) are drawn from official police and social agencies' records. This study shows that woman-battering is not confined to the ghetto; that women who endured battering more than once had a variety of individual circumstances guiding their responses and their responses differed somewhat by social class; and that techniques of physical abuse employed by their spouses differed to some extent along class lines.

Summary

This has been a review of some of the most frequently repeated statements encountered by the investigator from the very inception of field research. The myths and stereotypes outlined here were presented in a variety of expressions, but they evolved from similar ideas. They were repeated by doctors, nurses, lawyers, police officers, judges, school teachers, and strangers in a variety of locations, including one group discussion on a transcontinental airplane flight and a conversation with a night telephone operator taking a Western Union message. Presenting them here with responses from victims permitted exposure of victims' perceptions and explanations for them. Whether they are myths or not depends on the vantage point of the viewer. Based on quantitative survey data supplemented by qualitative data that enriches understanding, the investigator finds these popular assumptions are generally untrue. If this is the case, then their popularity and public acceptance serves to victimize the victims further by stigmatizing them or helping to keep them locked in their violent relationships. Examining common stereotypes in this chapter also exposed some of the resources and lack of resources of sample women, responses they received from agents of social institutions, and, to a limited extent, their traditionalism.

Chapter 4

VICTIMS AND ABUSERS: SOME CHARACTERISTICS

It is important to know more about the respondents who supplied the survey data to determine how representative or nonrepresentative they may be of the general population. Although the findings from tests to be performed later cannot be generalized beyond this sample because of purposeful sample selection and other limitations in the research design, it is best to have some background information to avoid unseen bias in sample selection. For these reasons, and because the broader focus of the investigation called for exposition of the sociocultural environment of battered women that may suggest reasons they stay with abusers, some demographic and other illuminative data from the survey sample are presented in this chapter.

Next will follow highlights of interviews with two men who have dealt extensively with men who battered their spouses. Even though this research project was not designed to include a sample of batterers, it seemed appropriate to find out as much as possible about them. It was decided at the onset of this study not to attempt to

TABLE 4.1   Sources of Survey Sample

Source Category	Percent	N
Women's Transitional Living Center	30.6	107
WomenShelter, Long Beach	5.4	19
Harbor Area YWCA, San Pedro	3.7	13
Emergency Shelter Program, Hayward	3.4	12
Santa Rosa, California	1.1	4
Women in Distress, Ft. Lauderdale, FL	42.5	149
Other shelters	3.7	13
Nonshelter volunteers	9.4	33
Total	100.0	350

interview abusive men, largely because of the possibility of endangering shelterees through direct contact with their spouses. In addition, it seemed unwise to attempt to study both sides of this social problem simultaneously. The major goal of the investigation is to study the victims and their perceptions of the problem and to study perceptions of community agents who come in contact with victims. But some of these community agents also come in contact with the batterers as well as their victims. Therefore, in addition to learning about abusive men through the women in this sample and by observing accused abusers in court room settings, interviews were also conducted with two knowledgeable men who deal directly with batterers and their spouses.

Sources of Survey Data

Survey questionnaire respondents were obtained from a variety of sources, as shown in Table 4.1. Inspection of this table shows that 42.5 percent of the sample came from a Florida shelter, 44.2 percent came from specific California shelters, 9.4 percent came from non-shelter volunteers, and the balance came from miscellaneous shelters.

Physical Characteristics

The following table provides physical descriptions of the women who responded to the questionnaire and the descriptions they pro-

TABLE 4.2   Physical Characteristics of Survey Women and Their Spouses

		Women	*Men*
Age in Years:	Mean	29.91	33.28
	Median	27.89	31.69
	Minimum	17	18
	Maximum	68	81
Height in inches:	Mean	64.07	70.09
	Median	64.08	70.11
	Minimum	57	62
	Maximum	71	79
Weight in pounds:	Mean	130.52	174.17
	Median	125.09	174.62
	Minimum	80	120
	Maximum	280	270

vided of the men who beat them. In the discussion that follows, it will be seen that these persons do not differ greatly from the general population on most characteristics.

AGE

Age of victims is considered an important factor because it is hypothesized that the older a person is, the more difficult it becomes to begin a new life or lifestyle. For approximately half the women in this sample, the possibilities of establishing new lives or lifestyles are less favorable than for those under 30 years of age. There are women in this sample as old as 68; 13 percent are age 40 and above. (Although no woman refused to tell her age, seven refused to tell their weight.) Even if they have no dependent children, these women almost surely face a decline in their socioeconomic status by separation from spouses. The earnings differential between men and women widens with age; it is greatest for those over 35 years old, and one-fourth of the sample women were 35 or older. Gainful employment and comfortable earnings are not likely if a woman enters the job market after several years' absence. Note the Veterans Administration's efforts to help men in this regard, despite the fact that many veterans were out of the job market for only two to four years.

The possibility of separating from their spouses introduces the question of financial independence, which is more difficult the older a woman becomes unless she has held full-time employment prior to the separation. Only one-third of the women were employed at the time they responded to the questionnaire; another third said they had been employed within the past year, but 27 percent (N = 95) had not been employed for over two years or had never been employed. For some of these women, especially the older ones, their best potential source of income is from the men who beat them. If a separating woman seeks alimony or spousal support, she must first prove to the courts that she has need and the husband has the ability to pay (Bersch, 1977:7). According to Bersch, this takes money—and in the case of high-income men it takes relatively more money for attorneys and accountants, particularly if the men are self-employed, such as doctors, dentists, and lawyers. In addition, the report of the National Commission on the Observance of International Women's Year states that only 14 percent of divorced or separated women are awarded alimony and only 46 percent of these collect it regularly; of all divorced or separated mothers, only 44 percent were awarded child support and of these only 47 percent collected it regularly (Bryant, 1977:24).

Two interviewed judges stated that they base child support payments on the father's income more than on the number of children or their financial needs. In no case would they set child support at or above 50 percent of a man's income, even if that meant the mother and children had to become welfare recipients to meet costs of living. One of these judges said that spousal support is viewed as temporary assistance in all cases, not a permanent financial burden for the man. He bases the amount of spousal support on the man's income and the length of support on length of marriage because older women are less employable. He believes that younger women have the responsibility to "hustle to get out there and get a job," even if they have young children in their care, so when he does award spousal support he sets it for relatively short time periods.

In sum, younger women face prospects of shorter-term spousal support (if any), and if they have young children, they have problems of obtaining good child care at reasonable costs. But younger women generally have the advantage over older women of better prospects in the job market. Older women, particularly if they devoted years to being full-time wives, housekeepers, and mothers, may leave abusive husbands with little or no spousal support, no job skills, and low employability. The film *Who Remembers Momma?* (produced by KERA-TV, Dallas-Fort Worth and the Dallas Chapter of Women in Communications, Inc.) documented well the dismal prospects of traditional, middle-aged women suddenly facing problems of financial independence and struggles for survival (Beyette, 1979).

HEIGHT AND WEIGHT

Physical size is also an important consideration because it is hypothesized that the smaller a person's size compared to an attacker's, the greater the vulnerability to attack and the less the ability to stop attacks or to fight back. Without going into elaborate detail, it should be noted that physical sizes of spouses listed in Table 4.2 are close to recent DHEW national statistics (Abraham et al., 1976). The mean heights of both men and women in the sample are one inch taller; the sample men are two pounds heavier and the women are 13 pounds lighter. Means in the national sample are based on persons between the ages of 18 and 74, with taller persons in the younger age ranges and heavier persons in the older ranges (Abraham et al., 1976). The greatest difference is found in the weights of the sample women, which may be due to error in estimation or deliberate underestimation because of a cultural preference for slimness in American women. On the other hand, since the national differential in weight means is 29 pounds for men and women and the sample differential is almost 44 pounds, this could lead one to question if men who batter women are those who take advantage of women least able to defend themselves or retaliate. However, this can only be provocative speculation, untestable in this study because focused sample selection precludes assumptions of population representativeness.

Nevertheless, the sample women are over three years younger and just over six inches shorter than their spouses, which does conform to national statistics (Abraham et al., 1976; Rawlings, 1978). The average sample woman is 5 feet 4 inches tall and weighs just over 130 pounds; her spouse is 5 feet 10 inches and weighs about 174 pounds.

The hypothesis stated earlier that size differential gives advantages to the bigger spouse is also based on an implicit assumption that men usually not only have larger size but are better trained in muscular development; thus, even at the same size, the average man has more muscular strength (Straus, 1978:449). Most of the sample falls in the normal range, but there are some exceptions: 12 women (3.6 percent) weigh over 200 pounds, and the heaviest woman weighs more than the heaviest man. There are some women in this sample who are not only heavier than average but are heavier even than their spouses. To try to understand why some heavy women could have been battered by spouses lighter than themselves, the three heaviest women's cases were examined for possible explanatory factors.

The heaviest woman is a 280-pound American Indian married to a 190-pound Caucasian ranch hand, who wrote that her husband "used me as a punching bag." This woman, married at the age of 21, entered her first marriage with a year-old baby and pregnant with another child (neither by her first husband). Her husband became violent the first time eight months after their marriage, but she lived with him for 13 years, bearing two children by him. When she left, her children ranged in age from 8 to 14 years. She was threatened with a knife and a gun, but the weapon her spouse used on her was a club. She wrote that all the children were battered by her husband but that the most severe abuse was directed toward her eldest child (his stepson), whose head injuries required medical treatment. Yet the police would not file charges against him.

The next heaviest woman was 260 pounds, married at 20 to a 200-pound man, her second husband (both were Caucasians). This woman described her childhood home as "sheltered" and her major reactions to being beaten as "powerless, fear, alone." She wrote that her husband had threatened her life with both a knife and a gun.

The third heaviest was a 240-pound woman married at 19 to a 215-pound man (both American Indians) who was also threatened with a knife and gun during their 10-year marriage. This respondent, whose education included two years of high school, was assisted by a shelter staff member to complete the questionnaire. The first violent episode occurred three days after the wedding; the wife left her husband just after the youngest child was born and when the oldest of the five children was 10. She reported that her spouse once chopped holes in a car with an axe, trying to get at her as she was attempting to leave him. She said he abused all the children with straps, fists, and choking. The abuse culminated in the death of their second son by beating. The comments reveal that the boy

> had head split open—took to hospital—[boy's name] beaten until blood splattered all over walls. . . . She pressed charges—police got him—he went to court, pleaded not guilty. She and children would have had to testify against him in court, both were afraid to face him. So the court lessened the charges so that he would have to plead guilty. He was put in jail for 90 days and she had a chance to leave him and the town. They were afraid to testify because he threatened [the eldest] son that if his mother pressed charges he would kill son and mother.

These cases may give some insight into why even heavy women felt powerless to prevent or stop physical attacks. Although there were some deviations from the norm, the vast majority of these cases follow the usual pattern of men being larger than their wives, in some cases as much as 100 pounds heavier or even double their wives' weights.

Weapons Involved

The test instrument was incapable of measuring the relative strength of the spouses in the sample, but it seems apparent that even overly large women do not have much of an advantage (if any) over the men who beat them, particularly when the men used or threatened to use weapons and they do not reciprocate. In this sample, 180 women were threatened with weapons (57 percent, $N = 323$) which were evenly divided between gun and knife; 75 women had a weapon used on them (24 percent, $N = 317$). Weapons most frequently used were knives, both knife and gun, and "other," which included chains, clubs, chairs, lamps, wrenches, hammers, golf clubs, and assorted other objects. Of the 3.6 percent of women over 200 pounds, not many were heavier than their spouses (13.5 percent of the men were over 200 pounds). A glance at the individual cases of women over 200 pounds shows that weapons were involved in their spouses' violence to a greater extent than reported by smaller women. It may be that when a batterer has less advantage in size he is more likely to compensate with weapons. This idea was suggested in an earlier paper (Pagelow, 1978b) which hypothesized that the weapon serves as a "equalizer," giving power to the one who holds it. Along these same lines, when battered women fight back or try to defend themselves, they frequently use weapons. Seventy-nine women (24 percent, $N = 330$) report they threatened spouses with weapons; 26 women said they used weapons (8 percent, $N = 317$). Of the latter 26, two used a gun, 8 used a knife, 1 used both, and the remaining 15 used a variety of household items such as lamps, breadboards and so on. From the description of these weapons, it seems that most were used to throw rather than for hand-held contact.

To summarize the data presented thus far: The men generally have height and weight advantages over the women that are close to national averages. Even when the men are slight in build compared with women, most men in this country have greater muscular strength than women because of the cultural emphasis on masculine athletics in schools, participation in sports—particularly body-contact sports— and, for some, military training. When women are as heavy as or heavier than their spouses there can be no a priori assumption that additional weight represents muscular strength. In addition, it was found that the few very heavy women in this survey were likely to encounter spouses with weapons. Finally, it should be noted that the men were proportionately more likely to follow through on threats with weapons: Of the men who threatened, 42 percent used weapons; of the women who threatened, 33 percent used them.

Ethnic/Racial Composition

It is hypothesized that if a person is a member of a discriminated minority group, the fewer the opportunities for socioeconomic status above the poverty level and the weaker the English language skills, the greater the disadvantage. Table 3.9 showed that there were 70 minority group women (22 percent, $N = 348$), who had a double disadvantage in this society that serves to tie them more strongly to their spouses. As mentioned earlier, an unknown number of minority group women were excluded from this survey sample because of language difficulties. There can be little question that women unable to communicate in English are severely handicapped in seeking independence. Some women thus excluded were even further disadvantaged because they were not U.S. citizens and some were in this country illegally. For a few of these, the only assistance shelter staff could render was to help reunite them with their families of origin. In California, indications are that many Asian and Mexican women are kept virtual prisoners and slaves, living isolated lives of great fear and constant threats by their spouses of "sending them back"—without their children.

Despite exclusion through language difficulties, almost one-fourth of the sample are non-Caucasian women. This should not be taken to infer that higher proportions of minority women are battered because many Caucasian women were probably excluded from the sample, since they are more likely to have available resources to enable them to avoid going to a shelter. Many shelters admit only women with few or no resources or alternatives.

The fact that females, especially those of ethnic and racial minorities, are disadvantaged in this society is well documented (Current Population Reports, 1978; National Commission on Working Women, 1978; Terry, 1974; U.S. Commission on Civil Rights, 1974, 1979). For sample women to leave spouses represents a probable financial loss. Persons living in families with a female householder (no husband present) represent only 11 percent of the total U.S. population (the term "householder" is the modernized substitution for "head of household" or "head of family"; see Current Population Reports, 1978:10). Yet 36 percent of all persons below the poverty level and 55 percent of all poor children under 18 in this country live in female-headed families. In 1976, 27 percent of families living in poverty had white female householders, but for black female householders, the percentage in poverty was 58 percent (Current Population Reports, 1978). Even when they are employed full-time, women's wages are lower than men's, regardless of race or ethnicity, as may be seen in Table 4.3.

We can see that regardless of race or ethnicity, women on the average earn far less than men; in the case of Spanish origin females, their annual income is less than half that of white males. In 1977, men's income averaged $15,070 while women's was $8,814, or

TABLE 4.3   Full-Time Employment Median Income for 1977

Category	Median Annual Income*	Percent of White Males
White males	$15,378	100.0%
Spanish origin males	10,935	71.1
Black males	10,602	68.8
White females	8,870	57.6
Black females	8,290	53.9
Spanish origin females	7,599	49.4

Source: From the National Commission on Working Women, Center for Women and Work, Washington, D.C., 1978.
*Income includes earnings plus social security, investments, etc.

$6,256 less than men's (National Commission on Working Women, 1978).

Marital Status

Table 4.4 shows the types of relationships (marital or otherwise) sample women had with the men who beat them. To check for representativeness, it is of interest to see if this sample has about the same percentage of married/unmarried women as can be expected in the population of couples living together. Bird (1979:12) says that in 1970, about two percent of the couples in the United States (which numbered about 48 million in 1977, according to Rawlings, 1978) live together without marriage, which accounts for 960,000 couples. Glick and Spanier, using June 1975 national statistics, say: "The approximately 886,000 unmarried couples comprised about 1.8 percent of all couples living together" (1980:21). Whichever is correct, there appears to be a growing international trend toward couples choosing conjugal relationships without legal ceremonies (Reiss, 1976:87-88). Yet even with the growing popularity, it seems that this survey, taken during the last four years of the 1970s, shows a higher percentage of cohabitees than might be expected. The recent DHEW report on 120 battered women discloses that 12 percent of the respondents were single (Service Delivery Assessment, 1980:ix). It is possible that the oft-quoted statement of the marriage license being a hitting license (Straus, 1976:543) is somewhat of an exaggeration and that the more important factor contributing to violence is the process of shared living arrangements (Martin, 1976a:18).

TABLE 4.4   Relationships of Batterers to Survey Women

Response Category	Percent	N
Husband or ex-husband	80.5	281
Lover or ex-lover	18.3	64
Someone else*	1.1	4
Total	100.0	349

*These others were: brother, stepfathers, foster father, and father. In two of these cases it was determined that the women were beaten by a male relative after returning home to escape a battering husband. They provided data about the male relatives' abuse in accordance with the instructions written on page 1 of the questionnaire telling them to respond to the questions regarding "the man who most recently physically abused or was violent toward you."

It is hypothesized that if the couple is legally married, possibilities are greater of court-ordered child and/or spousal support, but being married also adds the expenses of obtaining a legal separation or divorce. As shown in Table 4.4, over 80 percent of these women were legally married to their assaulters, while 19 percent were not. Although a woman seeking spousal support is in a more favorable position if she was legally married to her spouse, a woman who is not married to her batterer is in a slightly better position under the law. She may, for instance, have her abuser legally evicted if she owns the residence or if it is leased in her name only (although a 30-day eviction notice carries its own set of hazards in some instances). Unmarried victims have greater protection under the law from rape and physical assault. In most states, a husband can rape his wife with impunity from the law (a spousal rape bill passed the California legislature and became effective on January 1, 1980). Although changes are occuring slowly, the ideas expressed by Bersch (1977:4-5) are still largely true for California and most other states in the nation:

> There is another area which presents a problem only to a married woman. That is the lack of legal protection from sexual assault by her husband. . . . Legally, a woman cannot be raped by her husband, even if she is separated from him and waiting for the dissolution of the marriage to be finalized. . . . It is impossible to determine the number of Californians who are raped or otherwise physically abused by their spouses . . . charges of this nature generally will not be brought by the

police department because the authorities view such incidents as personal matters. Unless the wife has been seriously injured or has required hospitalization, the police may refuse to intervene.

In almost all states, evidence must be stronger and physical injuries much more severe when an assault victim is the wife of the accused perpetrator of the crime than when she is not married to him.

It is hoped that this section provided the reader with insight into the composition of the survey sample. They do not differ drastically from average American couples on physical characteristics, except that the men outweigh the women more than usual. The size differential shows that these women cannot reasonably be expected to defend themselves from physical attack any more than can the average women in our society, so the fear they frequently say immobilized them is well grounded. Women of any age are likely to suffer financial consequences when they terminate conjugal relationships, but the older and minority women in the survey are even more constrained to stay because of dim prospects for financial survival. In addition, these data show that their spouses were proportionately more likely to both threaten and use weapons against them. All these factors undoubtedly interacted to keep them with their spouses after the abuse began.

Next, attention turns to interviews with two men who have considerable insight into the topic of woman-battering, the batterers, and their victims.

Reports on Men Who Batter

The first expert interviewed was Michael Wellins, a civilian employee of the only police department out of 26 in Orange County, California, that has a crisis intervention unit. This man has probably had more experience in dealing with batterers than almost anyone else in the nation, since he began his work as crisis intervention counselor in February 1976. In addition to dealing directly with victims and offenders shortly after the disturbance, Wellins has conducted training classes for police officers to help them respond most efficiently and safely to domestic disturbance calls. The program was so successful from the beginning that indications were strong that other police departments were going to establish similar units. But when the so-called "taxpayers' revolt" began, money that might have become available disappeared. In fact, Wellins began his work aided by a social worker and administrative aide; their positions have since been eliminated. Wellins also serves as a community educator, giving talks to service organizations, in schools and colleges, and at public meetings.

There is a distinction between the one-time explosive event committed by reactive abusers who explode under stress, according to Wellins, and battering committed by hard-core abusers he calls "chronic cases." Sometimes involvement by police officers is sufficient to deter further violence in the former. As he describes it, the legal system is a crisis system: It intervenes to settle crises in matters such as domestic violence and it also creates a type of crisis situation, such as when people are put in jail. For the explosive abusers, police response may be sufficient, but if not, they are amenable to treatment. There are many more of this type than the chronic cases, which Wellins also called the "Friday night brawlers."

Unfortunately, no records have been maintained by his unit, but Wellins's conservative estimate is that he has worked with about 110 couples where the men are chronic abusers. Cases come to him by referral from police, women call him for help and together they try to get the husbands to participate in counseling, husbands call because they want to locate their wives, or batterers are referred by the only shelter in the county, Women's Transitional Living Center (WTLC). In the last two instances, the victims have obtained shelter and their husbands desperately want them to come home; they will "do anything you ask" to get them to return. Counseling is frequently one of the conditions and Wellins is one of the few experts in this specialized field. He does not do court- or police-referred mandatory intervention; all cases are voluntary.

Wellins tries to get the men or the couples into therapy as quickly as possible and usually sets limits at no more than six sessions with him because he believes the men need long-term treatment with the same therapist. He then refers the men to the public Department of Mental Health (DMH), to semipublic family service organizations, or to private counselors. Frequently they will not follow through because of financial pressures. Even DMH charges, though on a sliding scale based on income, can be as high as $73 an hour. Many families have a high income but similarly high expenses, and may thus feel they cannot afford even the public services. If alcohol problems are also evident, the DMH does not handle these cases—men are referred to an alcohol abuse program first. A number of these have in-patient programs and, once more, many of the men cannot afford to be hospitalized for treatment. Even if they do get treatment for the alcohol problems, they quite likely will not be referred back to DMH for the violence problem. In other words, like the women Lynch describes (1977), the men also get "lost" in the system and may never receive the kind of help they need because of lack of networking among service organizations.

Chronic batterers have certain identifiable characteristics, according to Wellins. Basically, he stressed their lack of ego-strength, their high role expectations for themselves and their families, and that they cannot deal effectively with stress. Wellins mentioned certain characteristics that are similar to features described herein as traditional. When asked if he conceptualized batterers as very traditional men, Wellins said:

Yes, they are—they believe in segregated sex roles, divorce is unthinkable—but it goes even beyond. The difference is like people who can deal with lack of order as opposed to order; they have rigid boundaries . . . locked in . . . need for structure. Things are black or white, there's certainty, rigid expectations, rigid role models. This applies to both parties.

Wellins thus gave support to some of the theoretical propositions of Model II, primary battering, as well as Model III, secondary battering, as developed for this study. He believes the victims and abusers are highly traditional people, but they go even beyond his definition of traditionalism. Wellins said that the "profile" he would offer of batterers is compatible with the one outlined by Walker in her book, which is as follows:

1. Has low self-esteem.
2. Believes all the myths about battering relationships.
3. Is a traditionalist believing in male supremacy and the stereotyped masculine sex role in the family.
4. Blames others for his actions.
5. Is pathologically jealous.
6. Presents a dual personality.
7. Has severe stress reactions, during which he uses drinking and wife battering to cope.
8. Frequently uses sex as an act of aggression to enhance self-esteem in view of waning virility. May be bisexual.
9. Does not believe his violent behavior should have negative consequences [Walker, 1979:36].

When asked if he knew anything about childhood violence experiences of the couples he has counseled, Wellins said he does not delve deeply into their histories but leaves this for long-term therapists. However, the overall impressions he has gained from the men are that they (1) have a deep sense of inadequacy, (2) had authoritarian homes, and (3) had poor role models. As a result, they feel ugly about themselves, lack self-esteem, and try aggressive ways to maintain whatever self-esteem they have left. Wellins phrased their relationships with their women in these words:

"If I'm not worth anything and I want to maintain a relationship with you, I've got to do everything to try to control you, maintain you, corral you, because if I don't, then I'm going to lose you." I think that's one of the reasons you see the pathological jealousy of these men.

As for the women's childhood homes, Wellins does not believe they were beaten or saw their mothers being beaten but thinks they came from "restricted environments, passive homes; no violence but where they have expectations of violence; they never learned about how to deal with it." Further, he believes they may bring unrealistic expectations into conjugal relationships.

Wellins not only offered support to the proposition that the women he has counseled who were victims of secondary battering were highly traditional, structured women from authoritarian back-grounds, but he also gave much support to the negative institutional response proposition in the following areas:

(1) The need for police training for more effective handling of domestic violence calls, and more understanding of why victims often refuse to cooperate with the prosecution of their assaulters.

(2) The lack of interest on the part of the District Attorney's office to prosecute spouse abuse cases.

(3) That more attorneys are willing to fight for men's rights than attorneys who will wage as intense a battle for women's rights.

(4) That many therapists are pro-family and that even if they suggest alternatives such as separation or divorce, the orientation behind the therapist is going to win out. "The license says, 'Marriage and Family Counselor,' it doesn't mention 'divorce.' . . . A lot of therapists don't see themselves that way [as change agents], it depends on scope and training and orientation, so those become real issues for referral and other alternatives."

(5) That even his own unit, in the initial stages, probably failed to identify some cases of woman-battering because they are frequently concealed behind other problems. As sensitivity grew, Wellins realized that sometimes behind the initial cause for intervention (such as child abuse, incest, etc.) lies spouse abuse.

In sum, Wellins seems to have a depth of understanding for the victims as well as the abusers, although he believes that some of the chronic batterers are untreatable. He feels that these men may have serious personality disorders or are manic-depressives. He understands why some women cannot bear to leave when doing so means leaving behind certain cherished possessions they feel they "bought" with their pain and suffering. He also confirmed that of the men who had previous conjugal relationships, the majority beat those other spouses, although he learned this mostly from the women because the men tend to deny or to minimize their violence in current and previous relationships.

Finally, Wellins thinks that putting abusers in jail, at least initially, is perhaps a better deterrent to further violence than diversion into the public mental health system under present conditions, which include financial problems, overloaded staff, undeveloped protocol, and the lack of assigning cases to specific therapists for consistency in treatment. He believes that many men require the shock of confinement in jail to convince them that their violence will not be tolerated. But if a man is jailed once and returns to beat his wife again, the woman is in extreme danger and should be moved to a new location, because this type of man will continue until he kills her. For treatment Wellins recommends assertion training, stress management, reeducation (values), support groups for anger control, and *good* counseling. For prevention he recommends public education at all levels—including elementary schools—nonviolent child rearing promoting healthy self-esteem, and swift intervention when violence occurs.

The second expert interviewed was Wayne Blackburn, a licensed clinical social worker at a family service organization. Blackburn also receives referrals from WTLC as well as a variety of other sources and is one to whom Wellins refers batterers for counseling. Only once has a man voluntarily come to him for help to curb his violence; in the other cases, men come to him because their wives either left them or were threatening to leave. After two years of counseling families where spouse abuse is the primary concern, Blackburn conservatively estimates he has dealt with 150 cases. He expressed the feeling of earlier writers that (1) male batterers must be pressured into seeking help in the first place, (2) they tend to deny or minimize their violence, blaming it on the women, and (3) will only continue in treatment for as long as there is the desired goal of getting their spouses back home or of keeping them there. If the women refuse to reconcile, the men immediately terminate from the program. Blackburn sees a very high attrition rate in cases and expressed a sense of futility in trying to keep these men and their spouses in treatment long enough to know whether it has been effective or not. Sometimes he works with the husband and wife separately and then together until at some point they feel they no longer require counseling; sometimes they call to say the relationship is going much better. Other times the women will call later and say she is leaving the relationship; unfortunately, this severs contact and he cannot do a follow-up evaluation.

When it comes to his general description, Blackburn corroborated Wellins's major point of lack of self-esteem and need for assertion training and approval for both the batterers and their victims. In addition, Blackburn drew a specific image of these men that brought out these major points:

(1) They are men who adopt all the external trappings of an aggressive, controlling image but are dependent and out of control within. They frequently work in all-male environments, such as fire and police departments, the military services (particularly the Marines), and on construction crews (he estimates that two-thirds of the violent male spouses he sees are blue-collar workers).

(2) They are men who must live and work within clearly defined boundaries; the rules must be clear and unambiguous; they function best within set patterns and parameters.

(3) They are traditional family men: They have very rigid ideas of masculinity and femininity and sex-segregated roles. They are authoritarian and patriarchal.

(4) They tend to use primitive defense mechanisms—denial, projection, and aggression—as ways of dealing with emotional difficulties. They do not yield to change, introspection, flexibility, or decision-making.

(5) Concerning their histories, *all* the violent men Blackburn has counseled came from violent homes—some were extremely violent and involved in severe child abuse; they had no good masculine role models; they developed unrealistic expectations for themselves and their women. All that had a former wife or lover had also beaten these women (information directly from the men).

(6) Both partners use a form of bargaining in all matters where it must be an equal exchange, such as: "You do this for me and I'll do that for you." There is no really free, unconditional exchange; all transactions involve equal costs and benefits.

Based on these criteria, Blackburn's treatment is direct: He sets the rules and boundaries with his clients. The men *want* his help; their goal is to "keep" their wives. Blackburn makes a contract: There will be no violence during the time they are in treatment. Violation of the contract means Blackburn will no longer take the case, and the women are instructed to call the police and prosecute. So far, no one has broken the contract; Blackburn feels these men are accustomed to taking orders from "superiors," and they seem almost relieved that someone gives them an order to stop beating their wives. The counselor believes that men's attempts at introspection to find out *why* they become violent is of little value; even learning why cannot help these men to change their behavior because they are so rigid. Instead, he concentrates on building self-esteem, working on those interests in which they excel, and teaches both them and the women how to be more assertive. Blackburn tries to look at the causes of the stress in their lives and searches for ways the men can remove it; he presents alternatives so that when anger is aroused the men can divert it from their wives and take a walk, use a punching bag in the garage, or call the county domestic violence "hot line."

As for the women, Blackburn believes they sometimes trigger the violent behavior of the men by saying or doing things that remind the men of their mothers, which sends them into a rage. He feels these couples are attracted to each other because of mutual needs: the men are attracted to the women because of their yielding and loving concerns for their husbands' welfare, and the very features the women find most attractive about the men are those that predict violence. In other words, when Blackburn asks the women about what attracted them to the men in the first place, they usually say something like "He was so strong, dependable, unchangeable—I knew he was someone I could rely on, someone who would take care of me." When he asks them if they feel they are capable of taking care of themselves, they indicate that they need to have the strength of a man to feel like whole persons.

By these comments, Blackburn presents an image of a traditional American woman who has been socialized to feel exactly that way. In today's society, despite the feminist movement, the majority of women regard themselves as needing the strength of a man in order to survive and to be a "real woman." Blackburn believes that a particular type of woman searches for a particular type of man (and vice versa) and the result is battering. Yet women who do not feel they need to depend on a man's strength and can have fulfilling lives without such a man are probably still quite rare. In addition, some popular theories of the male selection process are that opposites attract and there is "personality need fulfillment" (Reiss, 1976:94-96). As Reiss explains,

There is no fully rational way on the basis of a year or so of knowing someone to predict the next fifty years, and yet this is exactly what our type of courtship institution demands. We go with a person for a period of time, feel that we are in love, and decide to marry. . . . Experience and examination can help, but certainty is impossible. What marriage in our type of courtship system involves, then, is a leap of faith, if I may borrow an existentialist term. We take this leap of faith despite the lack of sufficient proof, because of our intense love feelings [1976:99].

Considering the way both men and women are socialized in this country and that ours is a violent culture, probably the main reason Blackburn sees these people as out of the ordinary is that his caseload restricts the number of couples he can counsel. The investigator suspects that either Straus (1978) is correct when he estimates that one out of four couples experiences violence or Walker is correct when she estimates that "as many as 50 percent of all women will be battering victims at some point in their lives" (1979:ix). In fact, Walker argues against Blackburn's ideas that certain people search each other out and violence is a result: "Pairing up with a batterer must be considered *purely accidental* if *one out of two women* will be battered in their lifetimes" (1979:16). Two other psychologists who have worked with batterers, Ganely and Harris, tend to look for specific qualities in the men, not the women, because "it is our assumption that battering men will continue to be violent even if they change partners, unless a major change occurs within the individual men" (1978:6).

In any case, the work being done by people such as Wellins and Blackburn is important to all the people in violent families who need their services and to society as a whole. Working in a virtually uncharted area, they have had to learn how to deal with violent men and troubled families, relying on their own judgment, bolstered by a few empirical studies, such as this one, that reveal the perceptions of victims.

Chapter 5

RESOURCES, INSTITUTIONAL RESPONSE, AND TRADITIONAL IDEOLOGY

The focus of this chapter is on tests of the theoretical model outlined in Chapter 2 with data obtained from 350 questionnaire respondents. Model III, Secondary Battering, postulates three key variables that may explain why women who are battered by their spouses remain in these relationships after the first occurrence of violence, which is termed primary battering. The major hypothesis states:

> The fewer the resources, the more negative the institutional response, and the more intense the traditional ideology of women who have been battered, the more likely they are to remain in relationships with the batterers and the less likely they are to perform acts that significantly alter their situation in a positive direction.

Resources, institutional response, and traditional ideology are constructs operationalized by certain independent measures. Length of cohabitation after the primary battering occurs is the dependent variable: secondary battering cohabitation. Statistics presented here include some frequency tables, zero-order correlation matrices of variables in each of the three subsets, and regression analysis of the dependent variable on several independent variables.

The independent variables range from nominal to ratio level measures, but most are ordinal data. All nominal categories are dummy coded and some Likert-type scales are collapsed into nominal categories (such as positive, neutral, or negative). Effect coding is the system or type of coding used, such that: "the assignment of 1's, 0's, and −1's, where 1's are assigned to members of a given group, 0's to members of all other groups but one, and the members of this group are assigned −1's" (Kerlinger and Pedhazur, 1973). Effect coding was chosen because of several advantages for multiple regression analysis, the most important of which is that its use results in a regression equation that reflects the linear model (1973:121-126). These authors support the use of nominal (which they term "categorical") variables in regression analysis by any of three suggested systems of dummy coding:

> The principles and methods of multiple regression analysis . . . apply equally to continuous and to categorical variables. When dealing with a categorical independent variable, one can express it appropriately with dummy variables and do a regression analysis with the dummy variables as independent variables [Kerlinger and Pedhazur, 1973:107].

Other measures remain at the ordinal level, but multiple regression techniques have been utilized on ordinal data without introducing bias (Kim, 1975; Labovitz, 1970) and this procedure is generally accepted. In their text on multiple regression, Kerlinger and Pedhazur (1973:102) categorize all variables measured by ordinal, interval, and ratio scales as "continuous variables" because they contain numerical values that express gradations.

Regression analysis was chosen because these techniques allow examination of each of the individual independent variables to determine their effect on length of stay in violent relationships through bivariate regression. In addition, multivariate regression provides an overall summary of the three major constructs and tells how well they can explain length of stay. As Kerlinger and Pedhazer state:

Multiple regression is a method of analyzing the collective and separate contributions of two or more independent variables . . . to the variation of a dependent variable. . . . Multiple regression's task is to help "explain" the variance of a dependent variable. It does this, in part, by estimating the contributions to this variance of two or more independent variables [1973:3, 4].

It should be noted that these tests are restricted to explaining action/nonaction of only this sample because test assumptions of sample representativeness have not been met. Regression analysis is viewed herein as a general statistical technique to analyze the relationships between the dependent variable and sets of independent (predictor) variables; it is being used as a descriptive tool rather than an inferential tool (Kim and Kohout, 1975:321). This provides a view of overall dependence of length of stay on three sets of independent variables as well as the unique influence of each variable substantively hypothesized to provide explanation.

An extension of regression analysis and a logical next step in analysis of statistical data, path analysis, will not be performed on these data because path analysis requires causal assumptions and that "all the variables must have a definite time ordering" (Johnson, 1977:151). The individual variables that make up the three constructs—resources, institutional response, and traditional ideology—do not meet assumptions either of causality or of a definite time ordering.

Analysis begins with zero-order correlations of variables in each subset, starting with those operationalized to measure the first concept: resources. It would serve no purpose to provide an overall correlation matrix that includes all variables correlated with all others, since this would be an atheoretical exercise. It would result in a cumbersome, overly large matrix; and whether or not a resource variable correlates with a traditional ideology variable, for example, can answer no theoretical propositions, however interesting such correlations may appear.

A correlations matrix gives a picture of the degree or strength of the interrelationships of the variables, which provides valuable insights, as will be noted below. However, it is also a way to determine which of the variables are likely to provide the greater explanatory power in regression analysis. Blalock (1972:376) explains that we want to know the degree of the relationship as well as the form because there is no point attempting to predict Y from X if the relationship is very weak. He further states: "Sociologists are often primarily interested in discovering *which* of a very large number of variables are most closely related to a given dependent variable. In exploratory studies of this sort, regression analysis is of secondary importance" (Blalock, 1972:376).

Resource Variables

Table 5.1 shows the zero-order correlations of resource variables with each other and the dependent variable, Secondary Battering Cohabitation. Secondary Battering Cohabitation, Women's Age, and Age at Beginning of Cohabitation are coded by years. The dependent variable is a measure calculated from each questionnaire by noting the date of response at the top right of the first page, the respondents' present age, item I-1(a), and the date of witnessing spouses' first violent behavior, item I-3. The median length of stay after violence began was 4 years and the mean was 6 years; the range was from less than 1 year to 42 years.

Women's Age is derived from item I-1(a) on the survey instrument. Survey women are not representative of married women in this country because, compared with national statistics, they are younger and so are their spouses. Median age of sample women is 28 and of sample men is 32; whereas the median ages for U.S. wives is 42 and husbands, 45 (Rawlings, 1978:4).

Age at Beginning Cohabitation codes are obtained by computation of scale items I-1(a), I-2(a), and I-7. Most respondents inserted a date of marriage (day, month, and year), obviously a date they are unlikely to forget. Some who responded that they were "common law" wives also inserted a date, usually the year but sometimes giving the month as well. For the others, items I-7 with I-1(a) were used to code this variable. Respondents usually defined length of cohabitation in terms of weeks, months, or years, which provided a way to code more precisely Secondary Battering Cohabitation.

TABLE 5.1 Zero-Order Correlation Matrix for Variables Included in Resources—Secondary Battering Cohabitation Analysis

	1.	2.	3.	4.	5.	6.	7.	8.
1. Women's Age	1.							
2. Age at Beginning Cohabitation	.60*** (346)	1.						
3. Children's Age	.89*** (306)	.52*** (303)	1.					
4. Education	.14** (347)	.12* (343)	.10* (303)	1.				
5. Differences in Earnings	−.13* (219)	.05 (218)	.04 (193)	−.07 (218)	1.			
6. Husbands' Earnings	.31*** (200)	.12* (199)	.21** (174)	.28*** (198)	−.71*** (198)	1.		
7. Home Ownership	.38*** (337)	−.00 (334)	.34*** (297)	.26*** (335)	−.27*** (217)	.41*** (199)	1.	
8. Secondary Battering Cohabitation	.60*** (350)	.11* (346)	.55*** (306)	.03 (347)	−.26*** (219)	.26*** (200)	.47*** (337)	1.

*Significant at the .05 level or beyond
**Significant at the .01 level or beyond
***Significant at the .001 level or beyond

Unfortunately, several scale items should have been worded differently to make this kind of calculation unnecessary. For example, item I-2(a) more appropriately should have asked: "If you and the man who battered you lived together, when did you begin (or how old were you when you began) this arrangement?" In the same vein, to obtain simple coding for the dependent variable, Secondary Battering Cohabitation, a question might better have asked, "Exactly how long did you live with this man after the first time he was physically violent with you?"

Regardless of the indirect way of obtaining response codes, there are only four cases in which the woman's age at beginning of cohabitation could not be obtained. Survey women's ages for the variable Age at Beginning Cohabitation ranges from 13 to 56 years: One was 13 and two were 14, while one was 52 and the oldest woman was 56. Mean age is 23; median age is 21. This sample tends to be younger than national averages on ages at marriage; half of the survey women began cohabiting with spouses at or under the age of 21. This reflected national averages until recently; during this century, first marriage median age for women has fluctuated between 20 and 22 years. However, recent trends make this sample unusual; they are nonrepresentative for reasons explained by Rawlings:

> There have been recent changes in the proportion of persons who have been delaying marriage. Very few people marry in their teens. The relative rarity of teenage marriage accounts for the fact that in 1977, 98 percent of the men 14 to 19 years of age and 91 percent of their female counterparts had never been married [1978:3].

In this sample, 118 women (34 percent, as contrasted with national rates of 9 percent of females married under age 20) were aged 13-19 at the time they began cohabiting with the men who beat them. Only 28 were over 30 years old. In addition, many women were not entering marriage for the first time; 37 percent had been married at least once before, which increased their ages when they began cohabiting with the spouses who battered them. For comparison purposes, the women reported that 44 percent of their spouses had previous marriage(s); 83 percent of the women's prior marriages and 87 percent of the men's ended in divorce and the rest were terminated by separation or death.

Inspection of Table 5.1 gives particular insights into the strength of the relationships among variables. The strong correlation between Women's Age and Secondary Battering Cohabitation indicates that the older the women were at time of response, the longer they had stayed in the relationship after violence began. This may be more an overall indicator of the interrelationship of the passage of time, aging, and length of marital relationships than an indicator that older women stay longer with violent spouses. Women's Age and Children's Age also correlate strongly; both of these are associated with the passage of time: older women have older children. The other variables correlated with Women's Age also follow from a natural time ordering; that is, the older she is, the higher a woman's educational attainment and the higher her husband's earnings and home ownership.

There are problems with the variable Differences in Earnings (male spouses' earnings minus women's earnings) that are addressed shortly; but for the moment it will be noted that the negative correlation between Women's Age and Difference in Earnings indicates that the older the woman is, the less the differences between her earnings and her spouse's. This could reflect the salary increments that occur as a worker builds seniority, but they can hardly be expected to lessen the gap between a woman's earnings and a man's earnings. In fact, Bersch (1977) indicates that the opposite occurs: the gap widens with age. Additional questions may be asked regarding this particular correlation, because many older women are relatively new in the job market. Until World War II, women traditionally were expected to be full-time homemakers and mothers, and much of the increase in married women's employment has occurred since that time.

It was hypothesized that there would be a much stronger correlation between the Education variable and all the others. As may be noted, Education correlates well with all other resource variables at the significance level of .05 or greater except Difference in Earnings and Secondary Battering Cohabitation. This leads the investigator to suspect that there may be some other, unknown factors regarding educational level of sample wives that reduce its relationship to Secondary Battering Cohabitation. Its positive relationship with Secondary Battering Cohabitation is opposite to the hypothesized direction. This can be interpreted to mean that the higher the woman's educa-

TABLE 5.2   Educational Level of Survey Women and Their Spouses and
Percentage Comparisons of Survey Women with Men

Response Category	Women Per-cent	N	Men Per-cent	N	Women-Men Percent Disparity
Grade school only	5.2	18	14.8	50	−9.6
High school attended	25.4	88	22.2	75	+3.2
High school graduate	34.6	120	30.5	103	+4.1
College attended	26.2	91	15.1	51	+11.1
College graduate	6.3	22	9.5	32	−3.2
Graduate school/ advanced degree	2.3	8	4.1	14	−1.8
Unknown	—	—	3.8	13	
Total	100.0	347	100.0	338	

tional level, the longer she stayed; or, alternately, the less her education, the shorter time she stayed. However, since the relationship is so weak, the statistical probability is hardly greater than chance.

The educational backgrounds of survey women and their spouses are important to determine whether these couples are similar to other adult Americans. Table 5.2 shows the educational levels of respondents and their spouses and the percentage differences of sample women and their spouses.

Men in this country usually exceed women at both ends of the educational scale (proportionately more men are at the lowest level and at the highest level of educational attainment compared with women). Table 5.2 shows that sample men and women reflect the national trend, with fewer women having only a grade school education and also fewer college graduates or advanced degrees.

Perhaps even more informative as to how closely this survey sample matches statistics on educational achievement in the United States is Table 5.3, matching women's and men's percentages at different schooling levels to national percentages.

As may be noted, neither survey women nor men are as undereducated at the lowest category—grade school only. More men and women are high school dropouts, fewer graduated from high school, but more attended (but did not graduate from) college—particularly the women, who exceed national averages by 12 percent. At the

TABLE 5.3 Education of Survey Women and Men Compared with National Statistics

Response Category	Survey Women Compared with National Statistics			Spouses Compared with National Statistics		
	Sample Women	National Women*	Difference	Sample Men	National Men*	Difference
Grade school only	5.2	13.0	−7.8	14.8	18.0	−3.2
High school attended	25.4	16.0	+9.4	22.2	15.0	+7.2
High school graduate	34.6	45.0	−10.4	30.5	34.0	−3.5
College attended	26.2	14.0	+12.2	15.1	15.0	+.1
College graduate	6.3	8.0	−1.7	9.5	10.0	−.5
Graduate school/ advanced degree	2.3	4.0	−1.7	4.1	8.0	−3.9

*Table from Educational Level of Husbands, Wives and Couples: March 1977 Perspectives on American Husbands and Wives, Current Population Reports, Bureau of the Census (Rawlings, 1978:11).

upper levels of education, survey women and men have lower percentages than national averages.

Examination of Table 5.3 shows that survey couples have similar deviations from national statistics, which should not be surprising, as Rawlings explains: "Just as there is a tendency for persons to select marriage partners of the same race and age, husbands and wives usually have completed a similar number of years of school" (1978:11). Of course, these comparisons are based on frequency tables, not on a couple-by-couple basis, so there may be some individual variations. Survey women differ the most in that more are high school drop-outs, fewer are high school graduates, and more attended college. Perhaps the higher college attendance can be accounted for by the fact that approximately half of the sample came from women in California shelters where a community college education is available at practically no cost compared with some other states of the Union. Further checking showed that 31 percent of the California shelterees had attended college (17 percent higher than average); and when the Florida respondents were separated out, 19 percent of them attended college, which is still 5 percent higher than average. On the other hand, the Florida women and their spouses, as a group, showed lower educational achievement overall than the rest of the sample. Highest levels of education were attained by nonshelter volunteers.

A report presented to Department of Health, Education and Welfare Secretary Patricia Harris by a Service Delivery Assessment team shows educational levels in their sample of battered women different from either this sample or national statistics. The investigator was contacted in December 1978 by a program analyst for DHEW, who consulted on an intermittent basis since that time. Their sample of 120 battered women from a wide geographic area, according to their report (Service Delivery Assessment, 1980:ix-x), showed a much higher educational level among the women than their spouses. (Like this study, the data on the women's batterers were obtained from the victims they interviewed.) The report shows that 48 percent of the male spouses had less than a high school diploma, while only 20 percent of the females had this low an educational level (by comparison, it may be noted that 37 percent of the men and 30.6 percent of the women in this study had not completed high school).

But the DHEW sample reveals an even greater disparity in the "some college" category: only 13 percent for the men and 41 percent for the women, compared with this sample's 15 and 26 percent, respectively. In their study, 7 percent of the men and 8 percent of the women attained 16 or more years of education, compared with 14 and 9 percent in this study. Further, their report states: "A couple by couple comparison of the education level of each abused woman and her husband or boyfriend revealed that in 45 percent of the couples, the woman had received more education than her abuser" (Service Delivery Assessment, 1980:x). The data in Tables 5.2 and 5.3 do not show women better educated than spouses, but there are much fewer women at the lowest levels and there is less of a gap (favoring the men) at the highest levels of education than national statistics. In addition, these women were much more likely to begin a college education than either their spouses or national men.

Difference in Earnings is a variable derived from the men's earnings scale minus the women's earnings scale. It was hypothesized that the larger the difference between wage earnings in a family, the greater the power of the ones who contribute the larger amounts. This idea was suggested by Bird (1979), who notes that there are more egalitarian relationships in two-paycheck families where there is relatively little difference in the sizes of the paychecks. One writer explains the connection of money with power:

> The more of a family income a husband earns, the more likely he is to win family arguments; that a wife's share of power is proportionate to how much of the family income she puts in—so that a wife who contributes $6,000 to her husband's $8,000 has more power than a wife who contributes $20,000 to his $100,000 [Mall, 1979:x-8].

In addition, some early research by Blood and Wolf (1960) similarly pointed to the balance of power in marital relationships that is maintained by the person who contributes the greater resources to the marriage. The resource theory of power suggested by Blood and Wolf may indirectly explain both men's willingness to use physical force to maintain control (and their power) and women's powerlessness to prevent or stop the violence. Blood and Wolf's study found that husbands' power ranged from the maximum at highest earnings peak (working overtime with wife unemployed) to minimum at unemployed with wife employed. But even when both husband and wife were unemployed, the husband had more power than when he was working overtime and his wife was employed.

If these data support the hypothesis, then the greater difference between his earnings and her earnings should show a positive correlation between Difference in Earnings with all other variables except Education and Home Ownership. Not surprisingly, there is a (weak) negative correlation between Difference in Earnings and Education and a strong negative correlation with Home Ownership. What is perplexing and appears to challenge these assumptions is that there are strong inverse relationships between Difference in Earnings and Husbands' Earnings and Secondary Battering Cohabitation, particularly the latter. (Husbands' Earnings and Home Ownership are self-explanatory captions for variables coded by male spouses' monthly net earnings and the effect coded yes-no responses to home ownership.)

Why a greater difference in earning power is associated with shorter stay and vice versa is not readily apparent and is the opposite of the expected relationship. It is notable that Husbands' Earnings, which does not take into account a differential in earning power, has a strong positive correlation with Secondary Battering Cohabitation that is in the predicted direction. These data would appear to argue against Bird's ideas on power differences based on income differences. But the Blood and Wolf test of the resource theory of power shows that even an unemployed husband still has more power than his wife if she is also unemployed (1960:12). Their analysis looked only at husband's income and whether or not wife was employed, not taking into account the income differential. The variable Husbands' Earnings similarly reflects only the men's income and appears to support the Blood and Wolf (1960:13) finding that the husband's power varies directly with his income if we assume that husbands' earning power helped keep these women in their violent relationships longer than women whose husbands had less earning power.

The lack of correlation (in fact, the negative direction) between Difference in Earnings and Secondary Battering Cohabitation perhaps can be explained by a revision to the resource theory of power offered by Heer (1963). Heer interjects relative value of wife's available alternatives apart from the marriage and explains that

> the greater the difference between the value to the wife of the resources contributed by the husband and the value to the wife of the resources which she might earn outside the existing marriage, the greater the power of her husband, and vice versa [1963:138].

It is possible that some unemployed women or employed women with lower incomes opted out of their relationships sooner than better-employed women because they had less to lose. That is, they did not face prospects of giving up good jobs in order to obtain freedom from abuse. Many women interviewed at shelters were forced to terminate employment when they left home because they dared not show up at the workplace for fear their spouses would appear and create scenes or even commit further violence. These fears appeared to be well founded: almost all spouses know their mates' workplaces, hours, and ways to find out if they are still employed. But some women do leave home and attempt to hold onto their jobs. For example, one woman who left her husband but continued employment met her spouse during her lunch hour for a discussion supposedly about possible reconciliation. The discussion apparently did not go in the expected direction, for the woman's husband stabbed her to death before witnesses in a busy shopping center (Los Angeles Times, 1979). In addition, since the locations of shelters are kept secret as much as possible for the safety of all residents, women who continue employment while in residence must take extreme precautions to see that they are not followed while enroute.

For these reasons it is possible that women who have established career positions that provide them with relatively good income (thus a lower differential in salaries of husband and wife) are reluctant to sever, or will delay severing, their relationships with batterers because they know that one of the costs will be their own jobs and income. These ideas are presented because they may explain why women with less income relative to spouses may have less to constrain them and their alternatives may appear more positive than those of better-employed women.

The only other unexpected discovery among resource variables is the Age at Beginning Cohabitation variable, which has a negative relationship with Home Ownership: It was expected not only that these would correlate but that they would do so in a positive direction. That is, the older the women's age at beginning cohabitation, the more likely the new relationship includes homeownership because older people tend to have higher earning power than younger people, are more settled, and therefore the women would stay longer. Since it is no more than chance that they have any relationship at all, this item provides little insight. However, Age at Beginning Cohabitation indicates, through its inverse relationship with Secondary Battering Cohabitation, that older women entering relationships that become violent may remain in them for shorter time periods.

In sum, most of these resource variables correlated well and in the expected directions. As mentioned at the beginning of this chapter, a correlation matrix is useful for locating which variables are likely to provide greater explanatory power in regression analysis. The bottom row shows not only the strength of the correlations with Secondary Battering Cohabitation and statistical probability but also the N and the direction of the association. Table 5.1 identifies the variables that will be used in multiple regression analysis: Women's Age, Children's Age, and Home Ownership. Some of the responses were missing, which accounts for the variation in the N, the number in parentheses below each correlation. As can be seen, there are sizable losses in responses for variables correlated with Husbands' Earnings and Difference in Earnings, a subject that will be discussed later. Overall, since all correlations with Secondary Battering Cohabitation reach statistical significance (with the exception of Education), they appear to offer support for the resource variable in the research hypothesis.

Institutional Response Variables

The next zero-order correlation matrix, Table 5.4, shows interrelationships among institutional response variables. There are a number of scale items that attempt to tap both the respondents' efforts to seek help and the results of these efforts. Once analysis began, it became obvious that some scale items should have been worded differently for a self-administered instrument. Many respondents answered only the first part of the questions on help-seeking efforts but either did not answer the query on their perceptions of results or gave responses that showed they obviously misunderstood the point of the questions. A glance at Table 5.4 (the Ns are in parentheses beneath each Pearson correlation score) shows that there is a decided drop in the overall number of responses to the "help" items. These nonresponses weaken the model considerably, as will be seen later when regression analysis is performed on these data. For example, item IV-7(2): while 305 women answered the question of seeking help from the clergy, only 78 (26 percent) gave an affirmative response, and of these, only 66 gave answers that could be coded to the open-ended question following it. It is uncertain how the instrument might have been constructed to avoid these problems. It would be meaningless simply to ask respondents how they regarded the helpfulness of community agencies and agents if they had never called upon them for help. This is one of the problems encountered when relying on structured interview schedules, as will be discussed later.

All variables are coded in a positive direction so that yes responses to "ask" questions and affirmative responses to "help" questions are coded 1s; no's, negative, and neutral responses are coded −1s; and nonresponses are coded 0s. As can be seen in Table 5.4, Ask Psychologist and Help from Psychologist as well as Ask Marriage Counselor and Help from Marriage Counselor cannot be correlated because the "ask" items are constants in relation to "help" items. That is, all "help" variables are included in the tests only when "ask" categories are coded 2, so there is no variation in the "ask" items. Help from Clergy responses were so few that they were not entered into the Pearson correlation test.

The table shows that those who asked for help from clergy were less likely to answer affirmatively to Help from Lawyer (a variable that includes private lawyers, law clinics, prosecutors' offices, and the like). Those who regarded police response positively also regarded Help from Lawyer positively. There is a strong positive correlation between asking marriage counselors for help and seeking psychological counseling, but the helpfulness of psychologists shows a negative direction. On the other hand, women who believed they had

TABLE 5.4 Zero-Order Correlation Matrix for Variables Included in Institutional Response—Secondary Battering Cohabitation Analysis

	1.	2.	3.	4.	5.	6.	7.	8.
1. Ask Psychologist	1.							
2. Help from Psychologist	(a) (63)	1.						
3. Ask Clergy	.31*** (291)	−.14 (61)	1.					
4. Help from Lawyer	.13 (151)	.25 (36)	−.03 (151)	1.				
5. Ask Marriage Counselor	.32*** (288)	−.20 (59)	.19*** (291)	.04 (149)	1.			
6. Help from Marriage Counselor	.30* (40)	.27 (19)	.24 (39)	−.02 (28)	(a) (41)	1.		
7. Help from Police	−.15* (153)	−.14 (35)	−.09 (158)	.21* (107)	−.09 (153)	.43* (21)	1.	
8. Secondary Battering Cohabitation	.22** (301)	.16 (63)	.20*** (305)	.09 (155)	.14** (298)	.27* (41)	−.05 (163)	1.

*Significant at the .05 level or beyond
**Significant at the .01 level or beyond
***Significant at the .001 level or beyond
(a) Correlation coefficient could not be computed.

124

been helped by marriage counselors also showed that psychologists were helpful, although there were few in this category (N = 19); respondents to both items are so few that interpretations would be purely speculative. Those who turned to marriage counselors were also very likely to turn to the clergy for assistance. One variable that is interesting to follow is Help from Police, which, not surprisingly, is correlated positively with Help from Lawyer. However, the direction of all other correlations is negative, with the exception of Help from Marriage Counselor; but once more, the N is so small as to disallow any interpretations.

There is a weak negative relationship between Help from Police and Secondary Battering Cohabitation, but in this case the N is somewhat larger, although it still constitutes responses from less than half the sample (N = 163). This could be interpreted to mean that women who received help from police intervention were likely to stay a shorter time in their relationships; or, conversely, the longer a woman remains in a violent relationship, the more likely she is to encounter unhelpful police intervention. Qualitative data lead the investigator to suggest that the second possibility is very likely because interviews with police show that in violent relationships of long duration police officers are less inclined to offer assistance or exert effort beyond what is obviously required for performance of their duties to protect life. As "problem families" become identified, police responding to repeat calls from the same home become disenchanted with the idea that anything they do will be followed by victim action to effect change, so they tend to handle these "repeaters" with a detached, peacekeeping attitude. This is not to deny that helpful police intervention might also affect length of stay, because just knowing that the violence that occurred constitutes a crime of assault and battery may act as a catalyst to change. In addition, helpful police may serve to bolster a sense of worth and give added self-confidence to victims, which encourages them to seek nonviolent lives away from their spouses.

Overall, the matrix of institutional response variables shows interesting features of the data and problems inherent in the survey instrument and even of collecting data with structured interview schedules. Table 5.4 shows that the only useful variables for regression analysis in this subset are Ask Psychologist, Ask Clergy, and Ask Marriage Counselor because of their stronger correlations with the dependent variable (Secondary Battering Cohabitation) and their higher response rate. Thus, while searching for explanation of length of stay in violent relationships, we are limited to testing only with help-seeking behavior rather than with the more important question of the effects on length of stay from help obtained or denied.

A slim majority of the institutional response variables tested reached statistical significance with the dependent variable. With the exception of Help from Police, correlations between the dependent variable and all women who both asked for help and perceived that they received helpful response are in a positive direction. These findings appear to offer mild support for the research hypothesis. In other words, women who sought and received help from these agents of social institutions stayed somewhat longer with spouses—men they eventually left. Of course, another interpretation is that the longer a woman stays with a batterer, the more likely she is to ask for help and perceive a favorable response. Theoretical assumptions are that the former interpretation is more likely to be accurate. What is strikingly noticeable here is that the strongest positive correlation between length of stay after battering is with the variable Ask Clergy, which may be more an indicator that traditional, religious women turned to the clergy for guidance and as a result stayed longer with their abusers.

Traditional Ideology Variables

Turning now to the third major concept, Table 5.5 shows intercorrelations among variables hypothesized to measure traditional ideology. As mentioned earlier, traditional ideology is conceptualized as an internalized way of viewing the social system and one's own position in it from a traditional frame of reference that endorses the patriarchal-hierarchical family system, resulting in behaviors that conform to this outlook.

The relatively weak correlations among many of these variables indicate that there may be unmeasured variables outside the model; that there may be weaknesses in the theoretical propositions guiding

TABLE 5.5 Zero-Order Correlation Matrix for Variables Included in Traditional Ideology—Secondary Battering Cohabitation Analysis

	1.	2.	3.	4.	5.	6.	7.
1. Previously Divorced	1.						
2. Pregnant at Marriage	-.08 (298)	1.					
3. First or Only Child	.12* (336)	-.03 (302)	1.				
4. Traditional Parents	-.02 (338)	-.06 (304)	.01 (346)	1.			
5. Religious Family	-.03 (335)	-.02 (301)	.01 (342)	.18*** (344)	1.		
6. Number of Children	.15** (333)	.04 (297)	-.10* (339)	.06 (341)	.10* (338)	1.	
7. Secondary Battering Cohabitation	-.13** (340)	.03 (305)	.02 (346)	.13** (348)	.12* (345)	.35*** (342)	1.

*Significant at the .05 level or beyond
**Significant at the .01 level or beyond
***Significant at the .001 level or beyond

the study; or that the survey instrument was incapable of adequately measuring the variables. There are obvious limitations to attempts to gather these kinds of data through structured survey instruments, as well as in the particular instrument constructed for this study. It is suspected that even the most sophisticated questionnaire may fail to measure adequately some of the most basic norms and values people carry with them through life and the effects of these norms and values when expressed through behavior. Other studies have shown that there is inconsistency between respondents' expressed attitudes and subsequent behavior (Dibble and Straus, 1980). Fortunately, the investigator employed other qualitative data-gathering techniques that may provide greater insight and clearer explanations than if quantitative data-gathering tools were solely depended on. There will be further discussion on these points later.

Table 5.5 shows variable names that should be explained. Previously Divorced is an effect-coded variable that separates previously married respondents into categories of either divorced or separated (assumed to defy traditional norms) or widowed. A theoretical assumption was that traditional women who experienced an earlier marriage dissolution would be more likely to remain longer in a second marriage because of the presumed "failure" a dissolved marriage represents to many women (Bernard, 1975). Previously Divorced correlates strongly with Secondary Battering Cohabitation in a negative direction; yet there is a statistically significant correlation with the variable Number of Children, which is expected, since many divorced women in the sample brought one or more children by other men into their relationships with the batterers.

Pregnant before Marriage is an effect-coded variable that categorizes women who were pregnant or nonpregnant when they entered the violent relationships, with the theoretical assumption that the pregnant women may be somewhat less traditional. Coding of Pregnant before Marriage is in a positive response direction; therefore, relationships of Pregnant before Marriage with other independent (traditional) variables is expected to be negative. The interrelationships of Pregnant before Marriage with the other traditional concepts are all in the expected direction, which gives some evidence of internal validity of the items. It does not correlate strongly with Secondary

Battering Cohabitation, however, and it does not meet statistical significance with any variable in the matrix.

First or Only Child is an effect-coded variable that distinguishes first-born or only children in their families of orientation. First or Only Child was tested in response to a provocative and plausible idea suggested by Forer (1969, 1976) that first-born and only children are more likely to be traditional in their behavior because they are usually the recipients of parental traditional values (in addition, they may be authoritarian and, in the case of first-born, jealous and possessive). As Table 5.5 shows, First or Only Child is not strongly correlated with any of the other variables exept Number of Children and Previously Divorced and both of these are in directions opposite from the expected. First or only children females in this survey are somewhat more likely to have entered the violent relationship after an earlier marriage and are likely to have fewer children. It was hypothesized that if first and only children are relatively more traditional, then they remain longer in unhappy relationships because they would be more unwilling to break with the tradition of monogamous marriage and two-parent families. First or Only Child has a weak positive relationship with Secondary Battering Cohabitation, so these women tend to stay longer in their violent relationships than women not first-born or only children. A significant number of these first or only children had an earlier marriage that ended in divorce; and if first or only children are more traditional, this may help explain why these women tended to maintain their current relationships longer despite physical abuse.

On the other hand, it was hypothesized that traditional women tend to have more children; yet First or Only Children had fewer. A recent report may provide insight into the seeming contradiction. The study by Polit et al. (1980) focused on adult only children and generally found that many stereotypes about the only child are unfounded. The nonrandom sample selected by Polit et al. was divided into three groups: onlies, first borns, and later borns (1980:101). Their findings give no support to some negative traits attributed to onlies; in many respects they found no differences between the groups. On some measures, the onlies among these white, middle- and upper-middle-class Boston suburbanites were significantly different.

Compared with other first borns with siblings, and with individuals of higher birth orders, only children were found to have higher educational levels, higher occupational status, smaller families, and to be more secularly oriented. Female onlies were more likely to be working, to have planned their families before marriage, and to have been more autonomous in deciding to work [1980:99].

A substantial number of the survey women seem to be first or only children, although there are no national statistics available on birth order of the U.S. population, so representativeness cannot be checked. Frequency tables reveal that 23 women in this survey were only children, while 109 were oldest children in their families of orientation, giving a total of 132 (38 percent) who were first or only children. (Their families ranged from one to 18 children and one woman was the eighteenth child.) By way of comparison, many of the batterers appear to be first or only children: 328 women reported on birth order of their spouses. Frequencies show that 25 of the men were only children and 116 were first-borns, giving a total of 131 (40 percent) of the abusers who were also first or only children.

The other two variables, Traditional Parents and Religious Family, were tested with the idea that perhaps they might tap traditional/ nontraditional upbringing of survey women. Traditional Parents is a term used for parental marital status to denote conventionalism in remaining married to each other; it is derived from items I-15 and 16. If respondents' parents were still living together or were widowed, the variable is effect-coded 1; if not living together through divorce or separation it is effect-coded -1; nonresponses are zeroes. Religious Family is based on family of orientation religious service attendance, item I-21. There is indication of internal validity of these constructs, as Table 5.5 shows. There is a strong positive correlation between the two and both of them correlate positively with the dependent variable at the .05 significance level or beyond. Traditional Parents does not reach statistical significance with any of the other variables, but all correlations are in the expected direction. Correlations of Religious Family with other variables is the same except that it does reach significance with Number of Children. Self-explanatory Number of Children of survey respondents also correlates with other variables in the predicted direction and achieves strongest statistical significance with the dependent variable, Secondary Battering Cohabitation. Traditional women are expected to have more children in their families, perhaps because of religious convictions, especially if they belong to the more conservative denominations but also because motherhood is expected among very traditional women as being a primary purpose in life.

The correlation matrix of traditional ideology variables in Table 5.5 shows interesting features of the relationships. With the exception of Previously Divorced, all correlations with Secondary Battering Cohabitation are in the predicted direction and some reached statistical significance; thus, they appear to offer some support for the research hypothesis. The strong negative correlation between Previously Divorced and Secondary Battering Cohabitation may indicate that theoretical assumptions that previously divorced women are likely to remain longer with abusers because they have already violated a traditional norm by divorce are incorrect. It may be that the fact that their traditionalism was already lessened by a prior divorce, so that when following conjugal relationships became violent, they were more likely to sever it sooner than women who had never before gone through the separation and divorce process. Thus, even by correlating in the opposite direction from expectations, this variable may add support to the research hypothesis by showing that these are less traditional women who remained a shorter time period with men who battered them.

Regression Analysis

Table 5.6 shows simple regressions of Secondary Battering Cohabitation on individual independent variables from the three subsets. The table includes the N of both variables in each bivariate regression run, the R square, and the Beta. With the exception of resource variables, it seems obvious that the remaining individual variables in the other two subsets cannot predict length of stay for battered women. The only institutional response variables that have sufficiently high cases are those indicating that some women did ask psychologists, members of the clergy, and marriage counselors for assistance. All institutional response variables indicating whether or

TABLE 5.6   Simple Regressions of Secondary Battering Cohabitation on
             Individual Independent Variables

Variable	N	R^2	Beta
RESOURCES			
Women's Age	350	.36	.60
Age at Beginning Cohabitation	346	.01	− .11
Children's Age	306	.30	.55
Education	347	.00	.03
Difference in Earnings	219	.07	− .26
Husbands' Earnings	200	.07	.26
Home Ownership	337	.22	.47
INSTITUTIONAL RESPONSE			
Ask Psychologist	301	.05	.22
Help from Psychologist	63	.03	.16
Ask Clergy	305	.04	.20
Help from Lawyer	155	.01	.09
Ask Marriage Counselor	41	.07	.29
Help from Marriage Counselor	41	.07	.29
Help from Police	163	.00	− .05
TRADITIONAL IDEOLOGY			
Previously Divorced	340	.02	− .13
Pregnant Before Marriage	305	.00	.03
First or Only Child	346	.00	.02
Traditional Parents	348	.02	.13
Religious Family	345	.01	.12
Number of Children	342	.12	.35

not such help-seeking was rewarded have Ns so low that further analysis would not be useful (none of them even have a 50 percent response rate). The traditional ideology variables have a higher response rate, but they also appear to have very little individual predictive value, with the exception of Number of Children (of survey women).

For purposes of multiple regression, the three variables in each subset that have both strongest statistically significant Pearson product moment correlation coefficients and largest Ns are selected. Table 5.7 shows the three stepwise regression tables; variables are entered into the equation on the basis of their explanatory power, beginning with the one that explains most of the variance in the dependent variable.

TABLE 5.7   Multiple Regressions of Secondary Battering Cohabitation on
Resources, Institutional Response, and Traditional Ideology

Variable	N	R^2	R^2 Change	Beta
RESOURCES				
Women's Age	350	.355	.355	.41
Home Ownership	337	.425	.070	.29
Children's Age	306	.427	.001	.09
INSTITUTIONAL RESPONSE				
Ask Psychologist	301	.047	.047	.15
Ask Clergy	305	.068	.021	.14
Ask Marriage Counselor	298	.071	.003	.06
TRADITIONAL IDEOLOGY				
Number of Children	342	.124	.124	.38
Previously Divorced	340	.161	.037	− .19
Traditional Parents	348	.170	.010	.10

Quite clearly—and not surprisingly—the strongest set of predictor variables in these regression equations is the resource subset, which accounts for 43 percent of the variance in the dependent variable, Secondary Battering Cohabitation. The institutional response subset has a disappointingly low R^2 of only 7 percent, which means that 93 percent of the variance in Secondary Battering Cohabitation is unexplained. Traditional ideology variables have a somewhat greater explanatory power at 17 percent, but Traditional Parents only contributes one percent of the variance. It was anticipated that the variables in each subset would have shown a greater effect on Secondary Battering Cohabitation, but, as mentioned earlier, regression analysis is being used as a statistical technique for description rather than inferential purposes. The weaknesses in explanatory power or predictability are probably due in large part to weaknesses in the survey instrument itself that failed precisely to tap measures of each of the variables. However, it was not assumed that any of the theoretical constructs alone can answer the question of why these women stayed with their batterers. It was expected that they have a cumulative and interactive effect on such decisions. In other words, if an individual victim has positive resources but is very traditional and meets negative institutional response when she seeks outside intervention, each of these factors will affect her decision to stay or to leave. Conversely, if a victim is nontraditional, she is unlikely to be as deeply affected by negative institutional response and may decide to leave, even without adequate resources. The problem of making decisions about staying or leaving is undeniably and predictably complex, and these tests show that there are many factors outside the model that impinge on and influence the process.

Discussion and Review of the Variables

The Pearson product moment correlations provided an overall look at the variables and their relationships with each other. The matrices serve several purposes: they show strong correlations among variables and also directions of the relationships. In most cases the variables correlated in the hypothesized direction, but in a few others the correlations are in the opposite direction. One of these is Difference in Earnings, which has a strong negative correlation with Husbands' Earnings, Home Ownership, and Secondary Battering Cohabitation. Some of the unexpected inverse relationships of Husbands' Earnings with other variables were discussed earlier and will not be repeated here. Probably one of the major problems with both Husbands' Earnings and Difference in Earnings is that the correlations are based on a low response rate. Some spouses are unemployed; some women did not know the correct answers; while others may have simply guessed.

Many of the interviewed women had no idea what their spouses' monthly net income was, even though in most states, such as California, a husband's earnings are legally equal property of his wife. Even if the survey women did not know their spouses' take-home pay, they usually knew something about the law regarding marital joint income, and the investigator assumes that the women were more willing to guess on these items than to admit this information had been withheld from them. If they were employed, they probably used their own deflated incomes as a base point for their responses, which would give a downward bias. Many shelterees encountered during this investigation are very intelligent women who had been isolated from friends, relatives, and significant others for long periods. Once they arrived at shelters they found a warm, supportive atmosphere maintained by staff and other residents and possibly for the first time in a long while they found the freedom to interact on an open and honest basis with other women. Usually by the end of the first week of residence they were able to talk openly with other victims of spousal violence about many matters never previously discussed. Only after such interaction did most of them gradually realize the extent of control that had been exerted over them. Some reacted in shock, anger, bitter humor, or self-recrimination for not having realized this earlier or for having stayed so long in situations with so little personal freedom. To admit not even knowing her spouse's salary could provide even more embarrassment to most of these women than to admit, for example, being 30 pounds overweight or 35 years old.

Tables 5.8 and 5.9 show responses to employment items on the survey instrument by the women on their own employment histories plus the data they provided about their spouses. These tables provide a picture of the employment status of sample women and their spouses.

Only one-third of the women were employed at the time they responded to the questionnaire. As mentioned earlier, it is quite likely that a number of them had just terminated employment when they

TABLE 5.8   Present Employment of Survey Women and Their Spouses and Past Employment for Presently Unemployed Women

PRESENTLY EMPLOYED

Response Category	Women Percent	N	Men Percent	N
Yes	32.3	111	64.2	219
No	67.7	233	24.6	84
Don't know	—	—	11.1	38
Total	100.0	344	100.0	341

TIME PERIOD FOR UNEMPLOYED SURVEY
WOMEN SINCE LAST EMPLOYMENT

Response Category	Percent	N
Within 6 months	38.6	76
Within 1 year	17.8	35
1 to 2 years	27.4	54
2 to 5 years	7.1	14
More than 5 years	9.1	18
Total	100.0	197

TABLE 5.9 Present and Past Employment Income and Job Classifications of Survey Women and Present Income and Job Classifications of Spouses

MONTHLY NET INCOME OF
SURVEY WOMEN AND SPOUSES

	Women—Now		Men—Now		Women—Past	
	Percent	N	Percent	N	Percent	N
< $300	17.8	19	3.5	7	31.3	51
$300–$600	44.9	48	19.0	38	44.8	73
$600–$900	25.2	27	30.0	60	17.8	29
$900–$1500	9.3	10	29.0	58	4.9	8
$1500+	2.8	3	18.5	37	1.2	2
Total	100.0	107	100.0	200	100.0	163

JOB CLASSIFICATIONS OF
SURVEY WOMEN AND SPOUSES

	Women—Now		Men—Now		Women—Past	
	Percent	N	Percent	N	Percent	N
Domestic	11.7	13	—	—	10.1	20
Vocational	31.5	35	16.8	51	42.7	85
Unskilled labor	10.8	12	22.8	69	32.7	65
Skilled labor	—	—	21.8	66	6.5	13
Tech/mech	5.4	6	14.5	44	1.5	3
Clerical	22.5	25	—	—	—	—
Sales	1.8	2	—	—	—	—
Managerial	—	—	8.3	25	4.0	8
Professional	16.2	18	8.3	25	2.5	5
Self-employed	—	—	7.3	22	—	—
Student	—	—	.3	1	—	—
Total	100.0	111	100.0	303	100.0	199

took shelter residence. According to some sources, percentages of women employed in 1974-1975 ranged from 42 to 46 percent (Bryant, 1977).

Of the survey women then employed, 75 percent worked full-time and 25 percent part-time, which matches the Bryant statistics (1977:12). The distribution of earnings and job classifications of women previously employed is shown in the right two columns in Table 5.9. Of the 197 formerly employed women in this survey, two-thirds had held full-time positions. By comparison, only 5 percent of the currently employed men were working at part-time jobs. But only 57 percent of the sample provided information on spouses' income, as shown in Table 5.9, and 36 percent of those who responded on current employment said either their abusers were unemployed or they did not know (see Table 5.8).

Unemployment figures for the men seem unusually high, but the few women who explained the sources of the men's income if unemployed generally stated that they were receiving support from retirement or disability. These data should be viewed with caution for several reasons, the most important of which is the low response rate on some items. Another reason for caution in interpretation is that reports on the men's employment histories are derived indirectly through the female respondents and thus are subject to error.

Not surprisingly, the women are clustered in lower-level employment categories. Adding the 197 women who indicated they were employed previously reveals that 308 women (88 percent) of the sample have held paid employment at one point in their lives, about 40 percent of the currently unemployed within the past six months. The other 12 percent had never held paid employment.

Inspection of the currently employed income distributions in Table 5.9 shows that 78 percent of the male spouses had take-home pay of $600 or more per month, whereas about 63 percent of the female spouses took home less than $600 a month. In fact, for women now employed, only 37 percent of them had net wages of $600 or more. A net wage of $600 per month translates roughly to around $8,000 gross per year when standard withholding deductions are computed. According to the National Commission on Working Women (1978), "Women working full-time, year round in 1977 had a median income of $8,814 while men's income averaged $15,070. Women made 58.5 cents to every dollar made by men."

The record is even worse for previously employed women: only 24 percent of them exceeded $600 monthly net income. This may partly explain why the Difference in Earnings variable has a negative correlation with Secondary Battering Cohabitation. Obviously, 76 percent of the formerly employed women had low-income-producing employment, and if leaving a violent spouse means also leaving a low-paying job, the sacrifice may seem relatively minor.

While monthly net incomes of the women compared with the men skew in the expected direction, the women's is reduced even more by the fact that more of their current employment was part-time, compared with the men. The tables might have used only full-time employment of both men and women for more precise comparison. But on the other hand, these distributions are the net earnings of the women in this sample and it was intended to determine how much cash income these women and their men bring home each month. If a woman works part-time, it is quite possible that this is all the time she can spare away from her home and children, or perhaps it is the only kind of employment open to her. These are the actual incomes brought in by survey women, regardless of working hours, because that is what they have to depend on when they contemplate separation from their abusers. Part-time work included jobs such as chambermaid, kitchen helper at school, door-to-door selling, and so forth, the types of jobs that offer or require no more than part-time work.

Each of these independent variables could be further described to reveal the wealth of information survey respondents provided. The most that can be attempted here is to touch on a few to provide insight into these women's life circumstances that go beyond the statistical tests of analysis performed above. The major shortcomings of the institutional response variables is that while they contributed much information, they do not adequately answer the questions posed by these tests. Sometimes the problem is in low response rates; for example, only 155 women answered the question asking about law agencies (Help from Lawyer); only 99 said they sought help from psychiatrists or psychologists; 78 went to clergymen; and 51 went to marriage counselors. Of those who asked for help, 69 said they received helpful response from law agencies (mostly private attorneys and legal aid); 26, from psychological counselors; 18, from the clergy; and 21, from marriage counselors.

What these survey figures do not show—information that is much more revealing—was obtained through interviews and group discussions. As mentioned earlier, many of the women were socially isolated when they were living with their spouses, and relatively few attempted to make contact with community agencies that are supposed to serve clients with needs such as theirs. In some cases, the women would manage to get to a counselor or clergyman and almost immediately become disenchanted with the idea that the agents they met would believe them, be able to fully understand their situations, or be truly helpful. During group discussions the topic was frequently the types of reception they received from counselors when some of them actually revealed their problems. Their experiences during the first attempt at help-seeking were frequently so disappointing that they made no further attempts until they turned to the shelters for sanctuary. Many women felt that their help-seeking efforts only made their situations worse, particularly if their spouses found out about them. Quite a few were so controlled and confined by spouses that they saw no way to consult with an "outsider" without their husbands' knowledge. One woman told the oft-repeated tale of being kept at home with children, no car, and no money. Her husband would take her once a week to the grocery store where he would wait while she gathered purchases; when she came to the cashier he would write out a check; then take her and the groceries back home. Her nearest relatives lived over 500 miles away; they knew nothing of her situation.

Another woman came to the United States from Europe with her husband who became a wealthy farmer. During an interview, this woman said that her husband denied her money even for food for herself and her seven children (they could eat what was grown on the farm or do without, apparently). She told of the times she and the children went to the barn and searched for the place where he hid money from his cash sales; this was the way she managed to get money for the children and their clothes. Her only attempt to get outside help was through a private attorney, who she discovered was a Mormon, so his efforts went toward "patching up" a bad marriage. Years later, one night she attempted to get away on foot, but her husband organized the neighbors to search the fields for her by convincing them that his wife was emotionally unstable. She was found and returned home, despite her pleadings. This woman spent 26 years living with her abuser until finally one night, when she was attempting to protect her daughter from abuse, her husband kicked her so hard that his foot tore into her vagina and she had to be taken to a hospital for emergency treatment. This case history came from one of the sample volunteers whose abuse occurred years before any shelters for battered women had opened in California. She was finally able to obtain a divorce and has since returned to her native country.

The consensus of opinion during group discussions was that it was not worth the effort to turn to traditional helping agencies: Prosecutors were unwilling to prosecute; lawyers wanted money before beginning cases; ministers advised prayer and faith; and counselors generally concentrated on problems within the woman since they usually could not conduct couples counseling. Some women, of course, did receive concerned response from some social agents, but this often took the form of misdirected help or not enough help. Many community helping agents simply do not understand the multiple problems of battered women well enough to render adequate and appropriate intervention. In addition, there was the possibility of penalty by further abuse from spouses when and if they discovered that their women had "betrayed" them by telling outsiders.

Even when the victims were taken to doctors or hospitals for treatment for their injuries, many of them did not dare reveal the cause to anyone. Almost half the survey sample (N = 157) said they received medical treatment at least once (65 said more than once) for injuries suffered in beatings by spouses, but only 78 women said they told medical practitioners what had happened to them. But in addition, 102 women said they *needed* medical treatment after a beating but were unable to get it. The reasons they presented for not getting medical attention included no money or no transportation, but most (44 percent) said their spouses would not let them go. Twelve women indicated they did not want others to know what had happened to them.

As for police involvement, 193 women reported the police were called on one or more occasions; unfortunately, only 163 recorded the attitude or behavior of law enforcement officers toward themselves. Of these, only 53 had a favorable report; 78 were unfavorable and 32 said the police attitude and behavior was neutral. Group discussions with battered women and interviews with law enforcement officers indicate that these responses probably are an accurate reflection of the interaction during police responses to domestic disturbance calls, given that most police departments regard them as nonarrest calls that are highly dangerous for officers but for which they usually receive very little training.

The statistical tests of analysis on the traditional ideology variables appear to provide more information. In the survey sample, 103 (29 percent) of the women were divorced from a previous husband (Previously Divorced); 69 (20 percent) revealed that they were pregnant at the time they married the men who beat them (Pregnant before Marriage); and two-thirds of the sample had parents either still married to each other or widowed (Traditional Parents). The individual variable with the greatest explanatory power in regression analysis is Number of Children. To provide a clearer idea of the children produced by these women and their spouses, Table 5.10 gives these figures plus the number of preschool-aged children of survey women.

As for the number of children being an indicator of traditionalism, the statistical tests presented earlier reveal a strong positive correlation with Secondary Battering Cohabitation, and Number of Children is the strongest predictor regression variable in this subset. Theoretical assumptions were that battered women would have more children than average Americans, which would be an indicator of their traditionalism, as stated earlier. Yet, contrary to expectations, these women had fewer children than did women in the general population: 306 women had given birth to an average of 2.4 children. The average number of children for couples up to 25 years of age in 1977 was 3.4 (Rawlings, 1978:19-20).

If these women are highly traditional, as hypothesized, there seems to be no reflection of it in the number of children they produced compared with other women outside shelters. But compared with the other women within shelters, the more children mothers had, the

TABLE 5.10   Marital Histories and Dependent Children of Survey Women
and Spouses

PREVIOUS MARRIAGES AND DEPENDENT CHILDREN

	Women	Men
Previously married	127 (36%)	153 (44%)
Children by other spouse	125	253
Resident stepchildren	42	75
Children not living with biological parent	36	211
Number of children produced by 306 couples in sample of 350	607	
Number of dependent children of sample women	613	

YOUNGEST CHILDREN BY AGE AND BIRTH ORDER

	0–6 months	6 months– 1 year	1–6 years	total less than 6 years
1st child	11	18	105	134
2nd child	5	17	80	102
3rd child	4	6	34	44
4th child	3	21	20	44
5th child	1	8	5	14
6th child	1	1	4	6
Total	25	71	248	344

longer they stayed, which can also be interpreted the other way: the longer they stayed, the more children they produced. Perhaps their traditionalism is reflected in the finding that the more children they had, the longer they stayed, in the belief that it was in the best interests of their children to live in a two-parent family.

As Table 5.10 shows, 344 (56 percent) of the children of survey women are youngsters under the age of six, which can be a very strong factor operating to keep these women in their relationships (note that Children's Age has a strong positive correlation with Secondary Battering Cohabitation). It can also be noted that the vast majority of survey women with young children waited until their children had passed the first-year infancy stage before leaving home. However, prospects of establishing independent lives away from spouses for the majority of mothers who come to shelters are dim, in view of the lack of adequate and affordable child care facilities in this country. Certainly having very young dependent children contributes to the fact that between 20 and 50 percent of the women who come to shelters return to their spouses. Unfortunately, no records are available on whether the women who return home continue to stay there or eventually leave permanently. Most shelters cannot afford to do adequate follow-up on ex-clients and have rules against readmitting the same women for security reasons. Shelter operators are unwilling to take the chance that during the "reconciliation" period the women did not divulge the location of the shelter where they had stayed during their absence from home.

Summary

The hypothesis proposed to explain why battered women remain with their abusive spouses was tested with data obtained from a survey questionnaire designed for this study that was distributed to women in the United States for self-enumeration. A subset of individual independent variables for each of the three constructs—resources, institutional response, and traditional ideology—were analyzed by the Pearson product moment correlations test and bivariate regression. Three of the variables in each subset with strongest relationships to the dependent variable were then selected for multiple regression analysis. The dependent variable Secondary Battering Cohabitation was regressed on the three constructs using the forward stepwise inclusion procedure: each independent variable enters into the equation in single steps from best to worst. That is, the variable explaining the greatest amount of variance in the dependent variable is entered first and the variable that explains the least amount of variance in the dependent variable is entered last.

These tests were performed for purposes of description rather than inference, since test assumptions of sample representativeness cannot be established. Because this is a case study of women who say they were beaten by spouses, there is no assurance that they and their perceptions are the same, similar, or strikingly different from those of most battered women in this country. The attempt was to gain some understanding of this particular group of women, their backgrounds, their experiences, and their circumstances to see if the three theoretical constructs could help explain why they stayed with their spouses beyond primary battering.

The survey instrument provided a wealth of data that were useful for giving an overall impression of the women as a group: their perceptions of the violence, their attempts to prevent or avoid the violence, and the responses they received to their efforts to obtain intervention or assistance outside the home. But selected variables were unable to explain enough of the variance in the length of Secondary Battering Cohabitation to do much more than offer weak support for the research hypothesis. Why this is so is discussed in the next chapter, and some suggestions for improving the measures are offered next.

Chapter 6

WHY DO THEY STAY?

There are two major areas to be covered by this chapter. The first is a review of the research hypothesis tests on why women stay with batterers that was the focus of the previous chapter and some suggestions for improvements in the survey instrument. This is followed by other findings on the variables resources, institutional response, and traditional ideology that were not included in the quantitative measures but which may help supplement understanding of why victims stay. Second, as mentioned earlier, there will be tests of the hypothesis offered by Gelles (1976) to explain why battered women stay. Since statistical tests failed to provide strong support for the research hypothesis developed for this investigation, better understanding of battered women's complex problems may be obtained by exploring suggestions made by another researcher. As sociologists know, no single study can be expected to provide the perfect answers or to have found the "absolute truth" but we can learn something from each of many studies so that the various findings will have a cumulative effect in our search for knowledge and better understanding of social problems.

Tests of This Model and
Suggestions for Improvements

Quantitative data obtained by the survey instrument offered some support for the research hypothesis, but this was mainly through the resource variables. Since much of the variance in the dependent variable is unexplained, these tests can hardly be considered conclusive evidence to support the major hypothesis regarding reasons these women stayed with their batterers. The survey instrument proved useful for gathering much information in a relatively short time over a geographically wide area; yet it appears to have been unable to measure adequately two of the three key constructs. But while the questionnaire employed in this study was unable to measure adequately some of the independent variables, it led the way to suggestions for improvements.

For example, there might have been fewer institutional response items inquiring about help-seeking efforts and perceived responses, and the remaining items might have been worded more directly. In attempting to gauge response from medical practitioners, there were seven questions with eight open-ended follow-up items. These were devised in a step-by-step format leading from the use or need of medical attention to the response women received from health care specialists. In a similar manner, the items regarding police involvement required a number of forced-choice plus open-ended response categories, attempting to follow in temporal sequence from initial responses of police following an assault through the prosecution procedures to adjudication. These items not only contributed to the length of the instrument but also required more concentration, patience, and comprehension from respondents. Some of the women who did not complete the questionnaire before they left shelters met with the investigator and explained that they were unable to spend the required amount of time necessary to respond as they had hoped. These women were anxious to participate but had too little free time away from other responsibilities such as house meetings, job or apartment seeking, child care, and so forth.

The traditional ideology measures are particularly in need of revision. For example, item I-20 asking parental family religion presents only major religious denomination categories. Frequency tables show that 184 women (53 percent) were raised as Protestants; 104 (30 percent) were raised as Catholics, and the balance were raised in various other faiths or none. Although the majority came from a Protestant family background, this tells very little, since there is a wide range within this category from liberal Unitarians to ultraconservative Mormons and Southern Baptists. This item more properly should have asked and been coded into the full range of religious denominations before it could be a reliable and adequate measure of liberal or conservative-traditional religious training these women received. The Blumenthal et al. (1972) study on American men's attitudes toward violence, for example, separated Protestants into five categories: general, reformation, pietistic, fundamentalist, and other Christian, and found differences in each of these categories. Interestingly, on the approval of violence for social control scale, Jews indicated a low level of approval, whereas fundamentalists showed a high level of approval of violence (Blumenthal et al., 1972:51). All that was learned about religiosity of the women from the scale used in this study was general denomination; that almost half (43 percent) of the sample said their families attended religious services "very often," but only 19 percent described themselves as currently "very religious."

In addition, since traditional ideology is a construct largely referring to attitudes as well as behavior directed by attitudes, one of the better validated attitude scales already available might have been utilized, such as the FEM scale designed by Smith et al. (1975).

In sum, some components of the survey instrument might have been shortened to obtain more clear-cut measures of help-seeking efforts of the women and the usefulness of these efforts and the extent of women's traditionalism. In other areas response categories might have been extended so that more precise measures were available. Because the instrument was designed in the exploratory phase of the study, it covers a myriad of topics not addressed here but which may prove useful for later analysis. These include items on involvement or noninvolvement of alcohol and other drugs, suicide attempts, and sexual practices. The instrument has already provided data that proved helpful to activists lobbying for the passage of the spousal rape bill when it was before the California Legislature in 1979. Some of the frequencies of spousal rape reported by survey women and a random selection of additional comments were offered in testimony before the Criminal Justice Committee (Martin, 1979). Martin feels that the presentation of research data was impressive and convincing evidence that helped facilitate passage of the bill into law.

Other Findings

Nevertheless, it seems that almost no structured interview schedule could adequately gauge the depth and breadth of the women's experiences and feelings. In efforts to provide responses or opportunities for individualized open comments for various contingencies and the multitude of possible answers, the scale was perhaps made too complex for self-enumeration—at least, too complex considering the circumstances under which it was distributed and administered.

On the other hand, there are the qualitative data obtained through field research. For the investigator, being in shelters provided rich and full impressions and memories of countless battered women and their children in this country and abroad. Talking with some of the women when they telephoned to gain admittance to shelters, observing them as they moved in and as they settled into the routine of communal living, talking with an individual in her overcrowded sleeping quarters or with a group around the kitchen table while some fed babies in high chairs and others prepared meals, or with the entire group of residents sitting in the living room areas after the youngsters had all been put to bed—these are etched in memory. These experiences served to establish rapport and understanding so that the women very quickly communicated honestly and openly. Insight gained through these methods may be nonquantifiable but it is just as valid as any written statements—perhaps even more so. In addition to interaction with victims inside shelters as well as outside them, encounters with members of the helping agencies, law enforcement, judiciary, and legislators all proved to be other rich sources of data. Overall, these contacts, whether brief or extensive through in-depth interview, tended to confirm the perceptions of victims and shelter personnel. The sections below address key variables and provide supplementary data obtained through field research.

Resources

Although the tests of analysis using quantitative data on the resources subset produce strong correlations with the dependent variable and explain almost half the variance, they merely provide a description. The problem for these women is far too complex to be summarized by the variance explained by a few measures. The variable Education cannot predict length of stay because there are many other intervening variables outside the model. For example, merely having many years of education cannot predict employability for these women and many others in our society. And employability is an important factor in economic independence. In the final analysis, a good education may help these women obtain jobs, but even when they do, they will very likely receive lower incomes than men with the same amount of education. For example, 1970 statistics provided by the U.S. Department of Labor show that at every educational attainment level, women earn less than men. With just an elementary school education, women earn only 55 percent of median incomes of men with the same education; and at the highest level, 5 years of college or more, women still earn only 65 percent of the median incomes of men at the same level. A female college graduate earns only $621 more per year than a man with only 8 years of schooling and a mere $14 more than a male high school graduate. According to more recent reports, this large differential between income by education remains the same (Harrison, 1979:28) and overall the gap has been widening. In addition, regardless of education, there are more unemployed or underemployed women in this country than men.

Sometimes women are well educated but their skills are not marketable. One young woman the investigator knew a number of years ago was scheduled to receive the finest higher education possible. There was but one restriction: her choice of field could be music or fine art, for example, but must include nothing that could make her economically independent. Reasons for this were that her mother was then a top executive in a field dominated by men—insurance. This mother saw her own marriage crumble as she climbed the career ladder. The woman decided for her daughter that financial independence was a handicap for marriage, as she apparently blamed herself for being too resourceful rather than blaming her alcoholic ex-husband for his shortcomings. The daughter was an accomplished equestrian, she bred and trained show dogs and raised orchids, but she would not be trained to fix a faucet or handle finances.

One shelteree had a Master's degree in education but had not taught for 20 years. Her divorce was finalized while she was in the shelter. When the joint property was sold and divided, she received a check for $1,600 for her share after a 25-year marriage. The investigator saw both the check and the accompanying letter from an attorney.

One of the women who never went to a shelter (her husband finally divorced her) was a biochemist in Canada before her marriage 18 years earlier. Her husband would never permit her to hold paid employment. This woman's education and earlier employment were no longer useful in the job market in 1976; they were outdated. The only work she could find was bookkeeping at minimum wages of $2.80 an hour. Just before her husband filed for divorce, he mortgaged most of their possessions and the cash was never located. Their $80,000 house she had helped build was sold after the court hearing, and after the new bills were paid off with the equity, she received a relatively small sum as her share. Her husband's treasured coin collection somehow "disappeared," but he was awarded the boat. She received no spousal support and only minimum child support; her self-employed tradesman husband was able to conceal his true income. One of this woman's two sons had a learning disability that required special education, but she received no extra support for his schooling and transportation.

That boy's learning disability leads to another issue. One variable was somehow totally overlooked in the design of the survey instrument: health of dependent children. This was brought to mind when a letter arrived from a correspondent in Louisiana who has been working several years with a group trying to establish a shelter. She wrote: "By the way, what have you found out about sick children of battered women? We have noted a disproportionately high number of kids with handicaps, physical and mental, as well as the commonly noted emotional. Have you looked into this in your study?" During the pilot study it was obvious that there were many children who had medical problems. For example, Doris, the woman who died shortly after the interviews, not only had an incurable disease herself but her youngest child had diabetes. The wife of a ministry student discovered during her stay at a shelter that her 11-month-old son had epilepsy. In retrospect, it is clear that there were many women who had the additional burden of children with poor health; on an individual basis, this made their problems of independent survival seem almost insurmountable. Other impaired children noted were autistic, retarded, had sight or hearing deficiencies, and some had behavioral problems specialists would probably diagnose as emotional.

It is possible that children with mental or physical liabilities have an effect on their parents' relationships in five important ways: their handicaps may contribute to stress between parents to trigger the violence; they may tie the mother all the stronger into a dependency relationship, since she may not be able to take outside employment; this may serve to let the father know that no matter what he does, the women will stay; ill or disturbed children may actually keep the woman longer with a batterer because of their special needs; and they may even act to send their mother back to the batterer each time she leaves because she cannot carry the burden alone. On the other hand, it is also possible that some of these children are physically or emotionally damaged because of the pre- and postnatal beatings of their mothers. As the Louisiana correspondent quoted earlier wrote: "Lots of beatings [occur] during pregnancies."

In any case, this interesting variable, neglected in this study, should have been included. Undoubtedly many factors enter into battered women's decisions to attempt to get help, to leave, or to stay. While some of the most obvious resources were included in this study, it seems that many more inadvertently were excluded.

Institutional Response

Survey instrument items offered only mild support for the ability of institutional response variables to predict length of secondary battering cohabitation, but qualitative data offer strong support. The subset of variables that was selected for regression analysis is disappointing because it tells us only that some women turned to various community agencies, and those that did stayed longer in their violent relationships. Did these women stay longer because they received ineffective or no helpful intervention, or did such help-seeking have the reverse effect of sending them back into their situations that became even more difficult to terminate? The investigator is convinced that the answers to these questions are generally "yes." Rarely did these women find individuals who seemed to understand their requests and who responded appropriately to them.

An antagonist could suggest that these shelterees may have sat around in circles feeling themselves thoroughly victimized by society as well by their spouses. For example, one member of the board of directors of a regional shelter coalition asked the investigator when she addressed them in 1978: "What do these women *do* in shelters, besides sitting around crying on each others' shoulders?" There was very little of that kind of behavior; release from fear and pain seemed to have rekindled a sense of humor in victims so that the investigator experienced far more laughter and good humor inside shelters than tears or self-pity. One of the most enjoyable evenings in memory was a rainy night in London spent around the kitchen table at a Brixton shelter where a collection of residents gathered. The group consisted of about 16 woman, although the number fluctuated because some came and went, depending on needs of their children and their own schedules. In this group were women from Scotland, Wales, Ireland, Northern Ireland, Trinidad, the West Indies, and various parts of England. These women knew each other well, because battered women in the British Isles may have to live in a shelter for up to a year, waiting for government-obtained housing. Some of the repartee included one strikingly attractive Trinidad women's story of her fright at her first sight of a white person; this was countered by a redheaded Scot telling about her first meeting with a black person. And there were many other occasions of similar light-hearted banter, wit, clowning, and good times in shelters to disprove the cynics' suppositions.

There was, however, anger, and some of that was directed by the women at themselves for having tolerated their situations as long as they had. Much of it was directed at community agents and their lack of comprehension and the actual damage many of them had caused. Negative responses took the form of insulting behavior from nurses and doctors; counselors who tried to get them to lessen their hostility instead of looking at the causes of such hostility; and police officers who, by their refusal to arrest, showed their spouses that they had nothing to fear from law enforcement for their violence. The women's earlier negative experiences with community agencies had occurred largely in privacy or in small group interaction; once they recounted these experiences they discovered that such responses were common to most, which probably helped increase their rage.

But negative encounters with community agencies were not just a thing of the past: While at shelters most women must turn to traditional agencies for services. For example, they may need personal possessions from their homes for themselves and their children; for safety's sake, they must be accompanied by the police. Almost all shelterees must obtain emergency welfare payments initially, regardless of social class or husbands' income, because it may be months before they obtain any financial support from spouses. Women and children frequently require medical care for either emergency treatment or chronic ailments, so they must depend on county or public medical services that deal with itinerants and the poor. The women may need housing, jobs, education to prepare them for jobs, and/or child care. All of these needs must be served within the maximum 30-day limit set by most American shelters (one in Pittsburgh had a 6-day limit and one in Cleveland had a 7-day limit). To be effective, response from these bureaucracies must be swift—which it seldom is. Most of the shelterees do not know how to deal with the "system," and when it works for them, it is usually slow, insufficient, or ineffective (Lynch, 1977).

For this reason, one of the most important functions of shelters is to serve as advocates for clients: literally to push for faster and more appropriate response. One example where shelter staff had to intervene on behalf of a resident occurred during a visit to a shelter in a large eastern city. One woman had a young blind son who had been attending the only school for the blind in that city, which happened to be miles away from the shelter. Normally, the school sent a van to pick up students from their homes, but the mother was informed it would take about two weeks to effect a route change to the shelter. It was up to the mother to see to it that her son got to the school. There were only two ways he could be transported: by public transportation, in which case she would have to accompany him, or by taxi. As the mother had less than one dollar in her possession, a taxi was out of the question. She was terrified at the thought of accompanying her son to school via public transportation because she was convinced her spouse would be waiting for her to beat her up and force her to return home. The mother explained her plight to school administrators, who were unyielding: The boy *must* attend school because if he missed a certain number of days she would be reported to the authorities for contributing to the child's truancy. She firmly believed that if this occurred, her husband would present this as evidence of her "unfitness" as a mother in an expected child custody court battle. In this particular case, the executive director of the shelter had to intervene directly on behalf of the mother and her child so that rigid rules could be "bent."

These negative experiences are not unique to the women encountered in this particular study. They have been documented frequently since 1976, in the United States as well as other countries. For example, Anderson writes of her sample in the Netherlands:

In my material, one out of three women had tried to lodge a complaint. In one third of these cases the police refused the complaint. The police will tell the woman to go home and settle things with her husband, will warn her that the beatings will just get worse, will sometimes even ask what did *she* do to provoke the violence [1979: 3].

Evidence also comes from England in a study of case files of a social work department (Maynard, 1979). A team of four sociologists analyzed written reports and found that 36 percent of all cases handled by social workers contained some reference to woman-battering. They identified a "social worker ideology" that strongly supports the patriarchy and operates to the disadvantage of female victims. Some of the examples they present of social workers' advice are as follows:

To a woman who has been locked out of her house after being beaten: "I discussed Mrs. F's options with her, to go home, to try and find a bed and breakfast place for herself or to stay with friends." The social worker goes on to comment that for the Social Services to have provided something for the woman would have given her too much of an easy option.

"I had again to explain my position to Mrs. G. I said that I had to be seen to be a neutral. I was there to help all members of the family. This I would be unable to do if the impression was given that I sided with any member of the family."

"It is most important that this couple stick together for the sake of the children."

"Mrs. K appears to have to complain about something. . . . I wonder if she feels she has to produce some problem because a social worker visits" [Maynard, 1979: 4-5].

From the recent survey for DHEW comes a report showing much evidence that conditions are still basically the same as reported by the women in this study (Service Delivery Assessment, 1980). Their major findings include the following statements:

Most traditional service providers do not know how to treat the victims of woman abuse. They either *fail to identify* abused women in their existing clientele or *rarely have a protocol* to handle known cases. . . . In some communities, services for abused women do not exist or are inadequate due to *lack of funds* or *rigidly interpreted eligibility guidelines* [1980:1].

Abused women may need services at a time of crisis or over a much longer period of time, regardless of whether they stay at home or choose to live independently. . . . While we found a few traditional agencies that have been working for some time to improve their services to abused women, most did not respond adequately to women we interviewed [p. 5].

This report goes on to describe each type of agency or institution surveyed; for the most part, those investigators conclude that response to battering victims is generally inappropriate or less than adequate (Service Delivery Assessment, 1980).

One crisis intervention counselor confirmed the idea that advice and type of response given to victims is influenced to a great extent by individual agents' personal biases and the way they view their role.

Whether they see themselves as helpers to restore marriages in trouble or as change agents largely determines their response. This seems to be a reasonable assumption, and if this is the case, it helps explain why most victims feel they received negative institutional response until they came in contact with shelters and nontraditional community service providers. The original thrust for establishing shelters came from people in the women's liberation movement who, while they are not antifamily, are strongly opposed to the traditional form of the patriarchal family and women's inferior status in it. Until shelters opened their doors, most women had to deal individually with institutions about a social problem that was privatized. The social system usually operates to maintain the status quo. But when feminists turned the personal into the political, they questioned the entire social system as well as the traditional structure of the family. Their viewpoint of victims sees these women as victims of a social structure that endorses unequal relationships between women and men and restricts the options of women who have violent spouses. In accordance with basic feminist ideology, they struggled to open shelters so that these women might have access to alternatives and the freedom to choose among a variety of options.

Traditional Ideology

The women who enter shelters are most frequently traditional women who have maintained conjugal relationships over long periods despite violence and pain. One frail young woman attempted to encourage her husband to continue his studies for the ministry while he in turn beat her for his frustrations. She continued to pray for him while at the shelter and told the interviewer she strongly believed her husband needed her because she was the only one in his life who had ever seen the good that was in him. After two weeks she returned home with her two young children, including an 11-month-old epileptic baby, convinced her prayers were answered and her abuser had "reformed."

A Hispanic woman who could speak no English arrived at a shelter with a year-old baby. She lay moaning on a bed, feverish and ill, clutching a rosary. She was about 7 months pregnant and her most recent beating included kicks to her belly. Another shelteree who spoke a little Spanish was tending her, bringing liquids for the ill woman to drink and washing the perspiration away; and at the same time telling the interviewer that "God will take care of her." The ill woman had to be taken to the hospital the following day for treatment of both the flu and her abdominal injuries.

There is a certain amount of change that begins in most women shortly after they enter shelters, however. It is suspected that this change occurs mainly in the weakening of traditionalism to which they had subscribed, as they begin to question previously strong sentiments regarding women's position in the family.

It seems entirely possible that the theoretical assumption of strong commitment to traditional values of battering victims is correct—as long as these victims stay in their violent relationships. It may well be that one of the other two variables undergoes change to enable them to make the decision to leave; that is, resources increase or institutional response becomes more positive. In the case of women who came to shelters, the latter may be taken as a given. For the first time for most, they have a telephone number to call and people to deal with who not only understand their problems but are able to provide an appropriate response. It is only after removing themselves from the violent relationships that they may be expected to change deeply held values about their "proper" place in society. The investigator suspects this process begins as soon as they make the first contact with shelter staff and other victims; and by the time the survey women went through the introspective process of filling out the questionnaire, they had already started seeing their recent past in a somewhat different light.

It has been pointed out to the investigator by at least two sources that the survey instrument itself is a "consciousness-raising" tool. The executive director of the Florida shelter, Women in Distress, decided to adopt it as an "intake form" for shelterees because she and her staff decided it secured sufficient demographic statistics for the organization's purposes; in addition, the process led women to examine their lives in retrospect, which they found "therapeutic." In addition, a San Diego television producer asked permission to offer the survey instrument to the viewing audience at the end of his documentary on wife abuse because he felt it could act as a consciousness-raiser and catalyst to change for women viewers still living with batterers. The producer said the station received hundreds of requests for copies.

For most shelterees, the experience of making the decision to leave is traumatic, and they usually are in a state of shock when they arrive. Most shelters, such as Women's Transitional Living Center (WTLC), have a 72-hour "time-out" period during which the women are not to leave the premises and are not required to join in house activities. They are given "space" to think and deal with their emotions and have the freedom to talk to anyone but are encouraged to choose one of the understanding staff members. Because of usual overcrowded conditions in shelters, there is very little privacy and almost never isolation. Soon they begin engaging in communal activities and communicating with staff and other shelterees. There is a caring, sharing, and nonjudgmental supportive atmosphere in most shelters the investigator has visited. It takes only a short time for most women to realize that other women have had the same experiences and felt basically the same emotions. Class, racial, and ethnic differences that keep most women divided all but disappear inside shelters (Pagelow, 1979a). Even in Northern Ireland, torn by a civil war in which religion is the key distinguishing factor, religious differences cease to exist among shelterees, according to Middleton (1977): "The war outside stops when they walk through that front door. Many of the women develop warm friendships, and the children, too, that exist until they are again separated by government assigned segregated housing when they leave."

What shelterees had previously viewed as private, personal, unusual, or even bizarre experiences suddenly appear to be commonplace. One group discussion led one woman to exclaim, "It sounds like we're all talking about the same man!" These open forums are encouraged and sometimes facilitated by counselors experienced in leading groups. Although they are not structured specifically as consciousness-raising groups as used by early feminists, they accomplish much the same thing by focusing on common experiences and feelings. All residents are encouraged to participate, but even less verbal women are impressed by the range of perceptions and emotions shared by women around them.

Probably the most effective force for change occurs through peer counseling, where women meet on an equal basis (unlike the usual credentialed professional counseling, which tends not to be egalitarian interaction). When two or more women get together to communicate who have followed all the traditional guidelines for sex-appropriate behavior, have tried every way they knew to be good wives and mothers, and still were beaten by the men they were told to look up to, they begin a process of change. Their firmly held beliefs begin to crumble as they are called into question; they made a contract and somehow the contract was broken. Peer counseling is the preferred type of counseling in all European shelters visited, whereas in the United States many shelters are tending to become more and more "establishmentized." American shelters are now turning more toward using professionally trained counselors, whether at the shelter site or in traditional agencies. A few shelters that are less committed to feminist ideology even make individual counseling with public mental health professionals a mandatory condition attached to admittance into the shelter. Refusal to continue with counseling can then result in termination of residency. One shelter even had a male psychiatrist as a part-time staff member; a condition for admittance was psychiatric screening to determine if they could stay. Fortunately, that situation no longer exists at that particular shelter.

One point agreed upon by almost all mental health specialists is that most victims of secondary battering are lacking in ego-strength or have low self-esteem (Hilberman and Munson, 1978; Walker, 1978, 1979). This should not be surprising in view of the fact that most battering is preceded by psychological abuse, and almost all physical abuse is accompanied by psychological abuse. It must surely be difficult to maintain high self-esteem if the person with whom one has been intimate and cared for later deliberately inflicts verbal and physical injury. The victims feel humiliated and shamed, which is one of the reasons they hesitate to tell anyone what happens to them. As a result, one of the most commonly chosen forms of therapy for victims is one or another type of assertion training, basically intended to build self-esteem. Assertiveness is therefore a desired goal of both establishment therapists and nontraditional service providers such as feminist shelter operators. Regardless of their sponsors' guiding ideology, the effects on the women who receive good assertion training is similar: they learn that they have basic human rights they may protect and even demand. The outcome is that they are less likely to fall back into the mold of the passive, dependent, and highly traditional women they were originally socialized to be.

This review of the research hypothesis was expanded by the addition of qualitative data, and considerations for the improvement of the survey instrument were outlined. Now attention turns to the hypothesis offered by a sociologist who directly asked "Abused Wives: Why Do They Stay?" (Gelles, 1976). Survey data from this study are used in tests to see if they support this alternative model.

The Gelles Hypothesis

Gelles's book (1974) was one of the first empirical works in the United States documenting wife-battering in violent families. Shortly afterward, Gelles published an article on why he felt abused wives stay with their batterers (1976). The ideas he expressed received wide publicity and have been quoted (and misquoted) extensively since that time. In the article, Gelles states:

> Three major factors influence the actions of abused wives. The less severe and less frequent the violence, the more a wife remains with her husband. Secondly, the more a wife was struck as a child by her parents, the more likely she is to remain with her abusive husband. Lastly, the fewer resources a wife has and the less power she has, the more likely she is to stay with her violent husband. In addition, external constraint influences the actions of abused wives [1976:659].

The third factor mentioned by Gelles—resources—is one of the major variables of this study tested in the previous chapter, and these data offered some support. External constraint may be synonymous with institutional response, another key variable discussed earlier and tested; these data gave it weak support. Interest in this section focuses on Gelles's first two variables, severity and frequency of the abuse and the amount of childhood abuse victims suffered in their homes of orientation.

SEVERITY AND FREQUENCY OF VIOLENCE

This section focuses on the first of the three factors proposed by Gelles: "The less severe and less frequent the violence, the more a wife remains with her husband" (1976:659). Unfortunately, the authors of a recent article (Bass and Rice, 1979) misinterpreted the investigator's ideas expressed in an earlier paper and state that both Gelles and Pagelow find that severity and frequency of violence help explain whether or not victims remain with spouses. In fact, the investigator strongly disagrees in that paper with Gelles's assumptions:

> The differences are that the first two factors do not appear to carry enough weight with the respondents in my sample. Certainly if we consider only both extremes of this variable, it logically follows that at one end of a continuum, the least severe and least frequent violence is a complete absence of violence. It may be taken as a given that nonviolence is unlikely to send women to seek outside intervention, at least not for battering. On the other end of the continuum, constant fear of death, total violence, would motivate any sane person to seek help if she is able. *Severity and frequency has had minimal accountability for a decision to break the cycle of violence according to my data.* . . . One victim endured batterings by her husband for seventeen years until he died of a heart attack. . . . Another . . . suffered through eighteen years of almost continual abuse and virtual imprisonment until her husband finally divorced her. An Irish woman raised fourteen children and then left for England after frequent batterings during thirty years of marriage. On the other hand, some women leave a spouse after one slap; a slap represents different things to different people [Pagelow, 1977a:18-19, italics added].

Although this study was not designed to test severity and frequency of abuse, there are a few suitable measures on the survey instrument. Item III-1 asks for a description of injuries received from spouses; the question is open-ended, and responses were ranked according to severity of injuries sustained by sample women. A Spear-

TABLE 6.1   Spearman Correlations of Severity of Injuries and Frequency
             of Abuse

Severity/Frequency Correlations	rho	N
A. Secondary Battering Cohabitation		
Severity of injuries	.1325*	312
Pain scale	.0248	314
Frequency of attacks	.0559	314
Frequency/severity over time	.0269	282
B. Severity of Injuries		
Pain scale	.3256**	323
Frequency of attacks	.2199**	325
Frequency/severity over time	.0695	292
C. Pain Scale		
Frequency of attacks	.1837**	326
Frequency/severity over time	.1547*	292
D. Frequency of Attacks		
Frequency/severity over time	.3149**	293

*p < .01   **p < .001

man correlation test of the severity of injuries scale with length of
secondary battering cohabitation (length of cohabitation after the first
occurrence of battering) and other measures of severity and frequencies are shown on Table 6-1. The pain scale is item III-5; frequency of
attacks are derived from III-3; and frequency/severity over time are
category responses to III-16.

As can be seen, the only strong correlation with this model's dependent variable (A)—secondary battering cohabitation—is severity
of injuries, which is in a positive direction, contrary to Gelles's assumptions. The more severe the physical injuries of the women in this
sample, the longer they had remained with their spouses. This tends
to confirm earlier suspicions of no strong negative relationship between increasing severity and length of violent relationships; it also
appears that the more severe a woman's injuries, the more likely she is
to stay. This may fly in the face of common sense, but what it may
actually reflect (rather than an unmeasured desire or intent to leave) is
support for assumptions of this investigator and others that spouse
abuse increases in severity and frequency over time, as stated earlier.
When tested with the length of time these relationships were maintained after the first occurrence of violence, all correlations are weak

except severity of injuries. But it should be noted that they are all in a positive direction; each variable was coded such that higher rank represents increase. Although none of these is a strong relationship and three are not statistically significant, their direction indicates that the longer the cohabitation in a violent relationship, the more severe the injuries, the more intense the pain, the more frequent the attacks, and both frequency and severity tend to increase over time.

Unfortunately, the construction of the question on frequency/ severity (item III-16) precluded distinguishing clearly severity from frequency, since each response included a combination of both frequency and severity. This made the item difficult to scale precisely. Nevertheless, of 296 women responding to item III-16, 74 percent indicated that their beatings increased in severity, frequency, or both since violence began. Only 17 women (6 percent) said there was but one attack. This item does not correlate well with severity of injuries, but there is a significant correlation with pain and a strong correlation with frequency of attacks which may indicate that there is greater likelihood that as violent relationships continue, attacks occur more frequently and pain (not necessarily leading to injuries) becomes worse over time. If this should be the case, it might indicate that batterers learn how to inflict more pain without administering categorical (and visible) injuries to victims—for example, black eyes, broken bones, or permanent damage. The strong correlations between pain and severity of injuries, as well as frequency of attacks, help establish measurement reliability of these items.

In sum, these data offer no support for the first item of Gelles's three-factor hypothesis. On the contrary, they suggest that severity and frequency cannot predict length of stay. They do somewhat support the proposition that women who remain in violent situations are likely to be hurt more seriously and that while these relationships continue, the attacks occur more often and are more painful. Gelles's second factor will now be discussed and compared with survey data.

CHILDHOOD VIOLENCE EXPERIENCE
IN FAMILY OF ORIGIN

The term "the cycle of violence" has frequently been proposed in the literature (Gelles, 1976; Owens and Straus, 1975; Steinmetz,

1977a) and discussed from many speaker's platforms at professional and civic meetings. The cycle of violence was introduced to suggest a similarity between spouse abuse and childhood experience in violence of adult murderers (Leon, 1969; Tanay, 1969) as well as child abusers (Gelles, 1973; Gil, 1971; Kempe et al., 1962; Steele, 1977). When writers, public speakers, or even members of Congress refer to the cycle of violence, most do not separate out the different learning experiences of males and females. Popular assumptions are that children growing up in violent homes learn to become batterers or victims and these ideas may well affect future public policy.

For example, a Service Delivery Assessment team report was presented to DHEW Secretary Patricia Harris in February 1980. Listed on page 1 under the heading "Major Findings," the first item states: "The victims of woman abuse are all members of the family: the woman is the target but the man and the children are also deeply affected." The third subitem listed states: "They pass down the violence from *generation to generation* (1980:1; italics in original). In a personal letter accompanying a copy of the report, a program analyst writes: "The Department, and especially the Office on Domestic Violence, is now involved in addressing many of the problems mentioned in the assessment."

Another example is Gelles's assertion that "the more an individual is exposed to violence as a child (both as an observer and a victim), the more he or she is violent as an adult" (p. 662). This idea was also endemic to the theoretical propositions suggested by the investigator in an earlier paper (Pagelow, 1977c) as a factor explaining some men's adoption of violent interspousal behavior. Closely associated with the social learning theoretical perspective guiding this study, battering experience was introduced earlier in this book as a predictive variable for male spouses in the Primary Battering model.

However, the learned response of violence to anger or stress was not extended to explain female spouses' likelihood of becoming victims. Field explorations did not reveal a large number of women who came from violent childhood homes. In fact, the opposite was found: many interviewed women described homes with biological parents who were almost completely nonviolent. The image emerged of strict patriarchal families that might or might not include physical punishment seldom described as severe. On the other hand, women described their spouses' homes in ways that supported cyclical effects of growing up in environments where physical abuse was common through experience as either victims or observers.

Yet it is commonly assumed that female spouses are included in the cycle of violence; some suggest that whereas the male learns to batter, the female learns to be a victim. Gelles states:

> The explanation offered for this relationship is that the experience with violence as a victim and observer teaches the individual how to be violent and also to approve of the use of violence. . . .If experience with violence can provide a role model for the offender, then perhaps it can also provide a role model for the victim [1976:662].

Gelles therefore asserts: "Women who observed spousal violence in their family of orientation were more likely to be victims of conjugal violence in their family of procreation" (p. 662). Gelles bases this on the fact that 66 percent of 12 women in his sample who observed their parents' violence were later victims of violent attacks by husbands. Unfortunately, with Gelles's focused sample selection and small sample size (this actually represents 8 women out of 12), there are good reasons to consider such findings hardly more than happenstance. As evidence to support his assumption, Gelles presents the finding that of 54 women in his sample who never saw parental fighting, almost half (46 percent) were also battered by their spouses (p. 662).[1]

Gelles further states two reasons women experienced in childhood family violence are "prone to be the victims of family violence as adults." First, such women are more "inclined to approve of the use of violence in the family" and second, they are "more likely to marry a person who is prone to use violence" (1976:662–663). Gelles carries these ideas a step farther:

> Given the fact that being a victim of violence as a child or seeing one's parents physically fight makes a woman more vulnerable to becoming the victim of conjugal violence, does exposure and experience with violence as a child affect *the actions* of a beaten wife? [p. 663].

In answer to his own question, Gelles suggests two alternative predictions that either more experience or less experience with violence in family of orientation will cause women to seek intervention or divorce. The problem in studying Gelles's analysis and conclusions is that he does not always clearly differentiate the kinds of violence experience he is referring to, and only by careful perusal is it possible to discern what he actually found.

TWO KINDS OF CHILDHOOD VIOLENCE EXPERIENCE

Violence experience should be separated into two distinct categories: being a victim of parental physical abuse and observing one parent being physically violent with the other. Gelles sometimes, but not always, indicates a distinction when he refers to experience and/or exposure to violence which corresponds with victimization and observation, as categorized above. For example, referring to the findings of a stepwise multiple regression table, Gelles states that "violence severity in her family of procreation" is the best predictor of seeking intervention; the "level of violence in her family of procreation" is the best predictor of divorce or separation; and "how much violence the wife experienced as a child" is the best predictor of going to a social service agency (1976: 665). In addition, Gelles appears to contradict himself: "Thus, neither of the alternative predictions is strongly supported by the data on experience and exposure to violence" (p. 663); yet in his conclusions he states that one of the three major factors influencing the actions of abused women is: "The more she was struck by her parents, the more inclined she is to stay with her abusive husband. It appears that victimization as a child raises the wife's tolerance for violence as an adult" (p. 667). What this implies is that childhood experience in violence was important only if the woman was a victim of parental physical abuse but not important if the woman was an observer of interparental violence. Gelles's statement cannot be considered conclusive because both his statements and the tables of evidence he presents are ambiguous.

Theoretical assumptions underlying this study agreed with the learning of violent behavior later acted out by males but did not postulate that female childhood experience in violence could be a predictive variable in adult victimization or responses to it. Therefore, the study was not designed to test such propositions; but, due to its exploratory nature, some items were included in the survey instrument that could tap experience/inexperience in childhood violence for both the female respondents and their spouses. These are scale items I-17-19 for the women and II-7-10 for their spouses (see Appendix B); tables for responses to these scale items are provided below.

Next, the focus is turned to what effect, if any, childhood observation had on secondary battering cohabitation. But in this analysis of data from the survey sample, childhood experience in violence is conceptually and empirically distinguished between observation (seeing/hearing interparental violence) and victimization (frequency and severity of physical punishment and who administered punishment).

OBSERVATION OF VIOLENCE IN HOME OF ORIENTATION

Observation of parental violence is operationalized by scale items I-17 and 18 and II-7 and 8; frequencies are shown in Tables 6.2 and 6.3. Table 6.2 shows distributions in response to frequency of physical violence between parents; there was much less frequency of parental violence in the women's homes than in the men's. The table also shows that if the men's parents had been non-violent to the same

TABLE 6.2 Frequency of Observations of Interparental Violence by Survey Women and Their Spouses

	Women		Men		
Response Category	Percent	N	Percent	N	Expected Frequencies*
Never	57.0	175	29.6	66	127
Very seldom	10.4	32	9.9	22	23
Occasionally	15.3	47	17.5	39	34
Often	6.2	19	22.4	50	14
Very often	11.1	34	20.6	46	25
Total	100.0	307	100.0	223	223

(Chi-square = 56.76, df = 4, p < .001; t value = −5.38, p < .001, 2-tailed test on 201 matched pairs)
*Expected frequencies for 223 men based on 307 women's responses. The index of dissimilarity between percentages in women's and men's frequency of parental physical violence is 27.9%. This indicates that over one-fourth of the cases of one group or another (women or men) would have to be redistributed to make them identical (Johnson, 1977: 124-237).

extent as the women's parents, there would have been 127 (compared with 66) men who never saw parental violence. About one-third of the women had parents who were violent beyond "seldom," whereas 61 percent of the men's parents reportedly fell in the upper frequency range.

Table 6.3, shows responses to a specific question about observing mothers being beaten. Respondents reported on scale item I-18 that only about one-fourth of them ever observed their mothers being beaten by their fathers, whereas more than 50 percent of the women who reported on their spouses in item II-8 said the men observed their mothers' abuse.

The null hypothesis of no difference in families of origin was tested. The expected frequencies for 196 men based on the proportion of yes-no women's responses show a significant difference between observed and expected frequencies in these categories; thus, the null hypothesis is rejected.

These data appear to support the proposition that men who batter their spouses are likely to have observed interparental violence and mothers beaten by their fathers. Sample men were significantly more likely to have observational experience in violence in their families of origin than were sample women. At the same time, these data do not support the idea that women who are battered by spouses are likely

TABLE 6.3 Observation of Mothers Beaten by Fathers in Survey Homes of Orientations

	Women		Men		
Response Category	Percent	N	Percent	N	Expected Frequencies*
No	72.5	232	46.9	92	142
Yes	27.5	88	53.1	104	54
Total	100.0	320	100.0	196**	196

(Chi-square=63.91, df=1, p<.001; t value=−5.26, p<.001, 2-tailed test on 177 matched pairs)
*The index of dissimilarity is 25.6%.
**Instructions to respondents about data regarding spouses on page 4 of the instrument may well explain why there is a much smaller N for the item on spouse observation of mothers beaten or not beaten. Respondents were instructed to answer only items about which they were confident they were correctly informed. When items were being coded, any that signified uncertainty by a question mark(?) were coded into the "don't know" category in an effort to establish a higher level of confidence in the veracity of these data. Fewer responses on their spouses' observations causes pairwise deletions in computer analysis resulting in rejection of 143 cases.

to enter a conjugal relationship with a high level of observational experience.

It may appear that survey women overestimated the amount of interparental violence in their spouses' homes of orientation. For comparison purposes, the report by the Service Delivery Assessment Team for DHEW's Office of the Inspector General provides further information. The report states: "We spoke with 15 men who had been or still are abusers. *Most (73%) grew up in violent families,* where father abused mother and maybe the children too" (1980:3).

The variables measuring sample women's observations of parental violence (items I-17 and 18) were recoded into a combined variable, Observation of Violence; then the dependent variable, length of Secondary Battering Cohabitation, was regressed on Observation of Violence. Results of regression analysis produced an R^2 of only .008 and an analysis of variance F of 2.00 (not statistically significant). Thus, for this sample, observing violence in childhood cannot explain (or predict) length of stay with a battering spouse. Independent variables are coded such that positive coefficients indicate increasing rank and affirmative responses to yes-no nominal categories that are dummy-coded. In this test the beta weight was negative, indicating that, to some extent at least, females' observation of parental violence may result in a shorter length of stay with a battering spouse.

In sum, these data neither support not disprove Gelles's statement: "There is the suggestion that exposure to conjugal violence makes women *less tolerant* of family violence and more desirous of ending a violent relationship" (1976: 663). Without obtaining a representative sample of battered and nonbattered women, it cannot be established that observation of parental violence either propels women into violent relationships or stimulates them to get out any sooner than other women.

Violence Victimization in Home of Orientation

In an effort to determine whether a relationship exists between men's and women's childhood violence victimization experience, scale items I-19 for the women and II-9-10 for the men were inspected, and they provide interesting data. The first part of the ques-

TABLE 6.4   Frequency of Childhood Violence Victimization of Survey Women and Their Spouses

Response Category	Women		Men		Expected Frequencies*
	Percent	N	Percent	N	
Never	18.6	64	9.4	24	47
Very seldom	24.1	83	10.2	26	61
Occasionally	33.9	117	33.3	85	87
Often	12.8	44	25.1	64	33
Very often	10.7	37	22.0	56	27
Total	100.0	345	100.0	255	255

(Chi-square=48.21, df=4, p<.001; t value=−5.75, p<.001, 2-tailed test on 252 matched pairs)
*Index of dissimilarity is 23.6%.

tions asks the frequency of physical punishment. The responses are shown in Table 6.4.

It is important to note that some persons may question whether or not parental spanking and other forms of physical disciplinary acts constitute violence victimization experience. The investigator agrees with Gelles when he counters the "many powerful pro-use-of-physical-force on children norms in our society" by saying: "If one defines violence as an act with the intent of physically injuring the victim, then physically punishing a child is violent" (1976: 662). There is a growing contingent in this country that argues against training children in violence by physical punishment (Goode, 1971; Owens and Straus, 1975). Professionals and paraprofessionals dealing with the effects of childhood victimization appear to be adamantly opposed to physical punishment of children; for example, most shelter service providers forbid shelterees to slap, hit, or spank their own or others' children.

But the majority of parents in the United States resort to physical punishment of their children as one form of normative discipline (Dibble and Straus, 1980; Goode, 1971). If we assume that sample women are typical products of American child-rearing practices, then this test attempts to see if their spouses experienced the same frequency of parental physical discipline. The two columns on the right in Table 6.4 show the observed and expected frequencies of the men's childhood victimization experiences, based on the women's experiences. The null hypothesis of no difference is rejected because sample men were punished significantly more often than were sample women.

Still, frequency of physical violence alone is limited information. Much more revealing is Table 6.5 showing responses to questions on the kinds (degree of severity) of physical punishment experienced in childhood, scale items I-19(a) and II-9(a). As shown in Table 6.5, 231 women reported on the severity of their spouses' violence victimization, and the null hypothesis of no difference is rejected.

On the basis of women's responses, it appears that their spouses were significantly more frequently and more severely physically punished than they were. The difference may or may not have a direct bearing on later adult behavior and may merely reflect parents attitudes and expectations toward their male or female children. There are some indications that girl children are treated less harshly than boy children beginning in infancy (Belotti, 1975).

The only way to determine if the childhood violence victimization of sample women and men is out of the ordinary would be to compare their experiences with those of a representative sample of adult women and men. The relatively minor degree of violence severity of sample women does not appear to support Gelles's conclusions regarding the impact of women's childhood violence experience because most of these women remained with their spouses after abuse began (one as long as 42 years); but almost all of them eventually left their abusive spouses.

TABLE 6.5   Degree of Severity of Childhood Violence Victimization of Survey Women and Their Spouses

Response Category	Women		Men		Expected Frequencies*
	Percent	N	Percent	N	
None	7.2	21	5.6	13	17
Mild	27.4	80	12.6	29	63
Moderate	46.2	135	33.8	78	107
Extremely severe	19.1	56	48.1	111	44
Total	100.0	292	100.0	231	231

(Chi-square=52.63, df=3, p<.001; t value=−5.12, p<.001, 2-tailed test on 193 matched pairs)
*Index of dissimilarity is 28.8%.

172

One other test was made to see if the women's experiences of childhood violence could be a predictor of the length of time they stay with battering spouses. Items I-19 and I-19(a) were combined into a new variable, Violence Victimization, and the dependent variable, Secondary Battering Cohabitation, was then regressed on this variable. There is a weak negative relationship, with an R^2 of .015; analysis of variance produced an F value of 3.9, which is statistically significant at less than 5 percent. These tests appear to argue against Gelles's assumptions that "the more she was struck by her parents, the more inclined she is to stay with her abusive husband. It appears that victimization as a child raises the wife's tolerance for violence as an adult" (1976: 667). Correlations here are in a negative direction, indicating that the greater the childhood victimization, the shorter the length of stay. Sample women reported less severe and less frequent parental abuse, and those who were abused as children tended to sever their conjugal relationships sooner than did the others.

Responses to items I-19(b) and II-9(b), the questions asking "If you were (he was) beaten as a child, who usually did this to you (him)?" provide an interesting difference. Two possible hypotheses could be generated: (1) that both parents are equally likely to administer physical punishment or (2) that mothers are more likely to be physically abusive to their children because they generally spend more time isolated with children in the home. If mothers are the primary beaters, they might thereby create docile daughters and/or create resentment from sons who use other females as scapegoats when they reach adulthood. Suggestions regarding the latter possibility were made by some women during interviews and group discussions when they revealed their spouses' hatred for their (stern) mothers and sometimes sisters. These women felt that their spouses were venting pent-up feelings of rage and aggression against dominant women in their childhoods; that their men could never hit back at these women in their youth and were somehow transferring stored anger and revenge onto different females—themselves.

However, neither of these alternatives is supported by the data; the frequency tables are shown in Table 6.6. Quite clearly, the men were more likely to receive beatings from father figures than mother figures, while the women appear to have been beaten equally by mothers

TABLE 6.6   Administrators of Childhood Violence Victimization to Survey
            Women and Their Spouses

Response Category	Women		Men		Expected Frequencies*
	Percent	N	Percent	N	
Father figure	42.7	50	63.3	88	59
Mother figure	40.2	47	29.5	41	56
Both	17.1	20	7.2	10	24
Total	100.0	117	100.0	139	139

(Chi-square = 12.46, df = 2, p < .01)
*Index of dissimilarity is 20.6%.

or fathers. There is a lower response rate for the women's assaulters (N = 117) than the men's (N = 139), but this may be explained by the fact that the women were less likely to report an abuser because of less frequent and less severe victimization by parents. These data appear to support the idea that physically violent men are likely to have learned from same-sex role models in the home that physical violence is appropriate behavior for men.

Computer t-tests are not used because they would be based on only 53 cases: pairwise deletion rejected all cases except where respondents supplied data on both their own and their spouses' abusers. However, the null hypothesis of no difference in the sex of abusing parent was tested and rejected. The expected frequencies for the 139 men, based on 117 women's responses, are shown in the far right column in Table 6.6. When predicting expected responses for the women based on the men, the same large and statistically significant differences held.

In addition, the women were asked about assaults by men other than the spouses who battered them (item I-10). One-third said they had been victims of other men's assaults, but only 22 of the 350 respondents (six percent) reported the assaulter was a father figure (father, stepfather, of foster father).[2]

It is interesting to note that the sex of both the abusers and the victims does make a difference in later life, according to the Straus et al. study (1980). These researchers report that boys abused by fathers and girls abused by mothers tend to be strongly related to violence in adulthood.

Assuming that children tend to pattern their behavior most closely after the behavior of the parent of the same sex, this finding supports the role model theory of why some people are violent and others are not. Apparently we learn violence best from parents of the same sex [1980: 108].

There is an extra scale item regarding the men's violence victimization experience (II-10), and 51 percent of 228 women said their spouses received unusual or harsh punishment when they were children. Of the 103 women who provided an open-ended description, 68 percent identified the extreme abusers as their spouses' fathers. Details of abuse included such acts as breaking bones, knocking the child down stairs, beating him with whips or chains, forced eating, and tying him to chairs. Some described extreme mental abuse but no physical abuse.

To complete the picture of childhood violence experience, the response categories of items I-23 and II-15 were collapsed into positive, negative, and other (which included "varied over time") types of homes. The same question applying to her childhood home and his childhood home has eight identical categories, so that responses 1, 3, 6, and 8 are coded positive while the others are coded negative. Only 16 women used the "other" category for their homes and 9 used it for their spouses' homes; these generally included statements to the effect that at one time they were happy and at another time unhappy. Table 6.7 shows the collapsed responses and the expected frequencies for 280 men based on 336 women's responses. The women were about evenly divided on whether their homes of orientation were

TABLE 6.7   Overall Appraisal of Home of Orientation of Survey Women and Their Spouses

Response Category	Women		Men		Expected Frequencies*
	Percent	N	Percent	N	
Positive	46.7	157	16.8	47	131
Negative	48.5	163	80.0	224	136
Other (varied)	4.8	16	3.2	9	13
Total	100.0	336	100.0	280	280

(Chi-square=66.33, df=2, p<.001; t value=−6.29, p<.001, 2-tailed test on 274 pairs)
*Index of dissimilarity is 31.5%.

remembered positively or negatively, whereas 224 women described their spouses' homes negatively.

The null hypothesis of no difference in overall description of childhood home is rejected on the basis of these tests. Interestingly, the adjective most commonly chosen by the women describing their homes was "troubled" (N = 96) and the second most common was "secure" (N = 67). For their men, they chose "troubled" (N = 117) and "violent" (N = 65).

These data appear to offer no support or, in some cases, very limited support to suggestions made by Gelles regarding experience in violence in the home of orientation of battered women. On the other hand, background material supplied by sample women on their spouses' childhoods seem to indicate the men had much greater experience in violence both as observers and victims, which may tentatively support a major proposition in the primary battering model as detailed in Chapter 2. That model proposes a variable that may predict which men are likely to batter spouses: violence experience in home of orientation.

Summary of Tests of Gelles's Hypothesis

This has been a brief examination, by means of survey data from women in shelters, of two of the three variables suggested by Gelles to affect battered women's decisions to stay with or to leave their abusers (the other, resources, was already investigated). It is important to note that a more appropriate test of Gelles's hypothesis would include data from samples of both battered and nonbattered women. An even better test should include women battered once (primary battering) who were never battered again by the same man, plus women from the other two categories. This would provide an ideal test of the variables proposed in this study and by Gelles.

In any event, the tests using these data do not support Gelles's first factor: severity and frequency of the violence. As noted earlier, discussions with battered women in shelters revealed that some women endured years of extreme violence and severe injury before leaving, while others left after the first or second episode that sounded relatively minor. Some women never make the decision to leave, regardless of the severity and frequency; a few of these cases become public when the violence ends in the death of the woman or the man.

The data also do not appear to support Gelles's second factor: the amount of abuse suffered from parents as a child. In fact, they suggest just the opposite: Women in this sample who experienced greater parental abuse were likely to remain a shorter time after the first instance of spouse abuse. On the other hand, the data weakly support Gelles's suggestion that observing interparental violence may make women less tolerant of family violence and more likely to leave (1976: 663), although he rejected observed violence as one of his predictive variables.

Nevertheless, this examination has added interesting pieces of information to our scant knowledge about the complex issue of women-battering. For example, these women report less violence in their homes of orientation, both in terms of observation and victim-ization, than they report for their spouses. The administrator of physi-cal punishment for the women was as likely to be a mother figure as a father figure, but they say that their spouses were much more likely to receive physical punishment from father figures. In addition, their overall appraisal of their childhood homes was equally likely to be negative as positive, whereas they reported much more negative viewpoints for their spouses' homes. An unexpected finding was that the adjective most commonly chosen to describe their own and their spouses' homes was "troubled." However, the second most frequent adjective for the women's home was "secure" and for the men's home, "violent." As is quite common when using forced-choice categories, the question remains: What does the word "troubled" represent to the many women who chose it to describe these homes?

Obviously, this is one of many problematic areas in survey ques-tionnaires: attempting to choose words that carry the same meaning to both the researcher and the respondents—both in the instrument construction and in interpretation of responses. This is one of the sensitive issues associated with placing heavy reliance on sur-vey questionnaires (Dobash and Dobash, 1979: 253). In this study, fortunately, the instrument was only one of several data-gathering techniques.

Interacting with and interviewing battered women in shelters gave strong impressions that severity and frequency of the violence had very little to do with their decisions to stay with or leave their batterers. Also, their descriptions of their childhood homes were generally of nonviolent parents, although frequently they described strict parents, particularly overly protective or controlling fathers. In essence, their patriarchal, authoritarian homes may well have prepared them for inaction and inability to prevent or avoid the violence that occurred in their adult conjugal relationships.

Overview

Because the major variables hypothesized to explain why battered women remain with their abusers did not receive strong statistical support, this chapter further examined the survey instrument for reasons why some important concepts may not have been adequately measured. Qualitative data were then presented on the independent variables Resources, Institutional Response, and Traditional Ideology. These data are useful for supplementing and expanding on survey responses and appear to give stronger support to the research hypothesis. This suggests that the complexity of the problem will not yield easily to explanation through any individual study; rather, different studies may each contribute elements that become, in effect, building blocks to knowledge.

Since Gelles is a sociologist who had previously investigated intrafamily violence and specifically addressed the question of why women stay with abusers, his major hypothesis was tested with survey data from this study. Gelles clearly identified three constructs that were testable, unlike some other highly sophisticated theoretical models that are untestable with these data because their research parameters go far beyond the problem of women battered by their spouses (Straus et al., 1980). These data offered support to Gelles's first variable, resources (see tests in the previous chapter); gave no support to the second, severity/frequency of abuse; and appear to argue against the third, childhood victimization in homes of orientation. But these tests of an alternative model provided further insight into the lives of the women in this investigation, in addition to greater understanding and appreciation of the complexity of the problem, while we continue to search for answers.

Chapter 7

THREE CASE HISTORIES

To provide depth to the understanding of woman-battering, case histories of three women are presented here. They may not be representative of most cases of battering victims—in fact, in many ways they are unusual or even unique. On the other hand, individuals, like fingerprints, are distinctive, and most battered women feel that their lives are unlike anyone else's, particularly when they are still in abusive situations. However, these women share certain common experiences with all battered women: pain, fear, frustration, and help-seeking efforts that were largely unsuccessful. Repeatedly they turned to others in the social system and were ignored or sometimes faced increased abuse because of their efforts. The investigator wonders how many times readers have heard women's screams for help and have responded by turning up the volume on the television set or closing their windows to avoid being disturbed.

For Better or For Worse, Till Death . . .

This section concerns the case history of Anne,[1] whose life was marred and strongly influenced by violent men. She was beaten by her first husband, her second husband of 17 years beat her, and her son-in-law beat, and eventually killed, her daughter. At first glance, this case may seem to confirm three unproved but very popular assumptions many people have about woman-battering. The first of these assumptions is that battered women "seek out" battering men because of some personality factor or innate need—the Freudian-based ideas of female masochism discussed earlier. The second is that girls who grow up in violent homes learn to be victims, an assumption that was discussed and tested in Chapter 6. The third assumption derives from some of the recent research on victims of battering from which researchers sometimes diagnose characteristics of "passivity" among victims they interview and study after months or years of abuse. In essence, this type of ex post facto analysis frequently is undifferentiated from traits before the abuse, during it, or following it. People are unlikely to ask themselves if the women's passivity made them targets for abuse in the first place or if they became passive as a result of the abuse.

Whether or not this case history gives support to these notions will be left to readers to decide for themselves. Was Anne a "victim-prone" woman—someone whose own weaknesses delivered her from the hands of one batterer to another? Was she a woman whose passivity led her into her situation and kept her there? Was her daughter so accustomed to violent men in her childhood that she was molded to be a victim of murder? It is hoped that the facts presented here will speak for themselves.

Anne was born in 1912 into a working-class family living in a midwestern city. Hers was a loving but authoritarian family. She was the second of four children, although her mother had children by an earlier marriage (her mother was widowed at the age of 21 when she had three children under the age of four). Anne's family life was probably typical of that era and place: parents struggled to pay bills, provide for their children, and raise them as good Americans. Parental control was strict, guided by fundamentalist religious beliefs. Whenever the children disobeyed rules, inside the home or out, they were "switched" by either parent. Anne never saw any other type of violence in her home. Her parents never fought; in fact, she can recall only one argument during the many years they lived together, and this was over whether to install a gas or coal furnace. Her father won the argument.

Occasionally Anne got into trouble with other youngsters because she was "different" from her siblings. Her eyes were brown, she was chubby, and her complexion was darker than her siblings who were lean and had blue eyes, as did both parents. She still remembers the pain of hearing a teacher tell her class that it is "impossible" for a blue-eyed couple to produce a brown-eyed child. Large cities in the early 1900s consisted of many distinct neighborhoods, very much like small towns, in which everyone knew everyone else. Anne was the target of teasing or ridicule and she fought back—only to be physically punished at home for not "turning the other cheek." She was carefully taught that girls must be ladies and never, never fight *anyone*.

In retrospect, Anne believes she was overly protected as a child. Her history suggests that these well-meaning, deeply religious, and loving parents literally set her up for victimization because of what she did not learn about herself and life. Sex was never discussed at home, so when other girls talked about being "sick" each month, Anne did not know what they meant. When her menses began, she was totally ignorant of what was happening to her body and had no adult whom she could ask. She had no idea how babies are conceived or born—all she knew was that they come from love and are a "gift from God."

At sixteen, Anne was a Campfire Girl and sang in the church choir with a neighborhood boy named Eddie, who was a member of the Boy Scouts. They frequently attended the same church, school, and scouting events but never dated. Anne was not permitted to date. On July 17, 1929, after attending Sunday night church services, Anne was lured to a garage to look at a car Eddie was fixing. There she met an ambush—an older boy and girl—who helped their friend while he raped her. It took a long time because Anne struggled and fought fiercely. She finally got home at 2:30 a.m. to be met by frantic parents who had called the police and had been searching for her everywhere. Her clothes were torn and dirtied and she couldn't tell anyone what happened to her. Her mother finally told everyone to leave her alone. Anne's mother spent the rest of the night with her, but there was little sleep and much crying by both. Anne had been threatened by Eddie and he told her not to tell anyone what happened because he already had it arranged to prove he was somewhere else at the time. The following day Eddie wrote her a note apologizing and saying that he loved her and wanted her for his own.

Rumors were flying in the neighborhood about teen boys being sent to a reformatory for raping local girls, a fact that must have impressed young Eddie. One month after the rape, Anne was leaving school to join her swim team for a competition in a neighboring school. Eddie drove up and told her that her mother had given him permission to drive her to the swim meet. He persuaded her to get into his car, but he drove out of the city to a small town across the state line. Leaving her in the car, he went into a house and soon came back with a certificate of marriage, saying to her, "Now you're married to me." Anne replied, "No, I'm not! You're crazy. I never got married to you and I never will. Nobody will ever believe you!" The document, with strikingly similar handwriting for both the bride and groom's signatures, cost Eddie $300, he later told her. All Anne wanted to do was get home before she got in more "trouble"; she felt certain Eddie would never be believed. Eddie drove them back to their city, but before taking her to her home, he stopped at the neighborhood grocery store with the forged document in his pocket. By the time he got Anne to her home, Eddie "discovered" that he had "lost" the marriage certificate in the store; it was picked up and read by their neighbors who were customers. The news spread quickly and although Anne protested that no marriage had occurred, no one believed her, including her parents.

Anne's mother noticed the girl was not well and a week later took her to the doctor who had attended her since she was little. When she was told that she was pregnant, Anne became hysterical. This was impossible—babies come from love and are gifts from God! When the doctor told her that they result from intercourse, she had no idea what the word meant. The doctor, a woman, sat with her a long time and slowly but sadly told her the "facts of life" while her mother waited in the other room. If they even thought of abortion, which Anne knew nothing about, no one mentioned it.

Now the matter seemed settled; there was no longer any question that Anne and Eddie were married. Probably with parental relief, the couple first lived at Eddie's home for a few weeks and then moved back to her parents' home, where Anne's daughter was born. Two weeks before the birth, Eddie beat Anne and broke one of her ribs. The couple moved constantly—Anne recalls moving seven times in 14 months—usually to avoid paying the rent. Eddie became a "weekend drunk," beating her frequently while sober or drunk. Anne suffered from rheumatic fever when she was 18 and the previously healthy girl became thin and underweight and developed a number of health problems, some directly related to the beatings she received. They may have contributed to a miscarriage that occurred when her second child was 14 months old, but doctors had told Anne she could not have more children without endangering her own life.

One time Anne woke up to find Eddie standing over her, ready to hit her with a shotgun. She rolled away as it came crashing down, the butt of the gun gouging a hole out of the furniture next to her pillow. Four times during those ten years Anne took her children and ran away, only to be forced back into the situation. During one of those escape attempts, Anne got a job and rented her own place, but Eddie found her and moved in with her and the children. On the fifth attempt, Anne and the children went to her parents' home. The following day, when she returned for the children's books and clothes, she found the place empty. Eddie had put everything in storage and moved away; apparently the relationship was over for him, too. By this time the girl was nine years old and the boy was five; the year was 1939. Anne and the children stayed at her parents' home and Anne found employment wherever she could. However, during this time, a man she had known and disliked since childhood began pursuing her. Fred was a "friend of the family"; some kin of the families were intermarried. Fred had strong racketeering connections, so when he publicly proclaimed Anne was "my woman," no one argued back. He followed her everywhere and the few times she dated were interrupted by Fred, who invariably appeared on the scene, yanking her aside and threatening the other men because "This is *my wife!*" Publicly, and despite Anne's protests, Fred dragged her away to his car while others looked on and did nothing to help her. Fred raped her in his car and even broke into her parents' home to rape her in her own room. She never dared call out or tell her parents because she felt they would believe she "invited" him, and besides, her mother was suffering from chronic illnesses.

A few months after her mother died in 1942, Anne left the family home and lived independently.[2] Fred continued his violent attacks, raping Anne on a number of occasions. Her only defense was to move from place to place hoping he would not find her. The longest she was able to avoid him was for three and a half months. No matter where she turned for help, no one would intervene or even listen. To her claims of assault or rape, Fred countered with claims that she was his wife and they merely had a fight for which she wanted revenge. Finally, just after her daughter's graduation from high school and departure from home, Anne received an eviction notice and concurrently discovered that she was pregnant through rape for the second time. She put her son into a boarding school.[3] Then, having no place to live and no one to help her, she gave up the struggle and married her rapist in 1947. Six months later a son was born and a year later, a daughter named Florence. Anne was beaten severely and constantly. She almost died at the girl's birth because her husband's signature was required for a Caesarean operation but he refused to sign. A doctor sent the police to Fred to coerce him into giving his permission, and at the last minute the operation was performed. The day Anne returned from the hospital with her new baby her husband beat her severely, kicking her in the abdomen and causing permanent internal damage.

Anne's life with Fred was filled with violence but no one would ever help; she believes it was because of his illegal activities and underworld connections. In the home in which they lived the longest, an ingenious cellar was connected to a basement in the adjoining building, where a "club room" was set up for gambling and a bookie joint. Some of the "visitors" who entered through their home to gamble were prominent civic leaders and city and state politicians, including the city building inspector. Some of Anne's daytime duties included making payoffs to bettors. One day when she was walking down her own street heading home, Fred drove up, got out of his car, and began beating her. He dragged her into their house while she screamed for help, in full view of a police officer who knew them both. He never intervened or reported the incident.

The day following a violent episode during which Fred beat her head with the butt of a handgun, Anne took the weapon in her handbag to the district attorney. She placed the loaded weapon on his desk, asking him to confiscate it because it was not registered. The district attorney refused to touch it, saying, "Get that out of here. I don't want to know anything about it." In despair, she rode home on the bus with her bag open, the gun in full view of other passengers, hoping someone would call the police so the gun would be taken away. Again, no one intervened. Anne made repeated attempts to get away, but Fred always found her and brought her back.

When her younger children were two and three, Anne decided to put some real distance between her and her husband so he could not find her. For more than a year she had been secretly earning little sums of money by baby-sitting, running errands, and selling her handiwork. She hid small change in Fred's dirty socks, then deposited the money in a bank; the bank book was hidden in the clothespin bag. Finally, she convinced Fred that her help was needed by a relative with a new baby in a state over 1000 miles away. Her husband grudgingly took her and the children to the train but became abusive publicly as she was leaving. She knew she would never return!

However, her relatives would not give her a place to stay when she arrived; one of them told her, "Who do you think you are? You get home to your husband, where you belong!" So she got on a bus and rode to another section of town and got off when she came to a neighborhood that somehow looked nice to her. She bought a newspaper to look for a job and housing and went to a health clinic to get medical care for the baby, who had a bad cold. There she was: a runaway wife, a mother with two tiny children, a small suitcase (after all, they were only going away to "visit"), looking at newspaper want ads, when she turned to a nearby police officer to ask directions. Anne still recalls with gratitude the kindness of this man who, when he learned something of her situation, asked her, "Wait right there, I think I can find someone to help you." It was 8 o'clock in the morning and she had no place to go, so she waited. For the first time in her life, Anne found people willing to help. The officer returned with a local

city official who took her and the children home to meet his wife. The
couple not only gave the refugees a place to stay, but the wife baby-sat
the children while Anne worked at a job the husband found for her.
Anne recalls this time as the happiest in her life. She loved her job and
felt great pride in being able to pay room and board to the couple who
befriended her. For the first time she felt good about herself, capable
and strong. However, her happiness was short-lived.

Three months after beginning her new life, free of pain and fear,
Anne and the children were returning from a day at the park when one
of Anne's relatives got on the same bus. It turned out that this woman,
who had refused Anne a place to stay, had recently married the
pharmacist at the drug store where Anne had taken her daughter's
prescriptions to be filled (neither Anne nor the druggist knew of their
relationship by marriage). Now Anne knew that she had been "found"
and she begged her relative to keep her whereabouts secret from the
rest of the family "back home." But the relative angrily said, "What
right do you have, doing what you're doing? The mail has piled up for
you at home, your brothers and father have been calling us, looking
for you. They want you to come home." It was not long before Anne
began to receive letters and phone calls from her relatives in the other
state. She described it this way:

> They told me I had to come back, that he was driving everyone crazy.
> They were all scared of him; he had been going around like a mad
> man, threatening all of them. He told them he'd kill them, or set fire to
> their homes, anything, if I didn't come back. They told me it wasn't
> fair—that he was *my* problem—that it was up to me to come back and
> straighten things out with him so he'd leave them alone. I refused, no
> matter what. I never wanted to go back.

> But then one day my stepmother called me to tell me that my father
> was in the hospital—he had been hurt, she said. She inferred that his
> being hurt had something to do with Fred although she didn't say that
> directly. What she didn't say was that my father was in the hospital for
> a hernia operation. She said, "You better get home—he needs you." I
> felt so guilty—they had been working on my guilt for a month—I
> figured it was my fault that something bad happened to Dad. My
> brothers sent me money for the return fare; I packed up the children
> and went back. Fred was supposed to meet me at the train but he wasn't

there. I took a cab back home and Fred was there, just waiting for me. He gave me the worst beating of my whole life the very night I returned. I never tried to leave again; I knew it was hopeless.

After four months of freedom, Anne was back in her private hell and never tried to escape again. Her marriage to Fred lasted 17 years until just before he was scheduled to be tried on criminal charges (unrelated to his violence), when he died of a heart attack.

Fred had never beaten the children—in fact, he took special pride in his daughter Florence. The children wanted their father's love but they feared his temper and were nervous when he was around; they never knew when he might turn on their mother. The older child was asthmatic and had a learning disability that required special tutoring. The girl was beautiful: blonde hair, blue eyes, charming, and intelligent. When she was 20 years old, she gave birth to a daughter who was fathered by a man to whom she was engaged; she discovered before the child was born that he was already married. Florence supported herself and her daughter and was proud of her independence. She was a loving mother; as the child grew they shared many activities and hobbies.

In the meantime, Anne's health became worse, and although she was unable to hold paid employment, she did not qualify in that state for disability and medical assistance. When her granddaughter was about three years old, relatives in another state asked Anne to come baby-sit their children while they traveled. Anne went and after her services were no longer needed, she decided to stay in the new state because the weather was milder. Later she discovered that under this state's laws, she qualified for needed medical expenses. She had a number of very serious operations, some of which required months of bed rest. When she was 63 years old, Anne underwent open heart surgery and was not expected to live much longer. All her internal organs were damaged in one way or another by years of abuse.

During this time Florence began a relationship with a man who had a long history of violence. She had been given the family home, and eventually Ralph moved in with her and her daughter. Anne does not know how this arrangement occurred, but she is convinced that her daughter feared the man and did not dare resist him. There was suspicion that Ralph had been involved in a shooting along with two other men; one man was killed. The dead man had a relative who witnessed the shooting and was going to testify against the three men; he was found shot to death. According to letters and telephone calls to her mother, Florence felt certain that Ralph would be found guilty after he was charged with the crime and she would no longer have to fear him. But the case against him was dropped and no one has ever been tried for the crime. About six months later Florence and Ralph were married, to everyone's surprise.

Anne returned for a visit later that year and found that Florence was living a life of violence and terror. Despite Anne's pleas and offers of help, Florence refused to leave her home. During her short stay Anne witnessed threats and domination by Ralph, including one time when he rode his motorcycle through the house, breaking everything in his path. Once when the two women and child were in the house, he shot to death a neighbor's barking dog but no complaints against him were lodged with the police. Unable to do anything to help, Anne unhappily returned home.

Florence continued to provide financial support for herself, Ralph, and her daughter; he remained unemployed, although Florence and her mother believed he was dealing in drugs. Finally, one night Ralph beat Florence badly and went to bed. The following morning the little girl came downstairs to find her mother lying on the couch, blood all over her head, unconscious but with her eyes open. An ambulance and police were called, and Anne flew to be with her daughter. Florence remained in a coma for six days in the hospital, never recovering consciousness, until she died a year and a half after marrying the man who killed her. She was 27. According to a newspaper account, "Mrs. _____ was admitted to the hospital . . . in convulsions, and died after brain surgery was performed to relieve a cerebral hemorrhage." Neighbors told Anne that when the ambulance and police were busy with the victim, Ralph told them over and over that he hit Florence; they had heard the sounds the previous night.

Ralph was first charged with assault and battery and released on bail. While Florence lay in the hospital he sold all the household furnishings and the family home. When she died, the charges became more serious but he remained free on bail. The death certificate listed death by homicide from assault by spouse; cause of death: "fractured skull with herniation of brain." Anne's oldest son took her seven-year-old granddaughter into his custody and Anne returned home, only to go back to her home town for Ralph's trial six months later.

Ralph was tried and convicted on manslaughter charges. The newspaper report says that Ralph "testified the he had accidentally injured his wife [when he pushed her]. She must have struck her head on a piece of furniture or on the floor, he said." The small article, buried within a big city newspaper, also said: "The jury deliberated for just more than one hour before returning its verdict yesterday in the two-day trial." The sentence: six months in state prison.

Fighting Back Through the Courts

> They are so very careful to protect the rights of the defendant but nobody worries about the rights of the victims.

The woman who made this statement was standing outside a courtroom in a southwestern state. She had left her home halfway across the continent and an ailing 70-year-old husband to testify in a civil suit lodged by her and her daughter against a man who had battered them both. Her frustration at that moment was based on the fact that after one day of hearings on the case, it was now being placed before another judge at the request of the defendant. That was not the only frustrating factor in this case, only the most recent in a series that stretched over a year and a half since the two women had filed suit against Martin, their abuser.

The trial was scheduled to begin the previous day at 9 a.m., but, as is usual in courts of law, the time schedule means only that plaintiffs, defendant, and their counsel must be in attendance. They went to one courtroom, where a judge asked the estimated time needed for presenting arguments. The plaintiffs' attorney, Patrick, said, "no more than three hours" and the defendant, representing himself, said it would take less than that. Next, the judge asked both parties if they would waive a jury hearing. The plaintiffs, Sue James and her mother, Mrs. Davis, had been given the right to jury trial. Patrick advised his clients to waive the jury, because calling and swearing in a jury would take much more time than he felt was warranted by the case. He also mentioned that juries are likely to be swayed by emotions rather than facts of law, and since most people believe men have a right to hit their wives, he did not believe they would find a jury sympathetic toward them.[4]

Since both the women had to leave their homes and loved ones to appear in court in a city in which none of the parties currently lived, they accepted their counselor's advice and waived the jury, as did the defendant. Cost was also one of the important factors in the women's decision; they had already invested thousands of dollars in pressing for trial, long-distance phone calls, attorney's fees, travel, and lodging.

The judge then assigned them a courtroom and told everyone to appear at 2 p.m. That took care of the first morning. The plaintiffs' attorney left immediately to attend to other business and returned late. Both parties entered the courtroom and at 2:30 the judge opened the trial. Testimony had been presented for about two hours when she recessed the case to hear others that were waiting. When that was finished, the judge called counsel into her chambers. In this instance, since the defendant was representing himself, Patrick and Martin left the courtroom to confer with the judge while the two women waited and wondered. After awhile Patrick and Martin returned to the courtroom. As he was sweeping up his papers hurriedly, Patrick told his clients that the judge had offered the defense an opportunity to decide if he wished her to continue to hear this case or ask for another judge. Martin had asked for another judge.

The reasons for this were not made clear to his clients, who were asking questions as Patrick rushed down the stairs and toward his car in the parking lot. Before they had many answers, he said he had urgent business at his office but they should return to the court the next morning.

There seemed to be one reason for the judge's offer to the defendant, a reason that was later deduced and confirmed. As a community leader and distinguished citizen, the judge's life outside the courtroom includes involvement in a number of civic and philanthropic organizations. One of these is a shelter for battered women and their children where she is a member of the governing board. Because no judges want to make themselves targets for attacks, especially of judicial bias, the judge came to the decision that it was best to reveal this aspect of her personal life, in case the defendant was not aware of it. That way, he could decide for himself if he felt this involvement could lead to bias against him and his case. By his request for another judge, it was obvious that Martin believed he would be subjected to discrimination.

The two women were angry and upset because they had seen no "special favors" granted to them during more than two hours of testimony. In fact, it appeared to them that the judge was "leaning over backward" to help Martin present his own defense and in questioning witnesses, despite constant violations of procedure. Martin had received the court's permission to represent himself because he said he had no money for counsel—and besides, he had represented himself before. Nevertheless, every time Martin said or did something improper, he pleaded the court's indulgence because of ignorance. When he began his cross-examination of his ex-wife, Martin turned to the bench and said, "Your Honor, I'm not sure I know how to proceed." The judge then patiently gave him instructions. Earlier, when Patrick was questioning his own witness, the judge herself objected on behalf of the defendant to one question asked.

The women were furious to learn that another judge was to hear the case, not only because of the lengthening of the trial time but also because they felt that judges' knowledge of social problems outside the courtroom should not be allowed to preclude them from hearing cases related to those same problems. In essence, they believed they had been discriminated against by the judge's having given the decision to the defendant. They felt it was not fair to them to be denied one judge who apparently was concerned about battered women and turned over to another judge who possibly was unconcerned about these victims. Sue angrily made this analogy:

If having a judge who knows and understands what women go through with violent men leads automatically to discrimination against a defendant then all judges should have to be ignorant of what goes on in the world. By that kind of logic, if understanding leads to empathy and that leads to judicial bias, then only judges who have no understanding of human behavior should be allowed to sit on the bench—get rid of all the rest! How do we know how many of these male judges approve of wife beating because they do it themselves? Here at least we had a good chance that we had a judge who didn't beat *her* wife!

It may be obvious that this case history differs sharply from the one presented earlier. The setting is contemporary and the major characters are young, attractive, well educated, upper middle class— typical of many seen on yachts, at tennis, golf, and country clubs, and at charity events. They are, in fact, the kind of people most likely to be described as "the beautiful people." Yet their relationship, despite its glamorous setting, was a stormy one covering three years from its beginning to the courtroom conclusion.

According to Sue James, with confirmation on some points and additions from Mrs. Davis, the major facts are as follows. Sue had an interesting job that required some travel and her knowing all the "right" people. Martin, 30 at the time, moved in a circle of fashionable friends and drove a bright-colored, very expensive sports car. Both Sue and Martin held executive-level positions; Sue had been with her firm for more than five years. They met and dated for about nine months. Then, early one Sunday morning, Martin persuaded Sue to accompany him on a drive to a city about 500 miles away to meet some friends. During the ride an argument developed, then yelling. Sue says that Martin was driving at 100 miles an hour, holding onto the steering wheel with his left hand (he is left-handed) while using his right hand to punch and slap her. At one point he stopped his car along the long stretch of open highway, dragged her out of the car, and continued beating her, bloodying her nose and bruising her upper body. Throwing her back into the car, he continued the high-speed drive while threatening her that he was going to kill both of them. By the time they got to his friends' house she ran in calling for help. Finally she made her way to a place where she met a police officer. She asked him to take her complaint but he advised her to report the assault to the police department where she lived. Two officers accompanied Sue back to the house where Martin was staying to retrieve her suitcase. He threw it at her, striking her with it, at which point one officer said, "Calm down, Buddy." No record was made of the report in that city.

Sue had no cash with her but purchased a flight home with a credit card. The following day she went to a doctor and did not go to work. The next day she asked her local police to take a courtesy report to be sent to the other city and to have her assailant arrested, but no action was taken.

After that Sue tried desperately to avoid Martin but to no avail. He would wait for her in her company parking lot or stalk her near where she lived. About two months later, when Martin was waiting for her at the parking lot, a bitter argument developed and he beat her again. Once more she called the police to report the attack but nothing happened. The pattern of stalking, harassing, and threatening went on, she said, until about four months after the first beating when Martin showed up at her home. She went out to talk with him and then they both went to where her parents were staying and caring for her eight-year-old son. Mr. Davis answered the door but refused to admit Martin; they had never met, but Sue had told her parents about his behavior toward her. Martin pushed the door open and forced his way in, shoving Mr. Davis several times as the older man tried to protect his family. An argument ensued, and Martin grabbed the little boy and held him "like a sack of flour under his arm." Mrs. Davis tried to grab the child away and Martin wheeled around and struck Mrs. Davis so that she hit the wall and fell to the floor. Sue called the police while her ill father went to the kitchen to look for some kind of a weapon with which to defend his family. At that point, Martin went out the door. When the police arrived, the women claimed Martin was hiding in the bushes nearby. This time he was charged with assault and battery (taken away without handcuffs), booked, and shortly afterward released. Sue says he was detained only two hours.

Three weeks later, on the evening of the day Martin was arraigned on assault and battery charges, Sue found him waiting for her inside her car after work, although she had taken the precaution of parking her car in an enclosed parking garage rather than in the company parking lot. Sue was forcibly held prisoner there for three hours; Martin refused to let her go. He said he would never go to jail because she was going to marry him and then she could not testify against him. Sue said:

> He told me that "You're going to get me out of this. If you don't marry me and drop the charges against me, I'll show you that you haven't seen any violence yet."

Frightened and feeling totally helpless, Sue gave in; she describes what happened to her as kidnapping. Martin drove them in her car to another state where the marriage was performed quickly. The "marriage" lasted exactly three weeks and every day was filled with violence, threats to Sue and her son, and pressure for her to convince her mother to drop the charges. On one occasion, Martin took Sue to an isolated spot and threatened to pull her teeth out one by one. Her screams brought two young men, who helped her escape. A few days later, Martin left on a short business trip, but after a series of threatening telephone calls, Sue said:

> On the day he was to return, he called me and raved and ranted for a long time. I realized then, that I had to leave because I knew my life was in danger. At that point, I threw what I could into my car, literally walked out of the house, with my pet cat under my arm, went to my son's school and literally walked him out of his classroom. We got in our car; I gathered up my parents at their apartment, told them to throw what they could into their car and we drove [over 2,000 miles away] where we lived for nine months. I had left all of my belongings.[5]

The case against Martin was dismissed because neither Sue nor her mother appeared in court; they were too terrified of Martin to return. Sue lived in the other state for almost a year under an assumed name. She obtained a divorce and about a year after the first assault returned to her former place of residence, where she and Mrs. Davis filed a civil suit for damages against Martin. By law, each was limited to asking $5000 in damages. It took 18 months of calling, filing, and postponements before the case finally was placed on the court calendar and the hearing began.

What transpired during the course of the trial was a series of events that frequently worked to the disadvantage of the plaintiffs. For one thing, it was obvious that Martin had some knowledge and/or experience in law and courtroom procedure which he initially admitted when asking the first judge to permit him to represent himself. Once given that permission, Martin committed a number of acts and made statements that were clearly out of line; when censured by either of the two judges, his excuse was his inexperience. Both of the hearing judges appeared to give more leeway to the defendant than they did the plaintiffs' legal counsel, which may have been motivated by a sense of fair play to compensate for the defendant's "disadvantage."

Martin obtained his "disadvantage" by telling the bench that he was impoverished, unemployed, and near ruin because of Sue's legal and verbal harassment. Martin appeared in court dressed to match the financial description he offered while Sue was attired in the latest expensive fashion.[6]

Despite the benefits Martin seemed to derive from representing himself, the female judge also scolded him on a number of his breaches of courtroom etiquette. Even after being told by the judge that questions were improper or irrelevant, Martin continued to ask by rephrasing them during his cross-examination of the witnesses. On one of these occasions the judge said, "I don't see the relevancy of that. Ask your next question." The next time she said, "This has no relevance to an assault and battering case. All we're interested in are assault and battery *that day*." The third time the judge's voice was sharper when she emphasized each word: "Mr. _____ , ask your next question. *Please*." Later, when Martin was badgering his ex-wife, the judge snapped: "Don't argue with the witness. Ask your questions." Finally, when Martin was clearly making insinuations about Sue's moral character, the judge pointedly remarked to Martin's explanation of inexperience:

> I understand you and I am *not* underestimating your intelligence. Naive you are not. I will give you as much leeway as I can within the confines of the law. But do not step out of line again. Do you understand what I am saying?

A short time later, when Martin's questioning had gone afield once more and Sue's attorney had not objected, the judge intervened by saying, "You are getting away from the issue."

Mrs. Davis was next examined by Patrick and then cross-examined by Martin. Both her own counsel and Martin moved in closer to Mrs. Davis when she was on the stand because of her hearing impairment. Martin not only paced during his questioning, but he had a tendency to move in as close as possible to the witnesses, which seemed to cause both women discomfort, if not consternation.

Finally, the case was recessed, followed by the events described earlier that led to the hearing the next day by another judge. Martin started off on the wrong foot by grumbling to the bailiff and then to the new judge about how much time was wasted with the earlier judge. Although the hearing was set for 10 a.m., the judge entered the courtroom at 10:53 because he had been reviewing the file in his chambers. Apparently Martin said something negative in a low voice to the judge about the judge who had stepped down from the case because there was a sharp retort: "Do not question the neutrality of the bench."

Again stating his poverty, Martin asked permission to represent himself and was allowed to do so. The judge said, "I'll help you all I can but I can't represent you." All parties agreed once more to waive the jury, but when it came to admitting into evidence the testimony given the previous day, the defendant said there might be some objection on his part and he spent some time reviewing documents before agreeing.

Sue was back on the stand for more cross-examination when Martin turned to the judge and asked to make a statement in which he claimed harassment by the two women and asked for dismissal. The judge told him to take his complaints to another court—this was not a harassment suit, this was an assault and battery case.

Throughout the trial, the defense was conducted in the same manner as many members of the bar might have conducted themselves: (see Strick: 1978) pacing, gesturing, raising objections, studied reading of documents, disputing dates on documents, and charges (and services) listed on doctors' bills. The judge conceded that only statements referring to "physical well being" would be admitted into evidence but none referring to beating.

A sergeant arrived with police records and photos of Mrs. Davis's injuries; he was put on the stand so he could return to other duties.[7] During his cross-examination, Martin asked the sergeant, "Did you ever see Mrs. Davis before these pictures were taken?" When the officer replied "no," Martin said, "You didn't see her two days earlier so you don't know if she had any bruises then, do you?" The officer admitted he did not.

When Martin resumed his cross-examination of his ex-wife, he turned to the judge and said, "I'm a little nervous, your Honor." Then he continued questioning, introducing many issues outside the case, Patrick finally objected and his objection was sustained. Mrs. Davis was returned to the stand for further cross-examination, during which one of Martin's questions was objected to and the judge explained to him his error. At another point the judge helped him rephrase the question so it could be allowed. When he questioned Mrs. Davis about the source of her income, the judge snapped at him, "What difference does it make?" When Mrs. Davis was unable to hear a question (asked while he was pacing) the judge ordered Martin to speak louder. At one point, Martin wandered too close to the bench, causing the bailiff to approach him saying "Mr. _____ , stay out of that area!" At another point, Martin pleaded with the judge to allow him to continue asking questions already declared irrelevant.

Finally, at 3:45 on the second day, the defendant was sworn in and took the stand. At 4:05 the judge took over the questioning of the witness from Patrick and then recessed until 4:27. Shortly after 5:00, after Martin once more asked for a dismissal that was denied, he took the stand as his own witness.[8] When he asked about procedure, the judge said, "cover anything you want about this case." With almost no interruption from the plaintiffs' attorney, Martin presented his defense, giving a long account far afield from the major issues that the plaintiffs had been restricted to: two particular instances of physical violence. Martin was uninterrupted when he introduced hearsay evidence: statements from Sue's analyst and reported threats on his life such as he heard: "she's in hysterics, she's got a hit man—she was out to hurt me." He talked about Sue's problems with the Internal Revenue Service, her job, her former employer, her travels, his highly respected former employer. Throughout, the defendant turned in his chair and looked directly at the judge, speaking only to him, pleading for understanding. As his emotional pitch grew higher, he began appealing to the judge, his voice breaking as he said, "How long will this be going on?"[9] Then he began crying as he was saying:

I'm a Leo. I can't stand being in jail. I was locked up; I had to call the
woman I love who had to bail me out. The happiest day in my life was
. . . [the day Sue and her son left town]. My woman is seven years
older than me, she supports me; I'm bankrupt. My woman has stood
by me through all this while these two have tried to ruin my life. I've
lost everything because of her; can't you make her stop?

The judge asked Martin if Sue beat him and he said "yes;" the
judge asked if he beat Sue and he responded "no."

Patrick concluded his brief summation by saying: "I think the
behavior of beating women should not be condoned." Martin made a
long, very professional summation after asking if he could respond to
the points made by plaintiffs' attorney. The judge responded, "It's
entirely up to you." He hinted that Mrs. Davis had used makeup to
create the bruises, wondering if the police officer knew cosmetology.
Standing with hands on his hips, Martin referred to himself in the
third person, saying: "Mr. _____ does not have the habit of beating people up . . . if I saw a woman being beaten beside the road I
would certainly stop to help! Nobody stopped to help. [Pointing to the
judge] You'd stop, I'd stop, [pointing to Patrick] he'd stop."

Switching suddenly from anger, he turned emotional again and
with a crack in his voice said, "I beg the judge's indulgence. I've been
under a terrible strain. She cost me a job. Because of her, we live in
constant fear for our lives."

The judge concluded the proceedings saying he would take the
case under submission and would reach a decision within 10 days but
reminded litigants it takes longer to process.

About four months later, the plaintiffs were notified that they had
won the decision; Martin was found guilty of assault and battery.[10]
What was the judgment levied against him out of the $10,000 suit?
Less than $1,000 total for both plaintiffs, slightly more than their
documented medical expenses.

In The Child's Best Interests

This last section details the case history of Donna and her struggle
to get custody of her only child, Danny. The final stages of this case
have not reached conclusion, but for the present the mother has legal

joint custody after four years of experiences with police, attorneys, lawyers, and judges. If having obtained joint custody can be considered a victory, Donna does not believe any credit should go to the legal system. In fact, just the opposite: Her son is living with her *in spite of* the lack of assistance from professionals associated with the courts, with the exception of her own attorney.

Briefly, Donna's background is probably quite average in many respects. The first of two children, she had parents who loved her and who never fought. She described her home life as secure. When she was disciplined, it was her father's responsibility to administer physical punishment. However, Donna's case gives support to the assumptions underlying the theoretical model on primary battering detailed in Chapter 2: when four months pregnant at age 18, she married a man not the father of her unborn child. Donna had the necessary characteristics of women likely to remain in relationships after the first instance of violence. As Model II proposes:

> It is hypothesized that if a woman has great willingness to invest in maintaining a conjugal relationship—if she is strongly committed to it for a variety of reasons, and if she firmly accepts traditional ideology—then she will neither retaliate nor terminate a conjugal relationship if she is battered.

The first time Kurt assaulted her three months after their wedding, Donna was surprised and hurt. However, he soon apologized, cried, and swore he would never hurt her again. Long before being interviewed, Donna wrote on the survey instrument her response to the question about the first instance of violence and what she did or felt about it: "My father spanked me and yet I knew he loved me. I was scared but I loved my husband so I believed him."

A young woman who disappointed her parents by a premarital pregnancy, now due to give birth in two months, has a very strong incentive for staying with her husband despite violence. First there were slaps or kicks for displeasing her husband, and this led to beatings that became more frequent and more severe over time. Donna tried to leave Kurt six times during the next nine years, the first time when Danny was a year old, the second time six months later. Once she left with the assistance of Kurt's sister, but the anger and threats of violence unleashed on his own family drove Donna back home. She knew she was endangering other people who wanted to help her with "her" problem. After that, Kurt always found her and brought her back.

Between his violent outbursts, Donna, Kurt, and Danny had a relatively happy home life, sharing many activities together as a family. They bought their own home and lived in a nice neighborhood. Donna had more than a year of college but Kurt refused to allow her to take outside employment. Kurt was a high school graduate and his supervisory job paid a comfortable income. Kurt accepted social fatherhood of Danny and wanted the boy to grow up "macho," so he rough-housed, sometimes hurting the boy. If the child cried or showed fear, Kurt became angry and was likely to fling him across the room. Some of Donna's beatings occurred as she was trying to protect her son from abusive behavior. Following beatings, Kurt frequently wanted sexual intercourse so they could "kiss and make up." The last thing in the world Donna wanted was sex, but Kurt insisted on his "rights." Like other interviewed women, Donna did not define unwillingness or nonconsensual coitus definable as rape, but sometimes she resisted and clearly recalls being raped forcefully seven times by her husband during those nine years.

On some occasions arguments preceded beatings; other times Kurt objected to expressions on Donna's face or what she said or did not say. Her beatings ranged from monthly to several a week; the length of time an attack lasted was from sharp slaps to prolonged beatings. Donna wrote: "If I screamed and cried loud, I got it worse." When asked if she struck back or tried to defend herself she said, "I tried a couple of times but it would be worse. I defended myself so I would not be hurt as bad." At one point, Kurt threw a pointed mechanic's tool at her that hit her knee; she was unable to walk for a week and has a permanent scar. She received other wounds such as severe bruises, cuts, and black eyes. When asked if she believed she deserved the beatings, Donna replied, "no" and explained: "I am a person, not a thing and I do not deserve violence from a man twice my size." At the time Kurt weighted 55 pounds more and was 10 inches taller than Donna; he also had served four years in military service, receiving an honorable discharge at the rank of noncommissioned officer.

According to Donna, Kurt's home life was also described as secure. He was the eldest of four children with devout fundamentalist parents who did not engage in violence. His father was considerably older than his mother and he died when Kurt was only 14 years old; physical punishment thereafter was administered by his mother, and, according to what Kurt told his wife, he was frequently punished for actions of his siblings. Kurt had no previous marriages, never used pleasure drugs, drank only occasionally, and was never under the influence when he beat Donna. She knows of no other violent acts he committed, and he was never charged or arrested for anything other than reckless driving. The police were called to their home on numerous occasions, but, while the officers were polite to Donna and talked to Kurt, no action was ever taken. Finally, the end of the relationship came when Kurt almost strangled Donna. She realized, "He's going to kill me! If I stay he'll kill me anyhow, so what do I have to lose? I may as well die trying to get away."

Donna left the next day while Kurt was at work, taking her son. She stayed with a friend and soon was in a supportive network of friends who not only helped her get employment but also drove her to and from work because she had no car of her own. But even with the kindness and understanding of friends, Donna's life was one of fear and running because Kurt seemed obsessed with getting her to return home. He went to her place of employment and created scenes; her employers called the police, but he left before they arrived so no charges were lodged against him. Because of threats of violence to her friends, she moved from place to place, putting Danny into one school and then another. But Kurt always found her and the threats, harassment, and intimidation—as well as beatings—continued. When her roommates were away, Donna would move around the apartments in total darkness, afraid to show her presence in case Kurt was lurking outside. When a roommate was home, she asked her to speak in whispers so no one outside would know she was inside.

Despite her best efforts, Donna found it impossible to avoid Kurt, who also demanded visitation rights with Danny. Once he had the boy, Kurt would take him to the place he was sharing with another woman, Sarah, and her two small children. Then he would return to Donna with flowers or other gifts, exerting charm and begging her to

reunite with him. After being refused, Kurt would dash the flowers to
the floor and stomp on them as he exploded into violence.

Finally, one day when Danny was away in Sarah's care, Kurt broke
into Donna's apartment. What followed was a three-day nightmare of
beatings, rape, and sexual abuse while Donna was kept prisoner,
under constant surveillance. Donna still cannot recall, three years
later, how she managed to escape because all she can remember is
driving her car toward a hospital one therapist had recommended.
She only knew she was at the brink of a mental breakdown, so she
committed herself into the psychiatric ward.

Donna recalls this experience warmly. All new patients were given
the first three days to rest and become acclimated before beginning
group therapy. Donna made new and lasting friends among the voluntary patients, including one woman who had also suffered much
physical abuse from her lover. For the first time Donna felt safe,
despite constant phone calls from Kurt. Although she was assured
that no uninvited visitor could get into that section of the hospital, one
day Kurt and Danny appeared. Donna accompanied them to the
cafeteria because she wanted to reassure her son that she was "OK."
At the end of a short visit, Kurt asked Donna to "Come home so we
can be a family again." Donna said no and the boy asked "What about
me?" When Donna again refused, saying she had to return to her
ward, Kurt yelled out at the boy:

> She's crazy! Didn't I tell you she's crazy? She doesn't care about you or
> me, she only cares about herself! She's always been crazy, you know
> that. She's the one who's breaking up our family. She doesn't want
> you!

Donna wanted to stay longer in the hospital but now realized that
Kurt intended to carry out his threats to take the boy away from her.
She also realized that having been in a mental institution, even if
voluntarily, could be used against her in a custody fight. So, two
weeks after she committed herself, Donna signed herself out and
went to stay with friends. That same night Kurt showed up and
created a scene outside the house.

Donna began the struggle to obtain legal custody of her son by
going to an attorney reputed to be the best criminal lawyer in the

county and one who waged strong fights for his clients. After hearing Donna's description of the three-day imprisonment and sexual assault and rapes, this "very strong-looking man" turned to Donna and jokingly asked, "What did you do? Drink wine in between?" Donna said she left immediately and refused to pay the consultation fees she was later billed.

It seemed impossible to get help anywhere. For the past months, Donna had called the police on numerous occasions, but they said they could do nothing—it was a "civil matter" or a "family problem." Friends had been urging Donna to go to a shelter for battered women; they were all afraid of her husband's violence. When Danny was with her for a Christmas visit, Donna decided to go to a shelter. At first she resisted the counselors' urging to quit her job and apply for welfare because it is too dangerous for shelterees to go to a place of employment known to their abusers. Like so many other Americans, Donna believed it was a personal disgrace to go on welfare, so she continued to go to work with escorts accompanying her to her car. Just after leaving work one day, she saw a car in her rearview mirror that looked like her mother-in-law's. It was rush hour but she headed for a busy expressway, only to be stopped in traffic. Shaking and fearful, Donna sat in the locked car with closed windows; her mother-in-law got out of her car stopped two places behind, came toward her, and pounded on the windows and windshield saying, "Donna, be reasonable! He only wants to talk to you."

As soon as she could get clear of traffic on the expressway, Donna began driving at high speed, hoping either to elude her pursuer or to attract the attention of the police. Her old car locked into high gear, and despite speeding and fast lane changes, she was unable to lose the chasing car. It began hitting the rear of her own. Kurt pulled alongside and began hitting her car's side. Afraid she would be forced off the road into a culvert, Donna took an exit to head for a police station which, in her panic and uncontrollable high speed, she passed. Remembering a corporation's guard station nearby, she headed there. As she pulled up, Kurt drove up and stopped immediately behind her. He and his mother jumped out and explained to the startled men, "It's OK, nothing's wrong, officers. Except she's my wife and she gets like this—she's hysterical. We just want to take her home where she belongs." With her husband beside her door and his mother at the other, Donna screamed from within the car, "Help me! Call the cops! He hit my car and he's trying to kill me. Call the police!"

One man turned away to call the police and at that Kurt and his mother returned to their car and drove away. When police officers arrived and examined the dents, scratches, and paint marks on Donna's car, despite Donna's pleading, they refused to take a report, saying that this was a problem between husband and wife and they could not interfere. They said that the husband, as coowner of the car, can do what he wants with his own property. In addition, they could not prove the damages occured in the way Donna described.

After that event, Donna decided to take "charity," quit her job, and applied for welfare. After a month at the shelter receiving emotional support, making close friends among shelterees, and receiving counseling in law and community services, Donna left for her own home. Kurt was now living with his girlfriend, Sarah, in the same neighborhood. Donna brought another battered woman and her five children to her home from the shelter. She changed all the locks and then, with a female attorney who specialized in family law, she went to court to file for divorce, custody, and a restraining order. That first court experience represents the only clear victory for Donna but was the first of monthly court hearings for the next year, each one before a different judge. This time the restraining order legally evicted her husband from the family home and ordered him to stay beyond a certain number of feet from the house. Kurt was given all-day Sunday visitation rights. Although Kurt and Sarah lived only a few blocks away, Donna (always accompanied by a friend) took the child to one of Kurt's relatives for his father to pick up. Kurt became an "amusement-park dad" to Danny, taking him to all the places children enjoy most and feeding him the kinds of "treats" youngsters like to eat.

But the harassing, threats, and day and night phone calls continued. A month later, Donna and the woman who was living with her had a birthday party and some men friends were invited. After midnight Donna received a threatening call from Kurt that she better get her guests out of his house. A few minutes later, Kurt drove up as the men were leaving and threatened them.[11] Donna called the police because of Kurt's violation of the restraining order, but the officers again shrugged, saying this was a civil matter and that after all, "this is his home, too—there's nothing we can do. Go see a judge in the morning."

Donna did go back to court, but each time there was some reason for no hearing: Kurt's attorney would not appear, Kurt was unable to come, or the court calendar had been changed. Each appearance required Donna to take time off from work; Kurt worked nights so he lost no wages for time spent waiting in the court house.

About four months after the ruined birthday party, Donna finally accepted an invitation to join a group of friends for dinner and dancing. As she was leaving the place she came face to face with Kurt, who threatened all of them and created a scene. One of the men knew she was upset and feared to let her return to her home that night so he insisted on taking her to one of his relatives to spend the night. When she returned home the next day she found the interior of the house a shambles: furniture smashed, mirrors broken, doors kicked in from the inside. She estimated several thousand dollars in damages to her own furnishings, and some borrowed things were destroyed or stolen. There was no doubt that Kurt had wreaked this havoc because he pulled out their wedding cake decoration Donna had carefully stored away and placed it prominently atop a piece of paper that said, "Because I love you."

When the police arrived, Donna made the unfortunate mistake of telling them her husband was the perpetrator, whereupon they refused to pursue the matter. She demanded:

A crime has been committed here. What if I'm wrong? How can you be *sure* my husband did this unless you investigate? If you at least take fingerprints you may find it was someone else. Won't you please at least take fingerprints?

But the officers insisted that all the damage was done from the inside with no sign of forcible entry, so she was correct in her assumptions. Once more they told her that a man has a right to do as he pleases with his own property. Donna was again defeated—she had hoped that an official report and fingerprints would make useful testimony in court. She went to the police station in an attempt to file criminal charges against Kurt. Her report was taken and she was told the district attorney would get in touch with her by phone, but he never contacted her.

Donna's next action was to leave her home and destroyed posessions and establish residence with a male friend's relative. When her home was later sold, she and her male friend bought a home jointly and moved in together. Meanwhile, Danny was being treated royally by his formerly abusive father on each visitation Sunday and concurrently being told that his crazy, selfish mother was responsible for breaking up their happy home. During the rest of the week, Danny was living with a man not his father and subjected to house rules of conduct, chores, and homework by his mother, who was again employed full-time. After Sundays with his fun-loving father, Danny seemed to return home with increasingly hostile attitudes and questions. Yet Kurt's harassment, threats, and phone calls to Donna continued unabated.

Finally, Donna and her attorney decided that the matter of child custody should be resolved and Donna wanted no more visitation privileges for Kurt, who seemed to be instigating more and more trouble. Donna asked the court for psychiatric screening to determine the issue, feeling certain that an expert would show that she was a good mother and the boy's father was a destructive influence. The judge appointed a male court psychiatrist, who interviewed Donna, Kurt, and Danny individually. This was followed by a joint interview with Donna and Kurt. During that time, Kurt became enraged and began hurtling verbal abuses at her; Donna was convinced that the psychiatrist would see who was an "unfit" parent. Later, the court sent a female social worker to investigate their respective homes. Donna and her friend were interviewed and apparently her friend answered incorrectly when he said he was not actively trying to "act like a father" to the boy but wanted instead to gain his trust and friendship. He said he left discipline up the boy's mother. Donna also admitted that she spanked Danny when necessary and on one occasion used a thin strip of plastic from a toy that happened to be nearby that "makes a loud whooshing noise so it sounds bad but it doesn't really hurt."

The screening completed, all parties returned to court. The psychiatrist's report made no direct recommendation but he noted that the boy seemed to prefer his father and Donna was diagnosed as "unstable." The social worker's report said that because Danny would have to share a bedroom with two other children, including a girl one year his junior, and because both Kurt and Sarah worked nights, she recommended placement with the mother as "the lesser of two evils."

Upon questioning by the judge, Sarah promised that she would quit her night job to stay home with the children if Danny was allowed to live with them. Donna's friends and neighbors testified as character witnesses that Kurt had physically abused both the boy and his mother and would not serve as a good role model. Evidence was produced of both wife and child abuse. It was pointed out to the judge that the boy was not Kurt's biological son, but the judge felt that Kurt's acceptance of social fatherhood and attendant responsibility was highly commendable, superseding biological parenthood.

The judge's decision was to award custody to Kurt, permitting Donna visitation privileges on some holidays and every other Sunday. Donna was distraught; she could not believe what had happened. The boy was placed in his new home and transferred to another school. Sarah continued working at her job and the children spent nights at a baby-sitter's house where a total of six children slept in the same room. The "amusement-park dad" became the absent dad: the boy arose when his father was still sleeping and returned home from school after his father had gone to work. Donna refused to become an amusement-park mom or to engage in bribing her son with treats on visitation days. They spent their time together in the usual ways around the house, going for walks, and so forth. Before long, Danny wanted to stay with his mother and began resisting being returned to his father.

In the meantime, the relationship between Sarah and Kurt began to sour and Kurt became violent with her. Kurt's pattern of beatings, threats, and harassment were now directed toward Sarah, who had never believed Donna's claims of abuse. However, there was a difference: now when the police intervened, Kurt was arrested and he also lost his job because of violent behavior.

Eight months after a judge awarded custody to Kurt, he and his attorney met with Donna and her attorney. Kurt was now willing to turn Danny's physical custody over to Donna (at the urging of his attorney), but only if she would agree to his terms drawn up into a contract. There would be no demand for legal custody (Kurt wanted informal joint custody), no child support, and visitation privileges the same as those the court had given Donna, plus many additional restrictions favorable to Kurt. These terms were not agreeable to the boy's mother but her attorney convinced her to accept them.[12] It turned out to be a wise decision because four months later, after Kurt was in considerable difficulties with the law, Donna and her attorney returned to court and obtained legal joint custody and a low rate of child support (Kurt was now unemployed), which he never paid.

Kurt later left the area to escape the law and, as a result, Donna lived a relatively normal life with her growing son for almost two years. However, shortly before granting the final interview to the investigator, Donna's telephone rang in the middle of the night. Kurt had been picked up by the police and was calling from jail with more threats. Donna wonders how soon it will be when Kurt is once more free to stalk, harass, and intimidate his prey.[13]

Chapter 8

IS THERE A SOLUTION?

This investigation of battered women and their perceptions of spousal assault was not intended to include a study of the entire social system within which the principal characters exist. But as actors in a play performing their roles privately behind closed doors, it became obvious that they were following scripts largely written by others. The individual twists and flourishes of their performances were perhaps part of their own creative artistry, but the plots were largely written by their ancestors who built the stage, the theater, and the audience. This study learned about the socialization of the women, the resources they had or did not have, and how institutional representatives responded to them.

Implications

Until the recent drive by the shelter movement to alert individual women living lives of violence and pain inside their homes that they were not experiencing something rare that was probably their own fault, and offered them the services they needed to help them stop the violence, a study such as this would have been impossible. Ten or even twenty years ago there would not have been 350 women willing to expose the most personal and painful aspects of their lives to an unknown researcher. There would not have been the additional hundreds of women discussing with a stranger intimate details of their lives with men they had loved, regardless of empathy.

The reason all this was possible is because of the shelter movement which began in 1972 in England (the very beginning has been traced to neighborhood women who organized to protest high food costs), spread to the continent shortly afterward, and reached the United States by late 1975 and early 1976. Almost all the respondents in this study were only able to break the pattern of violence in their private lives because of this international social movement. It created a positive change in the institutional response variable; now these women had a safe place to go and alternatives were made available to them that either were not there before, were not perceived by the women as alternatives, or the women did not know how to use them. The shelter movement made sufficient impact on individual lives to make this study possible.

But in addition, the shelter movement has had an impact on the social system in a wide variety of cultures around the world. Beginning at the grassroots level, groups of women got together in these various countries, noted the prevalence of the problem, and decided to do something about it (some expanded their memberships to include men). They formed community groups, determined to improve the lives of victims of spousal abuse—women and children. They persisted in their determination, but there has been massive resistance from the social system that follows a peculiar and distinct pattern.

There is strong evidence that woman-battering has existed for centuries (Davidson, 1977a; Dobash and Dobash, 1979; Pleck, 1979), yet it took until late in the twentieth century for the public to acknowledge it or show real concern. In the mid-1800s, Mill wrote about the lack of rights of married women (1971); Cobbe wrote about "Wife Torture in England" in 1878; and it is clear that women have had so few rights that even Lady Randolph Churchill (Jennie Jerome, Winston Churchill's mother) by law could not refuse to have sexual intercourse with her husband, even though he had syphilis (Martin, 1970:135).

Yet everywhere a (usually) small but determined community group attempts to establish a shelter for victims of battering, women and their children, the response is the same. Regardless of their country of origin, or section of the country, the first response they receive is skepticism. They are always told that such phenomena may occur but "not here." They must first go out and prove that such a problem exists to the extent that it justifies the establishment of a shelter. Whether their appeals are to city councils, mayors, burgo-masters, boards of supervisors, or national governments—it makes no difference. These groups of concerned citizens must each begin the same process, usually without funds and on a voluntary basis, searching for ways to document the extent of violence against women in their own communities. They soon learn that hospitals keep no records and the police do not identify specific cases of wife assaults in their log books. In the United States, the FBI gathers crime statistics (Uniform Crime Reports) that include several forms of violence in a catch-all category in which cases of wife abuse would be found called "disturbance call (family quarrels, man with gun, etc.)" (1977). This category includes brawls between adult brothers or adults at social gatherings or a man waving a gun at his neighbors for walking on his lawn. In addition, when batterings result in death of one or the other spouse, the crimes are listed as homicides.

The process usually begins with community groups trying to inter-est established traditional helping agencies in contributing whatever data they may have and possibly sensitizing them to the issue; in the event they have no statistics to contribute (which they usually do not), they will begin to gather some data. Then efforts are made to raise enough money for a "hot-line" telephone staffed with volunteers, whenever possible on a 24-hour basis. Then begins the long, difficult role of community education. This involves a long series of public speaking engagements, organizing discussion groups, and visiting politicians and appointed officials to get whatever can be gained.

This process continues until finally either a concerned philanthro-pist offers the group a building at low rental (as occurred in Long Beach and Seal Beach, California, and Dublin, Ireland); members raise enough money among themselves to rent housing (as in Boston, Massachusetts, by a group of battered women pooling their welfare checks); a women's resource center is turned into a shelter (as in Pittsburgh, Pennsylvania, and London, England); they obtain some funding (as WTLC and most other American shelters); they "squat" in government-owned buildings scheduled for demolition (as many in England have done); or the government turns one part of a building over to them (as in Oslo and Brussels). Sometimes the government itself opens and staffs shelters, as in Helsinki. A group may open a shelter with little or no funding, such as one in Minnesota that had only community service center funds and used primarily a volunteer staff (Minnesota Department of Corrections, 1979:48-49). In other cities such as Copenhagen, a group called the Joan Sisters began with a rape hot line and volunteers and has been trying, since 1978, to obtain housing suitable for a shelter. A group in Louisiana has been trying to do the same for about three years. For a provocative analysis of the shelter movement and critique of "official cooptation," see Johnson (1981).

Obviously, many of these groups succeed in obtaining residential facilities regardless of the method used. But from that point on, they face a new set of problems, such as establishing their operating philosophy, obtaining staff and volunteers and training both, facing the daily crises of shelterees and their children, and at the same time looking for new funding to maintain their services.

In the meantime, victims and children pour into the new shelters, which almost always are filled to capacity within the first week of operation. This condition usually continues unabated thereafter. Some shelters try to find alternative housing, such as motels, for the most desperate women for whom there is no room; other, less critical cases are put on a waiting list. Most have more applicants than they are able to admit; zoning and other local regulations determine the total number of residents they are legally permitted to accommodate. For example, in Minnesota, where in 1979 there were seven shelters and another due to open, a Department of Corrections report stated:

> Several regions of the state have no shelter and, because of distance, are not adequately serviced by those in other regions. Even in areas

with shelters, many women are not able to make use of them due to lack of space. Of the 2,749 women statewide requesting shelter between January 18 and November 15, 1978, 2,136 or 79% were turned away. In the seven county metro area in which two shelters are operative, 85% of the women requesting shelter had to be turned away [1979:45].

In addition to the 613 women these shelters admitted and served, there were also 726 children. If the 2136 women who were turned away had the same average number of children, that would have meant 2530 children, bringing the total number of refugees from abuse in their homes to 4666 persons who could not obtain shelter. As of 1979, the range of funding per year from the Department of Corrections for these 7 shelters was from $62,500 to $12,000—and for one, nothing.

It seems that if only 15 to 21 percent of all needy applicants could be accommodated by other public health and safety services, elected officials and other persons in positions of power would act swiftly to remedy the situation. For instance, suppose a community had only one hospital and it had to turn away 85 percent of all prospective patients, or if 79 percent of all criminals given prison sentences could not be housed in the state prison. It has been estimated that it costs between $10,000 and $15,000 to maintain one prisoner per year (Bowker, 1978). These shelters operate on approximately $10 per day per resident, and there is a constant need to search for new sources of funding, some of which is accomplished by holding fund-raising events and submitting grant proposals. Yet, at the same time—and unlike most hospitals and prisons—shelters are also performing gratis other services beyond the shelters, such as in Minnesota:

> In addition . . . shelter staffs are involved in providing community education and information. During this period, 7,922 calls and 376 letters requesting information were answered and 610 visitors toured the shelters. Shelter staffs participated in 366 workshops and speaking engagements involving a total of 12,031 participants. Thus not only have essential services been provided in shelters to women who are abused, but also valuable community outreach on the issue of battering has been accomplished [Minnesota Department of Corrections, 1979:45].

This, then, is the process, repeated over and over, in the United States as well as other countries.[1] Dahl recently documented the case for the Scandinavian countries (1980); Sutton did the same for the British Isles (1977); Dussuyer has been gathering statistics for the same purpose in France since before 1977; and a women's collective in Helsinki that included Chris Tornroth and Kari Mattila and many others went through the same process for Finland. In 1978 there was no shelter for battered women and their children in Finland; a year later, according to Matti Joutsen of the Research Institute of Legal Policy, there were several. Some of the Finnish shelters are operated by the government and others, by feminist organizations.

The intriguing question remains: What are the implications of striking international similarities in response by persons in power positions at all levels of these societies to the widespread problem of women-battering and the groups of people who want to establish provisions to assist and protect victims of spousal abuse? The pattern is clear: (1) there is denial; (2) the burden of proof is placed upon the citizenry; (3) funding agencies are resistant to providing funds for victims of this particular crime; and (4) funds provided are always insufficient and short-term.

Several answers have been suggested. One of them comes from Rose (1980:521-523), who criticizes British sociologists for their almost faddish enthusiasm for the new urban sociology proposed in France by Castells. Although this new perspective takes into account the "collective actions of students, squatters, and other community groups" (1980:523), it totally ignores women's rights groups and their offshoot, the shelter movement, both empirically and theoretically. Rose asks these pointed questions:

> Yet if the collective actions of women are not part of the politics of reproduction, what are they? To ask this question is to raise both political and theoretical difficulties. For example, does asking it push the issue of material and ideological reproduction beyond its relationship to the capitalist mode of production and on towards a relationship with patriarchy? And if, in order to avoid the concept of patriarchy and the problems that it poses for a marxist framework, as it presently exists, what does the new urban sociology do with this major social movement? What conjuring trick is open to it? Can it dissolve the social into the personal? [1980:523]

Rose goes on to suggest that not only the government but sociologists as well tend to make women and women's issues invisible, and perhaps one of the reasons for this is that there is the real possibility of women "leaving the oppression of being unfree laborers. Within the capitalist society itself, the possibility is born of non-patriarchal relations between men and women" (1980:536).

Another suggestion for the invisibility of the problem of women-battering and the reluctance of power holders to both recognize it and use their power energetically to eliminate it comes from class lectures by E. Gartly Jaco in 1975 at the University of California, Riverside. During the course of this class on the sociology of deviance, Jaco shared with his students a typology he was developing that helps explain the reactions of others to acts that deviate from established norms. The typology looked something like this:

Jaco's Typology

NORMS

(Crescive, Out of History, Rather than Enacted)

INFORMAL $\longrightarrow$ FORMAL

| FOLKWAYS (habits) | MORES (morals) | LAWS (conventions) | INSTITUTIONS (marriage and family, religion, economic, political, education) |

Jaco explained that all behavior is on a continuum from conformity to nonconformity; that is deviation, but not necessarily deviance. There are degrees of conformity or individuality, and sometimes conformity and deviance can exist together. According to Jaco:

> It is important to link deviance to the norm that the behavior deviated from in the first place. Deviant behavior is a deviation from a norm that is negatively evaluated by a group with sufficient power to sustain their negative evaluation of it. If we want to know how people react to these forms of deviance, we must go to the kind of norm it was that was deviated from in order to know what kind of reactions there will be [Jaco lecture, May 26, 1975].

The imposition of social control or punishment becomes more severe the farther along the continuum from folkways toward institu-

tions. The village eccentrics, for example, may be laughed at and
remain on the margins, but they are tolerated. Mores are moral laws;
mainly they are customs everyone is expected to conform to, but law
is more formalized where what is expected is spelled out and so are
the punishments, according to Jaco. At the most formalized point,
institutions, each of the basic social institutions has a set of systematic norms derived from the values. Examples of deviation from the
norms of marriage and family are divorce, separation, child abandon-
ment, and so forth. Other important points from these lectures include the following: (1) Sanctions for violation of norms of the institutions are the most extreme because *basic values are being
threatened*; (2) Norms must be systematized and they must have
clout; there must be power to impose a punishment; (3) Norms
change with the power structure. In sum, there must be enough power
behind the norms to give them legitimacy and to impose sanctions for
violations.

These are the main points from Jaco's lectures that may explain
why persons in positions of power have been unwilling to impose
severe sanctions on batterers and unwilling to accept the identification of woman-battering as a serious social problem or even to uphold
existing laws to protect victims. As Jaco instructed, "look for the
norm that is being violated."

In this issue, there are two sets of norm-violators: the batterers who
abuse their wives and sometimes their children, and the victims and
their champions, the shelter movement. The first question is: What
norm has the batterer violated along this continuum? Actually, in the
United States and most industrialized nations, it is located somewhere between mores and laws. In the United States, for example,
laws in some states make wife (spouse)-beating a crime, but the
requirements for prosecution are usually much more than for compa-
rable crimes between strangers, the penalties are less severe, and they
are seldom imposed. In addition, there are many specific laws that, in
practice, are not enforced.

Not much earlier in this country's history there were other laws
regarding marital violence, but these laws supported the institution of
marriage and the family, and they were enforced. Men historically
had the right to use whatever force necessary to "discipline" their

families. Further, these rights were backed by the other four institutions. Dobash and Dobash explain it in these words:

> The husband had complete authority over his wife and was given the legal and *moral obligation* to manage and control her behavior. The use of physical coercion was simply one of the "legitimate" means traditionally used to achieve such control. The subordinate position of women in the family and in other social institutions throughout the 19th century [remained] despite their movement into wage work, and they remained the legitimate victims of domestic chastisement. The legal, political, and economic institutions were committed to, benefited from, and reinforced the patriarchal structure and ideology. It would have been inconceivable for them to have supported any other form of family relations. All institutions were organized along these lines and all people were socialized into the supporting ideology. . . . These ideals, and their accompanying practices formed the foundations of the subordination and control of women. *It is still true* that for a woman to be brutally or systematically assaulted she must usually enter our most sacred institution, the family [1979:74-75].

Walker (1979) also adds her support to these ideas: "Today, many men still believe their rights to rule their women are primary. This notion has been supported not only by religion but by the law" (p. 12). Even with the passage of time the remnants of "rights" and "duty" remain associated with men's "chastisement" of women and children in their families. Some newer laws have been written to protect the rights of women and children, but these are further down the continuum where their violation is not necessarily a threat to the institution of marriage and family.

Then which norms are the victims and the shelter movement breaking, or at least threatening to break? Now, following Jaco's guidance, the answer becomes quite obvious: these people are the real troublesome ones, because they are threatening two of our basic institutions—marriage and family. At least the power holders may presume that they are undermining very important institutions that have been engineered into their present forms by all the other institutions. Battered women, by making public their dissatisfaction with their private lives, may well appear to be deviants, since they are thereby attacking the myth of the happy family (earlier papers detailed this idea; see Pagelow, 1977b, 1981a). And shelter movement people, by demanding alternatives for victims that may include separation or divorce, certainly can be viewed as deviants attacking marriage and family. Looked at in this light, with the help of Jaco's typology and identifying the norms that have been broken, it is easy to see why both victims and victims' service providers have been met with negative institutional response while the aggressors have not received severe social sanctions.

It is possible that Rose (1980) is correct when she suggests that the women's movement and the shelter movement may permanently change relationships between men and women. An American researcher agrees with these ideas, as is clear in her statement:

> Man became the patriarch in religious and other matters and a repressive mode of living ensued, resulting in harsh cultural attitudes toward women. There are many, myself included, who believe that we are entering into a new social order which will overthrow patriarchy and replace it with an egalitarian society. Probably the reason the women's movement has elicited such great fear is that it is correctly perceived as the beginning of this revolution. A cornerstone, then, of the creation of a new egalitarian social order would be to reverse the tides of violence committed against women [Walker, 1979:12].

Perhaps both these and other writers are correct; but, on the other hand, maybe the power holders are overestimating the amount of influence the shelter movement can have on victims. Perhaps the patriarchy will remain intact and the traditionalism of victims will return them to their batterers or to other men who will batter them and the cycle will continue. We know that many women return directly home from shelters and we do not know how many more eventually return to their batterers after making an initial attempt at independent living. When women come to shelters, go through their programs, and then, after many telephone conversations with spouses pleading with them to return home, pack up their children and possessions and return to their batterers, shelter staff are very likely to feel that they have failed. Some shelter operators talk in terms of "success" or "failure" rates. Success is presumed to include women who manage to make the enormous transition from battering victim status to the establishment of an independent life without their batterers. Concerned staff feel discouraged and fear for the women and children who return home on simple faith. They know that promises of reformation are likely to be broken and that returning women are almost surely going to suffer more frequent and more severe violence in the future. Some funding sources and traditional community helping agents are also likely to view women who return to spouses as evidence that shelters are not providing sufficient reeducation for victims or, more important, that victims have exaggerated the abuse that sent them out of their homes in the first place.

European shelter providers chided the investigator during a conference in 1976 for this American tendency to view women who return to batterers on mere promises as representing failure. They feel we expect change to occur so swiftly in women that they can reject a lifetime of training, perhaps 25 or 35 years of socialization, after only a relatively few days of exposure to entirely new ideas. Andersen and van Crevel stated it this way:

> You Americans want instant everything! You have instant coffee and instant other things; you want change overnight. Your expectations for these women are unrealistic. How can you expect these women to reject everything they've been told their entire lives—by their families, their friends, their schools, their churches, their entire society—almost overnight? Change takes time—they will keep coming back to shelters and then finally they will be able to take that big step!

The investigator contends that these women, who helped establish probably the first shelter on the European continent (Blijf van m'n Lijf in Amsterdam) and who have worked on the woman-battering issue ever since, are quite correct. Women who return home are not "failures" in any sense of the word. If there was only a short history of abuse and their spouses recognize they have a problem and begin to correct it, there is a possibility of no further violence.[2] But these women had the courage to leave the first time; they were exposed to alternatives and new ideas; they found out that other people outside their homes can and do care for their welfare; they learned that they are not ugly "freaks" with a rare, individual problem. They may return to the men that abused them, but they do not return the same women they were when they left. They know they managed to leave for safety before and they know they can do it again, if necessary. There are people "out there" who want to help them. By the same token, their spouses know this, too, which may change some of their attitudes and behavior. If there is no solution but permanent termination of the relationships it will happen—but only after the women have done all they could to hold them together. If and when that fails, they will leave and not return.

Summary

At the conclusion of this long process of reviewing the literature, designing the study, conducting the investigation, analyzing the data, and writing this report, there are feelings both of accomplishment and satisfaction as well as recognition of ways all of these steps might have been improved. Some of the inadequacies of the survey instrument were discussed earlier, but the greatest improvement would be to have designed a longitudinal instead of a case study. If the sample could be reinterviewed over a period of years, it would add much more to our understanding.

It seems appropriate to add here some comments about the overall research project designed to study battered women's perceptions of spousal violence (see Appendix A). Much valuable information was gathered directly and indirectly through a variety of techniques from victims, their children, service providers, and community agents. The statistical tests of analysis helped to described the interaction of a variety of key variables, but they failed to lend sufficient support to the major hypothesis proposed to explain the length of time these women had stayed with battering spouses. However, by examining and analyzing both quantitative and qualitative data gathered in this study, a greater depth of understanding has been gained than if the study had relied entirely on one or the other. Based on the data accumulated by all methodologies, the investigator is convinced that strong and sufficient evidence was gathered to support the idea that the principal factors determining the length of time these women remain with spouses depends on their personal and material resources, responses of social institutions, and the women's degree of commitment to traditional ideology. The majority of the sample in this study were able to leave spouses because of the development of a new social institution: shelters.

Even with this change in institutional response, many of the women in this sample probably returned to resume lives with their spouses. It would be of benefit to all—but especially to women who live with batterers—if it were possible to reinterview these women. Important information could be gained through interviews conducted one or five years from now, although this would be a particularly difficult subject to study longitudinally.[3] With this case study and at the present time, it is only possible to estimate the probabilities of more violence for the women who returned which appear high, as well as the likelihood that most of these relationships will eventually be terminated by the decision of one or the other spouse. The study suggests that shelters provided insufficient change in the other two variables for shelterees who returned home to have made the successful transition to emotional and economic independence. When and if returning women's personal or material resources increase, or when and if they reject some of the traditionalism of their socialization, then they will be able to begin new lives without spousal violence.

As for the women in this sample who did not directly return to their spouses after leaving shelters, the benefits of positive institutional response plus rejection of some traditional values after reexamination and the personal/material resources obtained through community outreach services provided at shelters apparently gave them sufficient impetus to change their lifestyles.

Many battered women and service providers who work with them, after reading some of the papers written by the investigator, have made enthusiastic comments to support the theoretical perspective and research hypothesis of this study. In one form or another, they have repeated the following statement in a letter recently received from a service provider: "I continue to find your work the most enlightening and most directly applicable to both program planning and actual service delivery in my work. The three key variables you define *work*." Letters have been received from other service providers confirming the importance of the three factors hypothesized to be most important determinants in their clients' decisions to stay with or leave abusers. Many letters also have arrived from battered women asking for copies of papers written by the investigator and/or offering encouragement and thanks for doing this study. One of these letters arrived in 1979 from a Canadian woman, which reads in part as follows:

> I was one of the battered wives who for years screamed quietly so that the neighbours would not hear. I remember a very alert neighbour told me to scream *loudly* so that they *would* hear—I never forgot that bit of counseling. Recently I picked up Mrs. Pizzey's book in our local public library and laughed out loud at the title. My life for thirty years with my husband was a disaster—he died in 1971. It was a terrible experience for a naive, trusting, inexperienced, woman. I couldn't figure out what was the matter and no one would help me. He was a successful business man in his own lumber business and I was blamed for everything. . . . The conspiracy of silence in the medical, scientific and publishing circles has been successful. Psychopathy is more acceptable in a permissive society. Fortunately because the modern woman is *not* accepting rape and beating as her just due—we are being forced to study behavior and hopefully expose sick behavior. Probably many battered wives have husbands such as mine. . . . I am happy to see a sociologist interested—that is a good sign.

A year later she sent a newspaper clipping and wrote:

> Now we are getting a bit of the truth at last. . . . It was only yesterday (about 1945) that I packed my car with clothes, and blankets, and my little girl, and drove for miles to escape but there was nowhere to go and no one to help me. Thank God women have some refuge now. Some people will have to face the truth at last. Don't get discouraged, keep up your good work.

This study is not perfect—no study ever is. But it may add to what we have learned recently from other sources about this complex issue, and perhaps new ways will be developed to deal with it. In the second volume on men's attitudes toward violence, Blumenthal makes these introductory remarks that summarize the struggle for understanding:

> Social problems are by nature complex and this complexity leads
> directly to the difficult and often unsatisfactory nature of research on
> these problems. . . . It is difficult to think about complicated phenom-
> ena clearly; to do so, work must progress in stages [Blumenthal et al.,
> 1975:v].

One complaint some persons may make is that this study did not
obtain a sample of nonbattered women. Some social scientists attempt to study individual features, looking for differences between
women with battering spouses and those with nonviolent spouses;
they are welcome to such exercises. But this was not an attempt to
find out what is peculiar or "different" about women who are battered; the theoretical viewpoint guiding this study rejects the idea that
specific "types" of women are battered as opposed to another type
who are not. The investigator is inclined to agree with Walker when
she suggests that it may be no more than a matter of chance, since so
many women are battered in this society. What good would it do, and
what would we really learn, if we go through the process of attempting to obtain a sample of women we *positively* can identify (a dubious
assumption) who have never been beaten by a man in their lives?
Unless we have designed a longitudinal study, we cannot be certain
that the nonbattered women we used as a control group at one point
were not battered the following year or a few years later. Some of this
sample were never battered until 7, 8, or 15 years after living with the
same men; others were not battered by their first spouse and then were
battered by a second one. To insist on a comparison group would
accomplish little, because comparing women for individual qualities
or life circumstances is not the purpose of this study.

Rather, the purpose was to find out from women who had been
battered what their lives were like; what were their perceptions of
their relationships; what were their resources, help-seeking efforts,
and responses; what were their fundamental values and ideology; and
how long and why they stayed with violent men. These were the
research goals and that is what was accomplished. By contributing to
our knowledge in these particulars, it has served the purpose for
which it was intended. If we can gain sufficient insight into these
matters, change agents may use these findings to begin engineering a

social system where few men will beat their spouses, and those who do will learn that the first time is also the last time. Researchers do not make social policy, but many of us hope that our work will be useful in guiding such policy.

APPENDIX A

RESEARCH DESIGN

The research design and methods used in this study as a test of Model III, secondary battering, are presented here, beginning with operational definitions of the three major independent constructs and the one dependent variable. Next, the research design is described, followed by the research methods employed in this study. Finally, there is a discussion on the various limitations and advantages in this case study of the perceptions of female victims of spousal abuse regarding their violent relationships and why they stayed in secondary battering cohabitation.

Operational Definitions

There are three key variables in the major hypothesis of this study: resources, institutional response, and traditional ideology. The dependent variable is length of cohabiting time after primary battering. Alternatives of female victims to continued batterings by spouses were discussed earlier and the decision-making process model was presented in Chapter 2 in diagram form, Figure 2.1. Key variables were operationalized by numerous items on the survey questionnaire and additional measures were developed through in-depth interviews and observations. "Resources" was defined by the positive and negative, present and/or obtainable, material goods and personal capabilities, physical features, and pool of human actors in the victims' environments. Some of the items that measure resources are age, race or ethnicity, physical size, health, number of children and their ages, education, employability, earnings history, and several indicators of socioeconomic status. For example, a young white woman with no children who is well employed

would be considered to have considerably more resources than an unemployed minority woman over 35 years old with several dependent children.
The lack of resources was expected to predict longer secondary battering
cohabitation.

"Institutional response" was measured by the amount and type of support
and assistance available and received by battered women (or the lack of
support and assistance), as well as pressures exerted against victims by
institutions and their agents to confine them within their relationships.
Women in this sample were asked if they had contacted a variety of medical,
legal, social, or law enforcement agencies and, if so, what were the
responses and outcomes. If they did not seek medical, legal, or family
assistance, they were asked why not. Past efforts to terminate the violence
and their results are explored. If they had attempted psychological, marriage
and family, or ministerial counseling, they were asked for the kinds of
advice given and its usefulness. Negative institutional response was expected to predict longer secondary battering cohabitation.

"Traditional ideology," defined as a set of internalized beliefs in the
hierarchical structure of the patriarchal family and mutually exclusive sex
roles, was measured by responses to questions pertaining to traditional and
nontraditional values during in-depth interviews and by some scale items.
Women who felt obligated to remain with their batterers regardless of the
violence because of deep belief in the permanency of marriage through
irrevocable religious vows were usually quick to make this point clear during
interviews. Their families' tradition of stable marriages and disapproval of
separation or divorce was a further indicator. Scale items tapped religious
denomination and worship attendance of family of origin and the victims'
present degree of religiosity. Inquiries were made regarding number of
children in families of origin and birth order, as some researchers suggest
there is a correlation between birth order and traditionalism (Forer, 1969).
Traditional religions—such as the Roman Catholic faith, which bans both
birth control and abortion—may lead to larger families among the faithful.
In addition, Forer (1969) gathered evidence from a number of studies and
showed that the eldest (or only) child is more frequently the recipient of
traditional parental values than are children who may follow. Strong commitment to traditional ideology was expected to predict longer battering
cohabitation.

The dependent variable "secondary battering cohabitation" was measured by the actual time of cohabitation from the first instance of battery
reported by victims to the cessation of violence through their departure for
shelter residence or through other means, such as their spouses' departure or

SHORT TIME SECONDARY BATTERING COHABITATION	LONG TIME SECONDARY BATTERING COHABITATION
High Positive Resources/ Low Negative Resources	Low Positive Resources/ High Negative Resources
Positive Institutional Response	Negative Institutional Response
Low Traditional Ideology	High Traditional Ideology

FIGURE A.1   Predicted Effects on Dependent Variable of Three Key Concepts

death. The effect of these theoretical constructs on the time span of the dependent variable is suggested in Figure A.1.

Data obtained during the course of this investigation revealed characteristics about a sample of battered women that have been theorized about frequently in the scientific literature but never before obtained through empirical research. This study yielded a rich data base from a group of over 400 American women, plus approximately 50 European women, who claimed they were battered by their spouses. Their resources, institutional response, and traditional ideology were examined to see if—and how—these factors influenced the length of time they lived with battering spouses or if there were other variables that had a stronger effect on the maintenance of their relationships.

Research Design

This project produced a case study of woman-battering that approached the question of why violent relationships are maintained—sometimes for years—despite conflict, physical pain, and disruption in the lives of family members. The project was designed to tap several levels of sources of data about and from the victims and social agents to whom victims are most likely to turn for assistance.

The primary focus of the study was on the lives and circumstances of female victims of physical assault by spouses. Sample selection was necessarily nonrandom, since battered women are generally indistinguishable from nonbattered women in the general population; thus, there are unknown population parameters. Even with random sample selection of adult women in this society, because of the social undesirability of spousal violence and perceived stigmatization of victims it seemed highly unlikely that an investigator could expect respondents to answer intensely personal questions frankly and truthfully. This was particularly true in 1976, when the study was initiated, because until that time very little public attention had been paid to the topic and most women who had been or were being battered by spouses were very likely to feel shame and embarrassment regarding their "personal problem." The mass media (Bell, 1976, 1977; Gingold, 1976; Grambs, 1977; Marvin and Gropper, 1976; Wall Street Journal, 1976) have since helped to inform women in the privacy of their homes that the problem is widespread and occurs in the "best of families" (Davidson, 1977b). The International Tribunal on Crimes Against Women held in Brussels (Russell and Van de Ven, 1976) and the National Organization for Women in March 1976 called national and international attention to what may well be a universal phenomenon and denounced the beating of women by their spouses. In addition to meetings and conferences in this country and abroad that increased public knowledge, television networks and stations across the country began producing documentaries, talk shows, and prime-time dramas that have penetrated the "wall of silence" that had kept most battered women believing they were the only ones who suffered beatings at the hands of the men they loved.

For these reasons, a purposeful sample was obtained primarily from shelters in the United States (mostly California and Florida), although some interviews were conducted in shelters in England, Ireland, Finland, Norway, Denmark, Belgium, and the Netherlands. Some women not residing in shelters volunteered to join the sample after hearing one of the investigator's presentations on the topic or after reading about the study. These were generally women who had suffered beatings from spouses before shelters had been established in the United States and elsewhere. Most of these nonshelter volunteers expressed the desire to help both other victims and the study. For some of these women, it had been anywhere from 4 to 30 years since the events they described; some added the comment that this was the first time they had disclosed to anyone their painful experiences. Many of them were professional and business women of the middle and upper classes. For example, one woman described herself as "independently wealthy" during a long-distance telephone interview; another telephoned some months after the interview that she was departing for a chateau in her native Switzerland.

All respondents, both shelterees and nonshelterees, were volunteers who consented to participate after hearing an explanation of the nature of the study. Although there are a number of disadvantages in focused sampling (discussed in detail below), there are numerous advantages for the study of battered women. First, 90 percent of the sample was obtained through shelters for battered women and their children, which provided ease of access to many women identified as battered. Women who come to shelters are provided safety and support services and are not stigmatized, since their identities are not revealed to outside sources. The shelter sample obtained for this study reflects a wider distribution of social class than those obtained through official agencies such as police and traditional social services, which are usually overrepresented by people of the lower classes (Gelles, 1974; Kirchner, 1977a; O'Brien, 1971). (As noted above, the inclusion of nonshelter volunteers also helped to broaden the socioeconomic level of the sample.)

Besides those listed above, there are three other important reasons for obtaining a sample through shelters. First, these data are useful for policy makers and government funding agencies for decision-making purposes (Pagelow, 1978a). Second, the researcher is relieved from the responsibility of making value judgments as to who is or is not a battered woman, since all these women define themselves as battered. In addition, screening procedures for admittance in shelters generally filled to capacity were performed by staff persons who made the determination that these women fit the criteria for residency, had been battered by spouses, and were in need of protection from further abuse (see Ferraro, forthcoming). The self-selected nonshelter respondents who heard about the study and asked to participate identified themselves to the researcher as formerly battered women. Considering the length and sensitive nature of many items on the survey instrument and the painful memories interviews elicited, there is little reason to question these women's self-identification as victims of battering.

Third, the supportive atmosphere of most shelters, contact made in shelters that allowed these women to see for themselves (many of them for the first time) that other "nice women" were beaten by men they had loved, and the sharing of their hitherto unacknowledged "secret shame" with other women combined to set the stage for openness and complete honesty. Most of these women had lived relatively isolated lives; many had never admitted to anyone before, even close family members, what had been happening between themselves and their spouses; and a number had never before shared intimate details of their lives with "strangers." As a result, the pent-up emotions and unrevealed experiences found a permissive forum for self-revelation that encouraged honesty and full disclosure.

The other part of the research design included gathering pertinent data about woman-battering and the victims from social agents most likely to come in contact with victims. The community agencies and persons contacted include the following:

(1) Medical professionals: doctors in private practice, clinics and hospitals, nurses, hospital admitting staff, and emergency room personnel.
(2) Law professionals: judges, lawyers (including prosecutors, defenders, legal aid, and students), and legislators at the state and federal level.
(3) Law enforcement: police officers and chiefs, probation and parole officers.
(4) Social services: social workers, welfare officers, and child protective services workers.
(5) Counselors: psychiatrists; psychologists; marriage, family, and child specialists; and members of the clergy.

Selection of persons to provide data for this part of the study varied greatly. In some cases, selection was circumstantial—as, for example, hospital admitting staff, some law professionals, and some counselors. In many of these cases, the opportunity presented itself and it was grasped. In no case was a respondent selected because of an expected attitude or personality trait; in most cases the respondent was previously unknown to the interviewer.

One unsuccessful attempt was made, however, to include someone because of information at hand about his past professional response to spouse abuse. In this instance, an attempt was made to interview a judge who had awarded custody of two young male children to their fathers despite evidence that these men had beaten their wives repeatedly. In one of these cases, the man receiving custody admitted he was not the biological father of the boy born out of wedlock, and there was evidence that he had beaten the boy as well as his wife. After the appointment for the interview had been arranged, the investigator was instructed to telephone the judge for confirmation. When called, the judge flatly refused to be interviewed by telephone or in person and cancelled the appointment. Despite explanations about the study and its purpose and requests to reconsider his decision, the judge remained adamantly opposed to the meeting. In addition, the judge made thinly veiled inferences that the researcher might be unscrupulous enough to "sell" the judge's viewpoints on matters discussed to attorneys who come before his bench.

Representatives of all the above-listed professions were included, although perhaps more persons from a law background than law enforcement contributed data to the study. Substantial data were provided by a number of students serving internships under the guidance of the investigator, particularly the team of three nurses (Waterbury et al., 1976), who had greater and faster access to medical professionals via colleagues, doctors, and emergency room personnel.

It was deemed important to obtain data from representatives of various community "helping agencies," in view of the fact that official recordkeeping of spouse abuse is virtually nonexistent. In addition, while most of the investigative efforts were directed toward victims themselves with no control group, it seemed appropriate to gather as many data from other sources that would be expected to reflect a less emotional or detached viewpoint of the crime of woman-battering and its victims. In fact, since women battered by spouses traditionally have been defined by most people as deviants, the perspectives of victims were expected to differ from those of the batterers or social agents whom they were most likely to contact.

Some consideration was given to the idea of obtaining a sample of alleged batterers to participate in this study. This might have been possible to a limited degree, but for maintenance of confidentiality with the female respondents and because such contact could conceivably endanger the women or the investigator, no attempts were made to contact their spouses. Names and addresses of the alleged batterers were available through some shelters for most respondents, but contacting these men for interviews could generate even more danger for victims and other shelter residents. Actually, several accused batterers were observed during court hearings attended by the investigator, but there was no attempt made to interview any of them. It was uncomfortable enough to be on one end of a shelter's hot-line telephone when an enraged spouse blasted orders from his home to "get this crazy woman out of here—now—before I kill her!" The three-hour negotiation that followed trying to convince the man not to abuse his spouse further was convincing evidence that a sociological researcher is not necessarily qualified to be a war correspondent. In addition, in most cases batterers refuse to admit that there is any "problem," and if there is one, the problem is not theirs, and they withdraw from discussion (Snell et al., 1964). However, supplementary data were obtained through two Orange County (California) men who counsel male batterers who recognize there is a problem and who voluntarily seek professional help. Chapter 4 contains a summary of the interviews with these counselors.

Nevertheless, the main target sample obtained for this study was comprised of female victims of spouse abuse—all other data are supplementary. These additional data were gathered for purposes of validation and reliability checks and to gain further understanding of the social system in which victims operate. It would be counterproductive to attempt to approach battering from both an "insider" and "outsider" point of view in the same investigation. As Becker (1966:173) points out, it is possible to see the situation from both sides but not simultaneously. Becker explains the position adopted in this investigation:

It is in the nature of the phenomenon of deviance that it will be difficult for anyone to study both sides of the process and capture the perspectives of both classes of participants. . . . Practical considerations of gaining access to situations and the confidence of the people involved in any reasonable length of time mean that one will probably study the situation from one side or the other. Whichever class of participants we choose to study and whose viewpoint we therefore choose to take, we will probably be accused of "bias." It will be said that we are not doing justice to the viewpoint of the opposing group. . . . We shall be accused of presenting a one-sided and distorted view. But this is not really the case. What we are presenting is . . . the reality which engages the people we have studied, the reality they create by their interpretation of their experience and in terms of which they act. If we fail to present this reality, we will not have achieved full sociological understanding of the phenomenon we seek to explain [1966:173-174].

Methods

Data from battered women were obtained through a variety of techniques in order to obtain depth as well as breadth. In-depth interviews were particularly useful for case histories, for persons unable to fill out the questionnaire because of language or reading difficulties, for women who had unusual or complicated circumstances beyond the scope of the survey instrument, and for juveniles. Interviews were audiotaped when respondents were not inhibited by the recorder and gave their consent.

The other methodologies included unobtrusive observation, participant observation in discussion groups, records analysis, and a survey questionnaire designed for self-enumeration (Appendix B). With the consent of their mothers, some children contributed data either through interviews or by writing out statements about their experiences, observations, and feelings.

Unobtrusive observation techniques were largely employed while the investigator served as a volunteer on weekends and some evenings at the Women's Transitional Living Center (WTLC), a shelter in Orange County established in January 1976. This provided an opportunity to observe casually the interactions of the women with each other and with their children. Sometimes they came around "just wanting to talk"; on other occasions it was the children who searched for a listener. One of the duties of a shelter volunteer is to answer the office telephone (the number is publicly available but not the address). Occasionally there was a telephone call from a woman asking about admittance policy or one who wanted a referral because she "can't take it any more." (Crisis calls are always referred to the staff member who is on call each weekend.) Sometimes a mother whose daughter was living with a violent man would call for advice, other times it might be a daughter calling about her concern for her mother. A few times the caller was a man who demanded to know if his wife was there; such information could not be released, for the safety and security of the clients. An experienced staff member once observed that frequently they know the name of the next client who will call to seek admittance because her call is preceded by one from her husband demanding to speak with her.

Participant observation involved being present during discussion groups at shelters; they are held weekly at WTLC. Also attended were community discussions, such as the "Speak-Out on Wife-Abuse," a public meeting held in Long Beach, California in 1976 (Pagelow, 1976:6, 46). Every visit to a shelter in this country and abroad provided an opportunity for participant observation, with the exception of a shelter in Oslow, where the staff but none of the shelterees could speak English, the only language the researcher understands, unfortunately.

Official records kept by WTLC were available to the investigator for unobtrusive and comparatively objective analysis. These agency records included intake files, daily logs, night staff memos, and telephone counseling and referral notes. Monthly reports to funding agencies were also available. These are a compilation of demographic data on clients, including race and ethnicity, geographic areas of residence, social class, ages of mothers and children, as well as services and activities provided by the center. Also available were records of the departure circumstances of each client; that is, if she reunited with her batterer or made the transition to alternate living arrangements and, if so, how this was accomplished. Staff follow-ups are done whenever possible, and these records were also made available to the investigator.

A survey questionnaire was designed for this study (see Appendix B). The instrument was devised for several reasons: (1) to obtain a maximum amount of demographic and a wide range of other data from victims, giving them the opportunity to review the history of their relationships with the batterers and to explain their perceptions of the violence and their help-seeking efforts; (2) to gather data on the greatest number of cases possible in the shortest time, since each in-depth interview required from two to four hours or more; (3) to achieve uniformity of administration and to avoid possible interviewer bias; (4) to have a standard instrument suitable for other researchers to reproduce the study and thereby measure reliability; (5) to obtain extremely sensitive information with the least possible contamination from social desirability influence or acquiescent response set, since respondents were able to complete questionnaires in privacy and with confiden-tiality.

The instrument was pretested and revised twice before the final format was adopted. In keeping with the exploratory nature of this study at its inception in 1976, the questionnaire is comprehensive, detailed, and long. It includes one or more items measuring each of the key variables: resources, institutional response, traditional ideology, and secondary battering cohabi-tation (length of time cohabiting after battering began). The 12-page instru-ment is divided into four parts: (1) personal data, (2) data regarding spouse, (3) nature of injuries, and (4) institutional response. Coded choice responses were provided for both objective and subjective items, and open-ended questions provided opportunity for individualized responses.

It is important to note that although more than half the survey sample responded to the instrument without interviewer assistance, a subsample of 149 women from a Florida shelter for battered women usually had an inter-viewer administer the questions. The director and staff of this shelter de-cided that the instrument would be administered to the clients by staff for several reasons, including the fact that it was useful as a thorough and comprehensive intake form. However, inspection of instruments received from the Florida shelter reveals that there are far more nonresponses and much less detail in the many open-ended questions than in instruments returned from other sources. This differential in response rate suggests that the Florida women either found it more difficult to answer freely some intensely personal questions in a face-to-face interview or that the inter-viewers failed to report in detail each answer provided by clients. Since many of the missing responses included simple "no" or "yes" answers that merely required circling the numbers of categories, it seems that the first possibility is the more likely.

Unlike the Florida subsample, many of the self-enumerated 12-page questionnaires contained all responses and had written comments filling up all borders and open spaces. It also had pages attached, providing room for elaboration. The majority of the instruments (168) were received from shel-ters located in California; they were distributed to shelterees who responded on a voluntary basis. The remaining 33 were received from the nonshelter volunteers discussed above, bringing the total survey sample to 350 cases (see Table 4.1 for sources of survey sample).

The other part of the study that focused on social agents employed fewer methods in the field. The methodologies for gathering data from community and social agents were unobtrusive observation (such as "court-watching" mentioned above), participant observation in public and professional meetings addressing the issue of woman-battering, and semistructured interviews of various depth which varied depending on circumstances, such as willingness of respondents to be interviewed or situational factors.

Limitations and Advantages

There are several limitations in the study and in the survey instrument itself, as outlined in an earlier paper (Pagelow, 1979b). One of the most important is that, due to the impossibility of taking a random sample, this is a purposive, volunteer sample (both within and beyond shelter residence). Second, there is no control group. Third, the data are retrospective. Each of these conditions carries its own limitations on the appropriate types of statistical tests of analysis and inferences to be drawn, the most important of which is that these data are not generalizable beyond a self-selected sample of women who say they were battered by the men with whom they had lived. Findings cannot and should not be generalized to all battered women, for this is a population of unknown parameters.

In order to try to compensate for disadvantages in the research design—specifically, the nonprobability sampling frame—a variety of research techniques were employed. It should be stressed that this investigation yielded a wealth of information about a specific group of women and that these findings cannot be generalized to all women or to all women battered by their spouses. There may be 1.8 million wives beaten by their husbands in any one year, according to the statistics obtained in the Straus et al. study (Straus, 1978:445) based on estimates of 47 million couples in the United States at that time. Straus believes the figure should be much higher. He outlines a number of factors inherent in the study itself, plus the problems of recall accuracy and social desirability response set.

> These considerations, plus the higher rates in our pilot studies and informal evidence (where some of the factors leading to underreporting were less) suggest that *the true incidence rate is probably closer to 50 or 60 percent of all couples than it is to the 28 percent who were willing to describe violent acts in a mass interview survey* [1978:447; italics in original].

A recent government publication (Rawlings, 1978) sets the number of currently married couples in the United States at 48,002,000; therefore, if Straus is correct, there could be over 24 million battered wives in this country. Neither Straus nor the Rawlings report included the number of cohabiting couples in quasi-marriages without legal ceremonies. Keeping these factors in mind, we can safely assume that there is a large but unidentified population of battered women in this society.

The problems arising from nonprobability sampling is discussed by Blalock:

> The major disadvantage of nonprobability sampling is that we can obtain no valid estimate of our risks of error. Therefore, statistical inference is not legitimate and should not be used. This does not mean that nonprobability sampling is never appropriate. In exploratory studies, the main goal of which is to obtain valuable insights which ultimately may lead to testable hypotheses, probability sampling either may be too expensive or lead to fewer such insights. One may wish to interview persons who are in especially good positions to supply information. . . . Nonprobability methods are sometimes used when the purpose is to make generalizations about a population sampled. Such methods invariably either make use of the interviewer's judgment as to the individuals to be included or permit an individual sampled to be selected out of the study on some nonrandom basis [1972:527-528].

Selltiz et al. point out that, despite some disadvantages,

> sometimes there is no alternative to nonprobability sampling (even if informants are far from typical since:) . . . The choice here is between data that do not permit a statistical assessment of the likelihood of error and no data at all. . . . This does not mean that one is not concerned with the possibility of error; but one places one's reliance on the internal consistency of the data and its coherence with other things that follow [1976:536-537].

In the same vein, Babbie (1979) states that there are situations in which purposive, nonprobability sampling is required, and both Babbie (p. 196) and Blalock suggest building sensitivity into the research methods and that the research questions should be well thought out in advance. Babbie suggests there are

> situations in which it would be either impossible or grossly unfeasible to select the kinds of probability samples described above. . . . There are times when a probability sample wouldn't be appropriate even though possible. . . . Occasionally it may be appropriate . . . to select your sample on the basis of your own knowledge of the population, its elements, and the nature of your research aims [1979:195].

Therefore, although purposive sampling restricts somewhat the use of some tests of statistical significance for analysis of these data and restricts generalizability, the findings from this investigation still make an important contribution to our pool of knowledge and our understanding of a crime committed in privacy. It also provides clues as to why the women in this sample remained with their batterers as long as they did. The findings from this study may be compared, when possible, with other purposive samples of battered women elsewhere, and each case study may contribute additional insight into the problem. The additive effect of many select samples may be the best means to knowledge-building, provided limitations applicable to each are kept in mind when drawing conclusions. As Reiss says, "when there is so little research evidence, one must take the best available even if it is not perfect" (1976:217). In this study, every effort was exerted to make it the "best available."

On the positive side, a number of checks for reliability partly compensate for built-in limitations. For one thing, it is fairly well documented that 90 percent of the sample were actually battered; all these shelters screen prospective clients thoroughly for evidence of physical violence and need before admitting them, and the 10 percent of nonsheltered volunteers in the sample had nothing to gain by taking on the difficult task of completing a questionnaire for the study. The questions that naturally arise whenever there is a volunteer sample are at least partly answered through some of the other methodologies employed in the study, in addition to some of the items in the instrument that provided cross-checks for validity.

Since the investigator spent several hundred hours in shelter facilities, there were opportunities to cross-check at least demographic data for reliability; when this was done, there was almost 100 percent agreement between agency records and the self-reports. Although some people question women's willingness to reveal true ages and weights, visual cross-checks were often possible and were highly consistent with written and oral responses. In a society that places such importance on youth and slimness, it was remarkable how truthful the women's responses were, even when their answers were at odds with the "marriage gradient" (Bernard, 1973:35)— that is, women who said they were older, taller, or heavier than their spouses. Many women admitted being far overweight, and the upper fiftieth percentile was over 28 years of age. Women's willingness to reveal socially unattractive facts about themselves and to complete a long and difficult questionnaire (many women added comments that it had been a painful experience for them) both attest to the reliability of the instrument, since the questions asked obviously had great relevance for them (Selltiz et al., 1976:166).

There is no way accurately to determine response rate because of the way most of the shelters involved chose to distribute the instruments to shelterees. No records were kept on how many women were asked to participate but did not respond, nor on how many shelterees were not given the opportunity to participate. The Florida subsample is presumed to include all shelterees for a set time period at Women in Distress in Fort Lauderdale, since staff regularly administered the instrument, using it as an intake form. But distribution in California shelters to clients for self-enumeration was done by staff members and sometimes by volunteers on a situational basis. Most of these shelters are greatly understaffed; thus, distribution and collection were largely circumstantial, occurring during relatively quiet periods when there were no crises that took top priority. All shelters require a number of intake forms to be filled out on admittance by clients who usually have been in a state of psychological crisis for up to 72 hours. The investigator asked staff to distribute the survey instrument on the fourth day of their residency—to wait until clients had settled in and recovered from the crisis period. Sometimes staff remembered to do so and other times the pressures of in-house duties caused them to forget.

Because of these factors, there is no way to know if women who did not respond to the questionnaire were different in any significant ways from those who did respond, or the number of women who were given the questionnaire but who left without returning it to the office. In an effort to check for bias, some interviews were conducted with both survey respondents and women who did not respond to the survey instrument. There was no indication that the nonvolunteers were substantially "different" from volunteers. The basic difference between these women was that frequently those who did self-reports either had received a thorough explanation of the purposes of the study and thus they were more willing to comply or felt better skilled at expressing themselves in writing. The only bias from self-selection for self-enumeration that could be identified was from the exclusion of women unskilled in reading and writing English, which reduced the sample by an unknown number of Spanish-speaking and Asian women and others for whom English is a second language.

During the course of this study, whenever possible, women with language barriers were interviewed in depth and some group discussions were held with both English-speaking and non-English-speaking shelterees with interpreters present. The women who spoke English with difficulty or not at all seemed to share most important features in common with other shelterees, with the exception that perhaps they had even fewer resources available to them. This was not only because of cultural differences regarding women's relationships with spouses and families of origin but also because their nearest relatives often resided in countries many miles (and even oceans) away. For these reasons, although it was not possible to measure the weight of disadvantage due to membership in ethnic or racial minority groups, a basic assumption is that in this country such membership amounts to a negative resource. Chapter 4 shows the ethnic and racial backgrounds of the women in the survey sample.

The second major limitation in the study involves the lack of a control group. While having a group of nonbattered women for comparison purposes might have been desirable, it was decided at the outset not to attempt to draw one. Because of the sensitivity of the research questions, there appeared to be no way to assess whether or not all women included in such a sample could be identified as "non-battered" with any degree of confidence. Battering by one's spouse appears to involve socially defined stigmatization of the victims so that previously battered women might easily, by nondisclosure, be included in a control group. In the case of battered women, those whose "differentness is known about already or is evident on the spot" are the "discredited" (Goffman, 1963:4), such as the women in the shelter sample. But women who were or are being battered who have not sought refuge in a shelter are women who assume their "differentness" is "neither known about by those present nor immediately perceived by them"; thus, they are the "discreditable" (1963:4).

Use of a possibly contaminated control group for comparing battered and nonbattered women could lead to conclusions based on false assumptions. It seemed that this possibility would have invalidated any findings and was a less desirable alternative than having no control group at all. Previously battered women are almost invisible in the population, and revelation most often depends on the women's self-disclosure on sensitive topics only after rapport has been firmly established (see, for example, Russell, 1980 and Bowker and MacCallum, 1980). Some previously battered women approached the investigator from most unexpected backgrounds, such as a high-positioned employee of an important federal government bureau, a marriage and family counselor battered by her psychologist ex-husband, and a successful attorney.

In one sense, the community agents' sample serves as a comparison group, for many of the charges and statements of the women were posed in the form of questions to these people. Frequently the social agents provided data that—purposely or inadvertently—supported the claims of victims. To obtain some measure of representativeness of this sample of battered women, Chapter 5 compares demographic features of adult women in the United States today with those of sample women.

As for limitations due to retrospective data, most studies of woman-battering to date (Dobash and Dobash, 1978, 1979; Walker, 1978, 1979) and intrafamily violence (Gelles, 1974; Straus, 1978; Straus et al., 1980) have had to rely on respondent recall of events that occurred previously, whether within the prior year or the length of the relationships. However, while there may be some nonsystematic errors or distortion of events as to their occurrence, the traumatic effects these events are said to have had on victims seem to have left vivid impressions that victims insist are factual. Some checks have been made throughout the study to see if accounts change from one telling to another; they have remained remarkably consistent.

For example, one 15-year-old girl entered a shelter with a 21-year-old woman and the woman's two young children. Both were battered by the woman's husband, who had assumed the role of "foster father" to the teenager. The girl had been courted, seduced, and raped by the man in a bizarre series of events that resulted in the girl's mother, unaware of these events, entrusting the girl into the man's care for the assumed "stability" of a two-parent family. The man, incidentally, was a 47-year-old father of 13 children from this and two earlier marriages plus two illegitimate children. As coach of a junior girls' athletic team, he frequently took young girl team members on trips for athletic competition in other cities; he was a respected member of a suburban community.

Both the girl and the wife were interviewed and tape-recorded in separate rooms at the same time by the investigator and another researcher. Neither interview was scheduled in advance, but the histories both young women revealed were closely parallel. The events recounted were so bizarre that the girl's story was rechecked the following day with the explanation that the tape recorder had malfunctioned. The girl entered into her long account giving dates, times, places, and even doctors' names (she had spent two weeks in a hospital for internal injuries after one beating). Every possible method of confusing her was attempted, but her responses were identical to the previous interview. (After being reunited with her mother, who was also interviewed, the mother and daughter attempted to file criminal charges against the man for rape, statutory rape, and assault and battery, but the district attorney's office refused to prosecute the case. The man is still coaching the junior girls' team and his community reputation is unblemished.)

Sometimes preteen and teenaged children corroborated their mothers' case histories; some even wrote statements about their impressions of the violence in their homes. The only problem with victims' recall seemed to be in putting events into correct temporal sequence, particularly if they had been abused for a long period. However, that was not the case for one 65-year-old woman who had been beaten in two marriages; she presented names, places, and dates and provided documents to support her statements. Chapter 7 details her case history.

The major point is that these retrospective data appear to be sufficiently reliable and the best available to researchers in studying a social problem of this nature due to the privacy of the conjugal setting. Direct observation of violent acts is impossible, since it would involve an invasion of privacy, and contrived laboratory experiments yield data that are contaminated to an undetermined extent by the artificiality of the laboratory setting and response set.

APPENDIX B

THE SURVEY INSTRUMENT

Dear Friend,

Please permit me to introduce myself to you. My name is Mildred Pagelow, and I am a research sociologist and graduate student at the University of California, Riverside. I am conducting scientific research on the topic of battered women and related household violence. You have received this questionnaire because you have some personal experience with this subject.

We know that many women have been treated violently by men in this society, but until recently, hardly anybody has dared to talk about it. However, silence permits these assaults against women to continue unchecked. Only when enough people are willing to talk about it will we begin to understand what is going on, and only then will we be able to develop ways to prevent woman-battering.

My goal is to investigate it, to try to understand what has happened to you and other women. I can only do this with your help. I do not want your name or any other identification on this questionnaire which tells exactly who you are. Since being battered is a very personal experience, there is no way I can get the information without asking personal questions. Please do not be embarrassed; the information you give will be kept strictly confidential. If you, and many other women like yourself, will take the time and trouble to fill out this questionnaire, you will be making a valuable contribution to understanding of woman-battering. By being as frank and honest as possible in your answers, you will be helping many women, perhaps even yourself.

Scientific research, such as this study, may even prevent some of the violence in the future adult lives of today's children.

Please remember to date the questionnaire at the top of page one, and keep this letter when you return it, so that you will have my home address and telephone number, listed below. You are invited to call or write me six months from now, so that you can tell me how things are going for you—I really would like to know.

Every question on this long questionnaire is important. You may quit at any time, but I strongly urge you to stay with it to the end, answering each question carefully and fully. Thank you for your kindness—your help is really needed—I can't do it without you!

Sincerely, in Sisterhood,
Mildred D. Pagelow

DATE: _____

This questionnaire was written specifically for women who have been battered or physically abused by men with whom they have lived. These questions ask you about your experiences with a man you lived with, whether married to each other or not. For simplicity, the word "spouse" will be used for the man who most recently physically abused or was violent toward you. If your answers require additional space, please attach extra pages as needed.

1. Personal Data

For each question below, please circle the number or letter which gives your answer. Where there are blanks, please write out the answer. In some cases, a check mark will be asked for. If you don't understand the question, please indicate that, too.

1. What is your:
   a. Age: _____
   b. Height: _____
   c. Weight: _____
   d. Ethnic group:
      1 White, Caucasian
      2 Black, Negro
      3 Mexican-American, Chicana
      4 Asian-American
      5 Other (please specify): _____
      _____

2. Is your spouse (the man who battered or physically abused you) your:
   1 Husband or ex-husband
   2 Lover or ex-lover
   3 Someone else (who?): _____
      a. If you were married to each other, what was the date of the marriage? ____
      _____

3. When was the first time you saw him behave violently? (approximate date) ____
   _____

4. What did he do? _____
   _____
   _____

5. What did you feel or do about it? _____
   _____
   _____

6. Are you now separated from your spouse?
   1 No (if no, skip to No. 7)
   2 Yes (for how long?) _____

7. How long have (had) you lived with him?
   _____

8. Prior to this time, have you ever left him?
   1 No (if no, skip to No. 9)
   2 Yes
   a. How many times have you left him? _____
   b. What was the longest time you stayed away? _____
   c. Where did you go? _____
   d. Why did you return? _____
      _____

9. Have you ever been married to someone else?
   1 No (if no, skip to No. 10)
   2 Yes
   a. How did that marriage end?
      1 Divorce
      2 Separation
      3 Death
      4 Other (please explain): _____
         _____

10. Were you ever assaulted by any other man?
    1 No (if no, skip to No. 11)
    2 Yes
    a. What was that man's relationship to you? _____
       _____
    b. When did he assault you? _____
       _____
    c. What did he do? _____
       _____

11. Do you have any children?
    1 No (if no, skip to No. 12)
    2 Yes (if yes, please fill in the blanks below regarding your children)

	AGE	SEX	LIVE WITH YOU? (check if Yes)	IS THIS CHILD YOUR SPOUSE'S STEPCHILD? (check if Yes)
(1)	_____	_____	_____	_____
(2)	_____	_____	_____	_____
(3)	_____	_____	_____	_____
(4)	_____	_____	_____	_____
(5)	_____	_____	_____	_____
(6)	_____	_____	_____	_____

12. Do you have any stepchildren who have made their home with you?
    1 No
    2 Yes (how many?) _____

13. How many children were in the family you grew up in? _____ (count yourself)

14. Counting down from the eldest, which number were you? _____

15. When you were 16, did both your parents live in the same house where you lived?
    1 Yes
    2 No (please explain: divorced, widowed, separated, etc.) _____
    _____

16. Are your parents now:
    1 Married to each other
    2 Separated
    3 Widowed
    5 Don't know
    6 Other (explain): _____

17. Was there physical violence between your parents?
    1 Never
    2 Very seldom
    3 Occasionally
    4 Often
    5 Very often
    6 Don't know

18. Did you ever see or hear your mother being beaten by your father?
    1 No
    2 Don't remember
    3 Yes (describe): _____
    _____

19. When you were a child, were you physically punished?
    1 Never (if never, skip to No. 20)
    2 Very seldom
    3 Occasionally
    4 Often
    5 Very often
    a. What kind of physical punishments?
       0 None
       1 Mild (occasional slap, etc.)
       2 Moderate (spankings, etc.)
       3 Extremely severe (beatings, etc.)
    b. If you were beaten as a child, who usually did this to you? _____
    _____

20. What was the religion in the family where you grew up?
    1 Protestant   3 Jewish
    2 Catholic   4 None
    5 Other (specify): _____

21. Did your family attend religious services:
    1 Very often
    2 Occasionally
    3 Seldom
    4 Never

22. Do you consider yourself today as:
    1 Very religious
    2 Somewhat religious
    3 Not at all religious
    a. If religious, what denomination? _____
    _____

23. Please pick the word that you think *best* describes your childhood home:
    1 peaceful   5 troubled
    2 sad   6 happy
    3 secure   7 violent
    4 hateful   8 loving
    9 other (describe): _____

24. What is the general condition of your health?
    1 Excellent (skip to No. 25)
    2 Average
    3 Poor
    a. If average or poor, please describe any condition(s) which cause your health to
       be less than perfect? _____
    _____

b. Do you have any kind of chronic physical condition for which you take *medically prescribed* drugs or other *medicines*? (circle as many as apply)
   1 Heart disease
   2 Epilepsy
   3 Diabetes
   4 Arthritis
   5 Migraine headaches
   6 Other (specify): _____

25. Do you use other drugs for pleasure or mood changes?
    1 Never (skip to No. 26)
    2 Occasionally
    3 Very often
    4 To the point where you may be addicted
    a. What kind of drugs? _____
    _____

26. Do you drink alcoholic beverages?
    1 Never
    2 Occasionally
    3 Very often
    4 To the point where you may be an alcoholic

27. Did you ever think seriously about committing suicide?
    1 No (if no, skip to No. 28)
    2 Yes
    a. What was the approximate date(s)? _____
    _____

    b. Was there a specific event which took place about that time that led you to think seriously about the possibility of committing suicide?
       1 No
       2 Yes (what had happened?) _____
       _____
       _____

    c. Was there a particular method you considered for taking your own life?
       1 No (if no, skip to No. 28)
       2 Yes (what was it?) _____

    d. Did you ever make an actual attempt at suicide?
       1 No (please explain what stopped you from making an attempt): _____
       _____
       _____

       2 Yes (please explain what happened): _____
       _____
       _____
       _____

       (Were you hospitalized or treated by a doctor?) _____
       (Did anyone try to find out *why* you did this, or give you counseling?) ___
       _____

28. Did you and your spouse engage in sexual intercourse:
    1 Very seldom
    2 Occasionally
    3 Often
    4 Very, very often
    a. About how many times a month? _____

29. Would you rate *your* satisfaction from sexual intercourse with your spouse as mostly:
    1 Extremely satisfying
    2 Satisfying (about average)
    3 Extremely unsatisfying (why?) _____
    _____

30. During interviews, some women mentioned some things about their sexual relationships with their spouses which they feel were unusual or strange. Are there any comments you feel are important to add?
    1 No
    2 Yes (explain): _____
    _____
    _____

31. What was the highest grade in school you completed?

Grade school:	1	2	3	4	5	6	7	8
High school:	1	2	3	4				
College:	1	2	3	4				
Postgraduate:	1	2	3	4				

    Highest degree held: _____

32. Did you have any other kind of education, such as vocational training, nurse's aide, etc.?
    1 No
    2 Yes (what kind?): _____
    _____

33. Are you now employed outside the home?
    1 Yes
    a. Job title, or what type of work do you do? _____
    _____

    b. Is it: _____ full-time or
    _____ part-time (please check)
    c. What is your approximate take-home pay—in other words, your income after taxes and other deductions, your net income per month?
    1 Less than $300
    2 $300 to $600
    3 $600 to $900
    4 $900 to $1,500
    5 Over $1,500

2 No
   a. Have you ever worked at a paid job?
      1 No (if no, skip to next page)
   b. When were you last employed? _____
   c. What kind of work did you do? _____
   d. What was your approximate take-home pay per month (your net income)?

   _____

   e. Was this _____ full-time or
                _____ part-time (please check)

II. Data Regarding Spouse

I realize you may not know all the answers to these questions asking you about the man who assaulted you, but I want you to answer all that you do know. If you really don't know, don't guess, just say so. If you *believe* you know, but aren't really positive, put a question mark (?) after your answer. Any other answers, then, I will feel that you have good reason to know you're right.

1. What is your spouse's:
   a. Age: _____
   b. Height: _____
   c. Weight: _____
   d. Ethnic group:
      1 White, Caucasian
      2 Black, Negro
      3 Mexican-American, Chicano
      4 Asian-American
      5 Other (please specify): _____

      _____

2. Was he ever married to someone else?
   1 No (if no, skip to No. 3)
   2 Don't know (skip to No. 3)
   3 Yes
   a. How did that marriage end?
      1 Divorce
      2 Separation
      3 Death
      4 Other (please explain): _____

      _____

   b. How long did that other marriage last? _____

   _____

c. Was he physically violent with another wife?

   1 No

   2 Don't know

   3 Yes (were you aware of this before you began living with him?) _____

_____

d. Does he have any children by a former marriage?

   1 No

   2 Don't know

   3 Yes (how many?) _____

3. How many children were in the family he grew up in? _____ (count him, too)

4. Counting down from the eldest, which number was he? _____

5. When he was 16 years old, did both his parents live in the same house where he lived?

   1 Yes

   2 Don't know

   3 No (explain: divorced, widowed, separated, etc.) _____

_____

6. Are his parents now:

   1 Married to each other

   2 Separated

   3 Divorced

   4 Widowed

   5 Don't know

   6 Other (explain): _____

_____

7. Was there physical violence between his parents?

   1 Never

   2 Very seldom

   3 Occasionally

   4 Often

   5 Very often

   6 Don't know

8. Did he ever see or hear his mother being beaten by his father?

   1 No

   2 Don't know

   3 Yes (describe): _____

_____

_____

9. When he was a child, was he physically punished?

   1 Never

   2 Very seldom

   3 Occasionally

   4 Often

   5 Very often

   6 Don't know

a. What kind of physical punishment?
   0 None
   1 Mild (occasionally slap, etc.)
   2 Moderate (spankings, etc.)
   3 Extremely severe (beatings, etc.)
b. If he was beaten as a child, who usually did this to him? _____
_____

10. Do you believe he received unusual or harsh types of punishments when he was a child?
   1 No
   2 Don't know
   3 Yes (describe): _____
_____
_____

11. Did he have physical fights with his brothers or sisters when he was a youngster? (If an only child, with other kids?)
   1 Never
   2 Occasionally
   3 Very often
   4 Don't know

12. What was the religion in the family where he grew up?
   1 Protestant   3 Jewish
   2 Catholic   4 None
   5 Other (specify): _____
   6 Don't know

13. Did his family attend religious services:
   1 Frequently
   2 Occasionally
   3 Seldom
   4 Never
   5 Don't know

14. Do you consider him today as:
   1 Very religious
   2 Somewhat religious
   3 Not at all religious
a. If religious, what denomination? _____
_____

15. Please pick the word that you think *best* describes his childhood home:
   1 peaceful   5 troubled
   2 sad   6 happy
   3 secure   7 violent
   4 hateful   8 loving
   9 other (describe): _____
  10 don't know

16. What is the general condition of his health?
    1 Excellent (skip to No. 17)
    2 Average
    3 Poor
    a. If average or poor, describe any condition(s) which cause his health to be less
       than perfect _____
       _____
    b. Does he have any kind of chronic condition for which he takes *medically
       prescribed* drugs or other *medicines*? (circle as many as apply)
       1 Heart disease
       2 Epilepsy
       3 Diabetes
       4 Arthritis
       5 Migraine headaches
       6 Other (specify): _____
       _____

17. Does he use other drugs for pleasure or mood changes?
    1 Never (skip to No. 18)
    2 Occasionally
    3 Very often
    4 To the point where he may be addicted
    a. What kind of drugs? _____
       _____

18. Does he drink alcoholic beverages?
    1 Never
    2 Occasionally
    3 Very often
    4 To the point where he may be an alcoholic
19. When he battered you, was he under the influence of: (circle as many as apply)
    1 Always alcohol
    2 Sometimes alcohol
    3 Always drugs
    4 Sometimes drugs
    5 Definitely no alcohol or drugs
    6 Don't know if alcohol or drugs were involved
    7 Other (explain): _____
20. Is your spouse a "dry alcoholic"—in other words, a man who used to drink very
    heavily, but who now doesn't drink any kind of beer or liquor?
    1 Yes
    2 Don't know
    3 No
21. Is your spouse a former drug addict who is now a nonuser?
    1 Yes
    2 Don't know
    3 No

22. Do you believe there is any connection *at all* between his use of alcohol or any other drug (whether prescribed medicine or not), and his use of violence toward you?

　　1　No
　　2　Don't know
　　3　Yes (explain): _____

　　_____

23. Do you know of any other violent acts he has committed toward other people, animals, or objects?

　　1　No
　　2　Don't know
　　3　Yes (describe): _____

　　_____
　　_____

24. Did he ever serve in the military forces?

　　1　No (if no, skip to No. 25)
　　2　Don't know
　　3　Yes
　　a.　What branch of the service was he in?

　　_____

　　b.　For how long? _____
　　c.　What was his rank? _____
　　d.　Did he have any combat duty?
　　　　1　No
　　　　2　Don't know
　　　　3　Yes (where?) _____

　　_____

　　e.　Was he injured while in the service?
　　　　1　No
　　　　2　Don't know
　　　　3　Yes (describe): _____

　　_____

　　f.　What kind of discharge did he receive?

　　_____

25. Has he ever been arrested on any charges *other* than assaulting you?

　　1　No
　　2　Don't know
　　3　Yes (what were the charges?) _____

　　_____
　　_____

26. Did he ever plead guilty to a crime, or was he ever convicted of a crime (other than assaulting you)?
    1 No
    2 Don't know
    3 Yes (what crime?): _____

    _____

27. What was the highest grade in school he *completed*?
    Grade school: 1 2 3 4 5 6 7 8
    High school   1 2 3 4
    College: 1 2 3 4
    Postgraduate: 1 2 3 4
    Highest degree held: _____

28. Did he have any other kind of education, such as vocational training, mechanics, etc.?
    1 No
    2 Don't know
    3 Yes (specify): _____

    _____

29. What is his job title, or what kind of work does he do? _____

    _____

30. Is he presently employed?
    1 No (if no, skip to c.)
    2 Don't know
    3 Yes
    a. Is this work: _____ full-time or
                     _____ part-time (please check)
    b. What is his approximate take-home pay—that is, income after taxes and other deductions, his net income per month?
       1 Less than $300
       2 $300 to $600
       3 $600 to $900
       4 $900 to $1,500
       5 Over $1,500
       6 Don't know
    c. If he is not now employed, what are the sources of his income? _____

       _____

31. Do (did) you and your spouse own the home you live(d) in together?
    1 No
    2 Yes (approximate value): _____

32. What is the distance between the home you share(d) with your spouse and any of your own relatives? _____

33. During interviews, some women mentioned that their spouses showed what they felt was a great interest in pornography. Does your spouse enjoy porno movies, books, magazines, etc.?
   1 No
   2 Don't know
   3 Yes (please tell what you know about it. If too detailed for this questionnaire, but you feel pornography may have something to do with your spouse's behavior, contact me at the telephone number on the cover letter.) _____
   _____
   _____

34. Finally, do you know of any reason *why* your spouse has been violent with you? (Write your comments below, and attach another page if necessary.)

III. Nature of Injuries

1. What physical injuries have you received from your spouse? Please describe as well as you can. For example: severe bruises on back and arms, broken bones (which ones), cuts, black eye(s), etc.,—whatever it was that resulted from a battering. _____
   _____
   _____
   _____
   _____

2. Did you try to hide your injuries?
   1 No (if no, skip to No. 3)
   2 Yes
   a. How did you hide your injuries? _____
   _____
   _____
   b. Why did you hide your injuries? _____
   _____
   _____

3. How often were you attacked?
   1 Once
   2 Occasionally (about how many?) _____
   3 Regularly:
      a. Once a month or less
      b. About once a week
      c. More than once a week
      d. Other (explain): _____
      _____

4. How long did an attack last?
   1 One blow
   2 Short time (less than 5 minutes)
   3 Sometimes short time, others very long
   4 Prolonged beating (describe): _____ _____
   _____

5. Below is a scale so that you can show about how severe you feel this (or these) attacks were. Please circle the number you feel best describes what happened. No. 1 is the *least* painful, and No. 9 is the *most* painful.

1	2	3	4	5	6	7	8	9
	(minor slap or shove)			(moderately severe)			(you felt he might kill you, or you became unconscious)	

6. Was there a particular part of your body which he usually struck?
   1 No
   2 Yes (which part?)
      a. Head, face, neck
      b. Upper torso (breast, arms, back, etc.)
      c. Lower torso (belly, genitals, legs, buttocks, etc.)
      d. Other (specify): _____

7. Were you ever sexually assaulted by him? (Forcible rape *is* an assault)
   1 No
   2 Yes (about how often?) _____

8. Were you pregnant at the time you married him?
   1 Yes
   2 No
   3 Not married to him

9. Were you ever battered by him when you were pregnant?
   1 Yes
   2 No
   3 Not pregnant during time you lived together
   3 Don't remember

10. In your judgment, what factors are responsible for causing the battering(s)? (Circle as many as apply)
    1 Argument over money
    2 Argument over in-laws
    3 Your pregnancy
    4 His jealousy
    5 Your jealousy
    6 Your housekeeping
    7 Child care
    8 Other (specify): _____
    _____

11. Did long verbal arguments go on before the attacks?
   1 Yes, always
   2 Yes, sometimes
   3 No

12. Did you say or do anything to trigger the attacks?
   1 No (explain): _____

    _____
   2 Yes (explain): _____

    _____

13. Did you say or do anything to try to prevent the attack(s)?
   1 No (explain): _____

    _____
   2 Yes (explain): _____

    _____

14. Do you think you deserved the beating(s)?
   1 No
   2 Yes
   a. Explain your response above: _____

    _____

    _____

15. Once an attack began, did you strike him back or try to defend yourself?
   1 No
   2 Yes
   a. Explain your response above: _____

    _____

    _____

16. Did the beatings increase or decrease in number and/or amount and type of violence since you began living together?
   1 Increased in number and increased in violence
   2 Increased in number but stayed the same in violence
   3 Didn't increase in number, but beatings got more violent
   4 Didn't increase in number, but beatings got less violent
   5 Stayed about the same
   6 There was one attack; no second time

17. Were you mostly beaten:
   1 By hand or fist
   2 By instrument (what kind?) _____
   3 By both
   4 Other (explain): _____

18. Were you ever threatened with a weapon?
    1 No (skip to No. 19)
    2 Don't remember (skip to No. 19)
    3 Yes
    a. What kind of weapon?
       1 Gun
       2 Knife
       3 Other (explain): _____

19. Did your spouse ever use a weapon on you?
    1 No
    2 Yes
    a. What kind of weapon?
       1 Gun
       2 Knife
       3 Other (explain): _____

20. Did you ever threaten him with a weapon?
    1 No
    2 Yes
    a. What kind of weapon?
       1 Gun
       2 Knife
       3 Other (explain): _____

21. Did you ever use a weapon on him?
    1 No
    2 Yes
    a. What kind of weapon?
       1 Gun
       2 Knife
       3 Other (explain): _____

22. What was your reaction to being beaten? (circle as many as apply)
    1 Surprise   9 Trapped
    2 Shame   10 Self-blame
    3 Fear   11 Depression
    4 Relieved   12 Humiliated
    5 Powerless   13 Guilty
    6 Unattractive   14 Outrage
    7 Revengeful   15 Confused
    8 Hatred   16 Alone
    17 Unworthy
    18 Other (specify):

23. If you circled three or more of the above, please choose the three words which
best express your feelings. Place them in order of importance below, with No. 1
being the strongest feeling, etc.
No. 1 _____
No. 2 _____
No. 3 _____

24. Did you ever go to a relative or close friend and tell them about the beating(s)?
   1 No (why not?) _____
   2 Yes
   a. Who did you go to? _____
   b. What did they advise you to do? _____
      _____
   c. Did they offer you any help? (describe): _____
      _____
      _____

25. Did you threaten divorce?
   1 No
   2 Yes
   a. Explain your reasons for the response above: _____
      _____

26. Was any adult present when the beating(s) took place?
   1 No (skip to No. 27)
   2 Yes
      a. Who was this person? _____
      b. What did they do? _____

27. Was there a child or children present when your beating(s) took place?
   1 No
   2 Yes (who?): _____

28. If there were children living in the home you shared with your spouse, were they
ever battered by him? (If no children, skip to next page)
   1 No (skip to No. 29)
   2 Yes (who?): _____
   a. Was the child-beating:
      1 Severe
      2 Moderate
      3 Mild
   b. Was a child or children beaten around the same time that you were attacked?
   1 No (skip to No. 29)
   2 Yes
   c. Was the child-beating directly connected with the attack on you? In other
      words, did the child somehow get into the middle of things, try to defend you,
      etc.?
   1 No
   2 Yes (what happened?): _____
      _____

The following questions are very personal, but please try to answer them as objectively as you can. Remember, your answers are strictly confidential, there are no "right" and no "wrong" answers, and no one is making any judgments about you. Please give the answers which best describe your treatment of your child or children.

29. Can you give an example of how you usually discipline your child or children?
    _____
    _____

30. Do you physically discipline your child(ren)? (spank, hit, etc.)
    1 No (skip to No. 31)
    2 Yes
    a. Please indicate how hard, and how often:

DEGREE OF PUNISHMENT	FREQUENCY
1 Severely (very hard)	1 Frequently (daily or more often)
2 Moderately (average)	2 Occasionally (about once a week)
3 Mildly (very light)	3 Seldom (less than once a week)

31. Has any child living in the household you shared with your spouse ever required the attention of a medical doctor or hospital care because of physical punishment given by you *OR* your spouse?
    1 No (skip to No. 32)
    2 Yes (please describe the injuries): _____
    _____
    _____
    a. Which one of you inflicted the injuries on the child? _____
    b. Was there any official action taken? (questioning, police report, charges placed, etc.)
       2 No (why not?) _____
       _____
       2 Yes (what happened?) _____
       _____
       _____

32. Has any child who lived in the household you shared with your spouse ever struck you?
    1 No (skip to next page)
    2 Yes
    a. How old was this child at the time? _____
    b. Boy or girl? _____
    c. What happened? _____
       _____
       _____

IV. Community Response

1. Did you ever receive medical treatment for injuries suffered in a beating from your spouse?
   1 Never (please answer a. only below)
   2 Once (answer b. through f. below)
   3 More than once (how many times?) _____
      (answer b. through f. below)
   a. If never, was there ever a time that you felt your injuries required medical treatment, but you couldn't go for care?
      1 No (if no, skip to No. 2)
      2 Yes (why were you unable to get care? circle as many as apply)
         1 No money
         2 No car or way to get there
         3 You didn't want outsiders to know
         4 He wouldn't let you go
         5 Other (explain): _____
         _____
         _____
         _____ (now go on to question No. 2)
   b. If you did receive medical care, where did you go?
      1 Hospital
      2 Doctor's office
      3 Clinic
      4 Other (explain): _____
      _____
   c. Did anyone where you went for medical care ask you how you received your injuries?
      1 No
      2 Yes (what did you tell them?) _____
      _____
      _____
   d. Did you *volunteer* to tell anyone what caused your injuries?
      1 Yes
      2 No (why not?) _____
      _____
   e. If you told them how you received your injuries, did they: (circle as many as apply)
      1 Advise you of your legal rights
      2 Refer you to police
      3 Refer you to a social work agency
      4 Refer you to a prosecutor
      5 Refer you to a marriage counselor
      6 Refer you to a psychiatrist

7 Treat you courteously and kindly

8 Seem indifferent

9 Seem to blame you, or embarrass you (explain): _____

_____

10 Give you any other kind of advice about what you should do (explain): __

_____

_____

f. If you went to more than one place for medical treatment for injuries, please
describe the places and how they acted toward you: _____

_____

_____

2. Did you ever report an assault on you by your spouse to the police?

1 No (why not?) _____

_____ (skip to question No. 4)

2 Yes, once (give approximate date): _____

3 Yes, more than once (please list below the approximate dates (month and
year) that you called for police protection. If there were two or three occasions, write the dates. If there were more than three, please include only the
three that stand out clearest in your memory)

	MONTH	YEAR
#1	_____	_____
#2	_____	_____
#3	_____	_____

If you called the police more than once, in questions b. to e. below, write after your
responses the *number of the attack* for which the answer best describes police
attitudes or behavior. For example, police response to call #1 may have been "polite
but firm," and for attack #2 their attitude may have been "sympathetic."

a. If you called the police during or after an attack, did they respond by coming
to the place where the battering occurred?

1 Always

2 Sometimes

3 Never

a. When they did not come, what was the reason given for not coming? ____

_____

b. Did they come:

1 Immediately   # _____

2 Quickly (less than an hour)   # _____

3 Slowly (more than an hour)   # _____

4 Did not come   # _____

c. If your spouse was there when police arrived, what was their attitude or behavior toward him? (circle as many as apply)
   1 Concerned and helpful   #_____
   2 Polite but firm   #_____
   3 Rude, hostile, or blaming   #_____
   4 Sympathetic   #_____
   5 Tough or aggressive   #_____
   6 Neutral   #_____
   7 Other (explain): _____
   _____

d. When police arrived did they (circle as many as apply)
   1 Arrest him   #_____
   2 Warn him   #_____
   3 Advise you of your rights   #_____
   4 Urge you to press charges   #_____
   5 Refer you to legal aid   #_____
   6 Tell you that you could go to a shelter for women   #_____
   7 Refer you to another social agency (which one?) _____   #_____
   _____
   8 Other (specify): _____ #_____
   _____

e. What was the attitude and behavior of the police toward you? (circle as many as apply)
   1 Concerned and helpful   #_____
   2 Concerned but not helpful   #_____
   3 Rude, hostile, or blaming   #_____
   4 Sympathetic   #_____
   5 Tough or aggressive   #_____
   6 Neutral   #_____
   7 Other (explain): _____ #_____
   _____
   8 Not helpful because: _____ #_____
   _____

3. Did you request that your spouse be arrested?
   1 No (why not?) _____
   _____
   2 Yes (what happened?) _____
   _____
   a. If he was ever arrested, did you press charges?
      1 Yes (what happened?) _____
      _____
      2 No (why not?) _____
      _____
      _____

    b. If he was arrested, and you pressed charges, did the case go to trial?

      1 Yes (was he convicted?) _____

      2 No (at what point were charges dropped?) _____

      _____

    Why? _____

4. If you went to any of the law agencies for assistance (district attorneys, lawyers, judges, etc.), what was their response to you and your problems? Were they:

   1 Kind and polite

   2 Rude or nasty

   3 Indifferent

   4 Insulting

   5 Understanding and helpful

   6 Neutral

   7 Did not go to any law agencies

   8 Other (specify): _____

   _____

    a. Did any law agencies give you assistance?

      1 No

      2 Yes (describe): _____

      _____

    b. Who did you go to? (for example, a private attorney, legal aid, etc.)

    _____

5. Did you ever go to any social service agency to request help?

   1 No (skip to No. 6)

   2 Yes (please list the names of the agencies and briefly note their response to you) _____

   _____

   _____

   _____

    a. If you are now, or have stayed, at a shelter for women, how did you learn about it? _____

6. Did you ever seek help from a psychiatrist, analyst, or psychologist and tell about the battering?

   1 No (skip to No. 7)

   2 Yes

    a. What kind of specialist did you go to? _____

   _____

    b. What was the outcome? _____

7. Did you ever seek help from a clergyman, and tell him about the battering?

   1 No (skip to No. 8)

   2 Yes (what advice did you get?) _____

   _____

8. Did you ever go to a marriage counselor for help and tell about the battering?
   1 No (skip to No. 9)
   2 Yes (what advice did you get?) _____
   _____

9. Have you gotten, or are you going to get, a divorce from this man? (If unmarried to him, are you planning to live separately?)
   1 Yes
   2 Unsure
   3 No
   a. Please explain reasons for the above response: _____
   _____
   _____
   _____

10. Do you believe your spouse earns enough income to support your children if you get a divorce?
   1 No
   2 Unsure
   3 No children by him
   4 Yes
   a. If yes, do you believe he will make child support payments?
      1 Yes
      2 Unsure
      3 No
      Please explain reasons for the above responses: _____
      _____
      _____

11. Do you believe you can earn enough income to support yourself and your children if you get a divorce?
   1 Yes
   2 Unsure
   3 No

12. Do you have any relatives who would be *able* to give you (and your children, if you have any), a place to stay?
   1 Yes (who?) _____
   2 Unsure
   3 No

13. Do you have any relatives who would be *willing* to give you (and your children, if you have any), a place to stay?
   1 Yes (who?) _____
   2 Unsure
   3 No

14. If you have been battered more than once, what are (or were) your reasons for continuing to live with him? _____

_____

_____

_____

_____

15. People are complex beings, and so is our society. I have tried to cover a lot of ground in hopes of understanding what goes on in individual lives. If there is any question NOT asked here which you feel needs to be asked, please help by telling what you think should be asked. Then, tell what your answer would be.

    In addition, if you think there are any special circumstances about your own life or situation which should be mentioned, please write it below. If you feel that would be too difficult to do, or this questionnaire hasn't given you the opportunity to really express yourself, please call or write me, and we can set up a meeting so you can talk about it. My address and telephone number are on the cover letter.

THANK YOU VERY, VERY MUCH FOR YOUR KINDNESS AND HELP. I WILL TRY TO REPAY YOUR KINDNESS BY WORKING HARD FOR A BETTER UNDERSTANDING OF VIOLENCE AND ITS CAUSES. MANY OTHER PERSONS BESIDES MYSELF BELIEVE THAT ONLY BY EXPOSING AND STUDYING VIOLENCE CAN IT BE ELIMINATED.

THE VERY BEST WISHES TO YOU IN THE FUTURE, AND I SINCERELY HOPE THAT THE BEST DAYS OF YOUR LIFE ARE AWAITING YOU. THANK YOU.

NOTES

Introduction

1. All names, of course, are pseudonyms to protect respondents' identities.

Chapter 1

1. For one of the most comprehensive and thorough reviews of the literature on woman-battering, see Dobash and Dobash, *Violence Against Wives: A Case Against the Patriarchy* (1979).

2. According to Middleton (1977), a man in Belfast, Ireland, who kicked his wife to death was tried on charges of manslaughter rather than murder because, according to the North Ireland courts, there was no weapon employed in the homicide.

Chapter 2

1. For a full discussion of male versus female spousal violence see Abrams (1978), Fields and Kirchner (1978), Pagelow (1978b), Pleck et al. (1978), and Steinmetz (1977b, 1978a, 1978b).

2. Battering is clearly distinguished from noninjurious acts such as pushing and shoving where the act is clearly not intended to inflict pain. Battering does not include nonphysical types of abuse such as intimidation, harassment, threats, or other forms of psychological force or coercion, unless they occur in conjunction with physical force or injury. Although such non-physical abuse is undeniably damaging, painful, and injurious, the scope of the phenomenon addressed herein has been restricted to bodily injury.

3. This sample includes cases of all these categorical relationships. One example is a respondent who fled from her battering spouse to the home of her brother, who battered not only her but her children as well.

4. "Sadomasochistic" practices may place a woman in the position of using (what she believes to be sadistic) practices necessary to arouse her partner's sexual drive; or conversely, arousal may depend on a woman playing the masochistic role. Clearly, when the "play" becomes painful or injurious to an unwilling spouse, or when one is physically forced into

actions repugnant or painful to him or her, then this interaction ceases to fall in the realm of sadomasochistic sex play and becomes something else—such as battering or torture—depending on the turn it takes. Steinmetz and Straus provide concise distinctions between "mutually enjoyable sexual violence" and "one-sided aggressive acts" (1974:10-13). For purposes of this study, sadomasochistic practices are excluded if they are mutually agreed upon for the purpose of sexual arousal and enjoyment.

5. "Mutual combat" is a term coined earlier (Pagelow, 1976:46) to describe activities engaged in by some couples that differ from woman-battering, in that neither combatant is a victim in the same sense as battered women are victims of frequently unprovoked, unexpected attacks from which they may (but usually do not) attempt to defend themselves. Mutual combat refers to situations in which couples are equally determined to do battle with one another and inflict as much damage as possible on each other—verbally, physically, or both—usually within certain implicit limitations. Situations like these appear to be a form of violent "play," albeit sometimes dangerous, between persons fairly matched in aggressiveness and hostility. The Cuber and Harroff (1965) study of couples married at least 10 years identified some couples who engaged in such activities; these relationships were typed "conflict habituated."

6. A neighbor once tried to evict her lover from the home she owned after a beating, but when the man told police he was her "tenant," the police said she would have to readmit him into her home until she had given him the appropriate 30 days notice to vacate.

Chapter 3

1. Throughout the text, all names are pseudonyms and other possibly identifying materials have been slightly modified. Whenever respondents' statements contain material that might endanger anonymity, the statements are altered. These measures in no way change the basic content or meaning but are taken to protect confidentiality and the right to privacy of respondents, in view of the highly sensitive nature of the subject matter.

2. One of the most celebrated weddings in the last decade was that of Princess Anne of Britain and Captain Mark Phillips. Televised for viewers around the world, the vows taken by the Princess included the traditional phrase, "love, honor, and obey."

Chapter 6

1. It is unclear where this N of 54 came from, since Gelles's total sample consisted of 40 violent families—that is, identified by social agencies or police as suspected or known to be violent—plus 40 neighboring families. Out of these 80 families, Gelles located 41 women who had been battered by their spouses.

2. Some of the father assaults may have been incest rather than battering, since some mentioned rape by father. Responses to item I-10 (2)a were categorized by age, and 15 women said their previous assaults occurred when they were less than 12 years old.

Chapter 7

1. Names and some details in this and the other case histories have been changed to protect the identity of the victims and their families. In no instance has any fact been introduced that goes beyond the cases, although some incidences have been eliminated because they might tie

too closely to a particular case due to public knowledge. In the case of Anne, official documents such as birth, death, and marriage certificates have been provided to the investigator, as well as newspaper clippings regarding some of these events. In addition, names of city, county, and state officials named by this respondent were checked in the city in which events occurred and were found to be correct.

2. Anne received no spousal or child support for the children from 1939 until 1945, during which time one of the children had serious medical problems, requiring operations which put Anne into debt for many years. The children's father went into military service, but it was not until 1945 that Anne began receiving allotment checks of $62 per month for the support of both children.

3. Anne paid for her son's boarding school by adding $20 each month to the military allotment check of $62.

4. While the plaintiffs' attorney may have been correct about his assumptions that jurors are unsympathetic toward beaten wives, there was another important feature he overlooked or ignored. This was not simply a case of a former husband and wife testifying against each other—it included a third party, Sue's mother. If jurors are swayed by emotions, their bias against the younger woman might have been counterbalanced by their sympathies for a pleasant-looking, white-haired grandmother of 69 with a hearing impairment.

5. Because of her hurried departure, Sue found she had to hire an agency to represent her to gain back her possessions. Martin returned to the apartment, resumed living there, insisting that the things were his; he was Sue's husband and everything belonged to him. The agency got a court order, hired a moving van, and put what they found in storage. Months later, Sue had her clothes and other possessions moved from storage to her new location. It was then that she found that Martin had destroyed a number of things, and many valuable objects and paintings he knew were important to her were missing.

6. It is commonplace for attorneys to "coach" their clients before trial begins, particularly, as in Sue's case, if they have never testified before. As Strick says, "prestand coaching in the privacy of your attorney's office is understood to be a large part of what you pay him for" (1978:45). Clients are frequently instructed in how to dress, what is expected of them, what they may and may not do in courts of law. Most important, there is the role they are to play, their demeanor, and the verbal and body language that will cast them in the most favorable light to jury and/or judge. Sue never received trial briefings from her lawyer. Her appearance was appropriate to her social class but, when pitted against a man who took an emotional, poverty-stricken, and humble approach to his defense, it worked to her disadvantage. By her clothing, posture, attractive figure, good looks, and emotional control, it was easy to cast her as an unfeeling mannequin. Certainly the image she presented could have been interpreted as someone incapable of the feelings of fear, pain, or uncertainty she tried to describe. In short, it was difficult for the listener to picture her in the scenes she described, although it was easy to imagine Martin as a hapless, poor man victimized by a hard, invulnerable, scheming woman.

7. The appearance of a police officer with records of the battery and pictures of Mrs. Davis's wounds came as a surprise to the plaintiffs because in the 18 months spent trying to bring the case to trial, that police department had consistently said that the records were "lost." In fact, just before the hearing on the first day, Sue had again called the detective who took pictures of Mrs. Davis demanding that they "find" the records, to no avail. She said he was hostile, saying that when the women did not appear in court, the pictures were destroyed, and hung up, as he did when Mrs. Davis called later. The following morning Patrick called the detective and threatened him with a subpoena if the documents were not produced.

8. On this point, it appeared that the defendant had a distinct advantage over the plaintiffs, who faced their questioners during examinations. They did not make eye contact with the judge,

who had a vantage point that allowed him to see only profiles. Half the time they were on the stand they were facing a man who had beaten them and responding to his questions. When Martin took his own defense, he did not face his accusers but rather addressed the judge directly with full eye contact and with little or no interference from the plaintiffs' attorney.

9. A sex-stereotyped role reversal occurred here: The man was highly emotional and weeping, appealing for sympathy from the judge. On the other hand, the women maintained composure and control almost throughout the trial. The main emotion Sue showed was intense anger at some points, particularly when responding, or refusing to respond, to some of Martin's questions. Her anger could easily have been interpreted as vindictiveness or spite; traditionally people expect women who have been victimized to appear frightened, pitiful, and to express emotions by tears. On the other hand, people traditionally expect men to maintain control and be unemotional; when they are not, the impression is that extraordinary circumstances very hurtful must have occurred.

10. An afternote: Sue was forced to hire another attorney in Martin's city of residence in order to get a stay on Martin's bankruptcy case. That attorney also watched the same courtroom antics/advantages of Martin representing himself months after the assault and battery trial. Both of Sue's attorneys said they had never seen such apparently simple civil cases maneuvered into drawn-out, time-consuming situations. In the meantime, Sue has suffered a series of illnesses, and her attending physician tells her that her present health problems may well be the result of the physical and psychological abuse she suffered five years earlier.

11. Interestingly, the following day Kurt telephoned Donna to tell her the names and addresses of the men who had been invited to the party. He warned her that he would "get" any men who came to "my house."

12. One event convinced Donna she had to obtain legal custody of her son. Shortly after her son was returned to her home the boy hurt himself, so she took him for emergency treatment at the hospital. Medical personnel would do nothing for him until they located his legal guardian, Kurt, and received his permission.

13. Between the time this was written and a telephone call a few days later, Donna discovered that Kurt was already "on the streets." His arrest was for drunk driving and he was quickly bailed out by a relative—before the police checked to see if there were any outstanding warrants for his arrest. There were at least two, including one for "jumping bail," on a previous charge. Donna now hopes that Kurt will leave the area permanently to avoid prosecution on multiple charges. But she continues to live in fear.

Chapter 8

1. There has been personal correspondence during the course of the study with groups and individuals involved in the movement in one capacity or another from all over the United States, including Alaska, Hawaii, and Puerto Rico, plus many of the industrialized nations. There are unconfirmed reports that one shelter has even been established in India.

2. Based on social learning theory, the longer the violence had occurred, the less the possibility of change. Many experts, including Walker (1979), agree that the likelihood of change for long-term batterers is extremely low.

3. Evidence of the difficulty of making later contact with women after they have left the shelter residence may be seen in the follow-up study conducted by Peterson (1980). This researcher attempted to establish contact with 237 women who had stayed at the YWCA Women's Emergency Shelter in Santa Rosa, California, during the previous two-year period.

Making up to five attempts to contact them over a seven-month period, she located 30 women willing to be interviewed. Peterson was able to obtain limited information from an additional 38 women through friends, relatives, and service providers. Despite difficulties, her efforts were rewarded with valuable information on the women's present situations and their evaluation of their experiences while staying at the shelter. This is the first follow-up study of oattered women and evaluation report on shelter services that has come to the investigator's attention. It has provided a much-needed data base for researchers, service providers, and policy makers alike. Peterson's report has been published in two volumes entitled: *Beyond Battery: A Follow-Up Study of Residents of a Womans' Shelter* (1980). Book One contains a look backward: evaluation of their shelter residency. Book Two consists of data on the present lives and future plans of the women.

REFERENCES

Abraham, Sidney, C. Johnson and M. Najjar
  1976 "Height and weight of adults 18-74 years of age in the U.S." Advancedata 3(November). Washington, DC: Government Printing Office.
Abrams, Susan
  1978 "The battered husband bandwagon." Seven Days, September 29:20.
Akers, Ronald L.
  1977 Deviant Behavior: A Social Learning Approach. Belmont, CA: Wadsworth.
Amir, Menachen
  1971 Patterns in Forceable Rape. Chicago: University of Chicago Press.
Andersen, Ingerlise
  1977 "Wife battering in the Netherlands: needs and incidence." Paper presented at the International Sociological Association Seminar on Sex Roles, Deviance, and Agents of Social Control, Dublin, Ireland.
  1979 "Battered women: the dangerous sex-role scenario." Paper presented at the IV World Congress of Sexology, Mexico City, Mexico.
Andersen, Ingerlise and Noor van Crevel
  1976 Personal communication.
Ardrey, Robert
  1966 The Territorial Imperative. New York: Laurel.
Babbie, Earl
  1979 The Practice of Social Research. Belmont, CA: Wadsworth.
Bandura, Albert
  1973 Aggression: A Social Learning Analysis. Englewood Cliffs, NJ: Prentice-Hall.
Bannon, Commander James D.
  1975 "Law enforcement problems with intra-family violence." Paper presented at the annual meeting of the American Bar Association, Montreal, Canada.
Bard, Morton
  1969 "Family intervention police teams as a community mental health resource." Journal of Criminal Law, Criminology and Police Science 60(2):247-250.
  1970 Training Police as Specialists in Family Crisis Intervention, U.S. Department of Justice. Washington, DC: Government Printing Office.

Bard, Morton and Joseph Zacker
  1971   "The prevention of family violence: dilemmas of community intervention." Journal
          of Marriage and the Family 33(November):677-682.
  1974   "Assaultiveness and alcohol use in family disputes: police perceptions." Criminol-
          ogy 12(3):281-292.
  1976   "How police handle explosive squabbles." Psychology Today (November):71-74,
          113.
Bass, David and Janet Rice
  1979   "Agency responses to the abused wife." Social Casework 60(6):338-342.
Bates, Vernon, assisted by Dyan Oldenberg
  1980   "Domestic violence and the law." Paper presented at the annual meeting of the
          Pacific Sociological Association, San Francisco.
Becker, Howard S.
  1966   Outsiders. New York: Free Press.
Bell, Joseph N.
  1976   "New hope for the battered wife." Good Housekeeping (August):94-95, 134-138.
  1977   "Rescuing the battered wife." Human Behavior (June):16-23.
Belotti, Elena Gianini
  1975   Little Girls. London: Writers and Readers Publishing Cooperative.
Bernard, Jessie
  1973   The Future of Marriage. New York: Bantam Books.
  1974   "My four revolutions: an autobiographical history of the ASA." Pp. 11-29 in Joan
          Huber (ed.), Changing Women in a Changing Society. Chicago: University of
          Chicago Press.
  1975   Women, Wives, Mothers: Values and Options. Chicago: AVC.
Bersch, Blanche C.
  1977   The Legal Status of Homemakers in California. Washington, DC: National Com-
          mission on the Observance of Women's Year.
Beyette, Beverly
  1979   "Mid-life divorce: modern tragedy." Los Angeles Times, April 18:IV-22.
Bird, Carolyn
  1979   The Two-Paycheck Marriage. New York: Rawson, Wade.
Blackburn, Wayne
  1980   Excerpts from an interview, March 31. Mr. Blackburn is a counselor in the Family
          Service Association of Orange County.
Blalock, Hubert M., Jr.
  1972   Social Statistics. New York: McGraw-Hill.
Blood, Robert O. and Donald M. Wolf
  1960   Husbands and Wives: The Dynamics of Married Living. New York: Free Press.
Blumenthal, Monica, Robert Kahn, Frank Andrews, and Kendra Head
  1972   Justifying Violence: Attitudes of American Men. Ann Arbor: Institute for Social
          Research, University of Michigan.
  1975   More About Justifying Violence: Methodological Studies of Attitudes and Behavior.
          Ann Arbor: Institute for Social Research, University of Michigan.
Boudouris, James
  1971   "Homicide and the family." Journal of Marriage and the Family 33:667-676.
Bowker, Lee H.
  1978   Women, Crime, and the Criminal Justice System. Lexington, MA: D. C. Heath.

Bowker, Lee H. and Kristine McCallum
  1980 "Women who have beaten wife-beating: a new perspective on victims as victors." Paper presented at the annual meeting of the American Society of Criminlogy, San Francisco, November.

Broverman, Inge, D. M. Broverman, F. Clarkson, P. Rosenkrantz, and Suzan Vogel
  1970 "Sex-role stereotypes and clinical judgments of mental health." Journal of Consulting and Clinical Psychology 34(1):1-7.

Brownmiller, Susan
  1976 Against Our Will: Men, Women and Rape. New York: Bantam Books.

Bryant, Barbara Everitt
  1977 American Women Today and Tomorrow. Washington, DC: Government Printing Office.

California State Department of Justice Felony Case Statistics Tables
  1975 State Department of Justice for County of Los Angeles (January-December) 1973.

Cobbe, Frances Power
  1878 "Wife torture in England." Contemporary Review (April):55-57.

Crosby, John F.
  1980 "A critique of divorce statistics and their interpretation." Family Relations 29(1):51-68.

Cuber, John and Peggy Harroff
  1965 The Significant Americans. A Study of Sexual Behavior among the Affluent. New York: Appleton-Century-Crofts.

Current Population Reports
  1978 Consumer Income: Characteristics of the Population Below the Poverty Level: 1976. Washington, DC: Government Printing Office.

Dahl, Tove Stang
  1980 "Domestic violence: crimes against women." Crime and Crime Control in Scandinavia, 1975-1980. Oslo: N. Bishop.

Dales, Alyce
  1977 Statement before the California Finance Committee.

David, Deborah and Robert Brannon (eds.)
  1976 The Forty-Nine Percent Majority: The Male Sex Role. Reading, MA: Addison-Wesley.

Davidson, Terry
  1977a "Wifebeating: a recurring phenomenon throughout history." Pp. 2-23 in Maria Roy (ed.), Battered Women: A Psychosociological Study of Domestic Violence. New York: Van Nostrand Reinhold.
  1977b "Wife-beating: it happens in the best of families." Family Circle (November 15):62, 68, 70-72.

Dewsbury, Anton R.
  1975 "Family violence seen in general practice." Royal Society of Health Journal 95(6):290-294.

Dibble, Ursula and Murray Straus
  1980 "Some social structural determinants of inconsistency between attitudes and behavior: the case of family violence." Journal of Marriage and the Family 42(1):71-80.

Dobash, R. Emerson and Russell P. Dobash
  1976 "Love, honour and obey: institutional ideologies and the struggle for battered women." Paper presented at the annual meeting of the Society for the Study of Social Problems, New York.

1978   "Wives: the 'appropriate' victims of marital violence." Victimology 2(3-4):426-442.
1979   Violence Against Wives: A Case Against the Patriarchy. New York: Free Press.
Dussich, John P.
    1976   "The victim ombudsman revisited." Paper presented at the Second International
            Symposium on Victimology, Boston.
Eisenberg, Sue E. and Patricia L. Micklow
    1974   The Assaulted Wife: "Catch 22" Revisited. Ann Arbor: University of Michigan Law
            School.
Faulk, M.
    1974   "Men who assault their wives." Medicine, Science, and the Law 14:180-183.
FBI Uniform Crime Reports
    1974   Crime in the United States: 1973. Washington, DC: Government Printing Office.
    1975   Crime in the United States: 1974. Washington, DC: Government Printing Office.
    1977   Crime in the United States: 1976. Washington, DC: Government Printing Office.
Ferraro, Kathleen J.
    1979   "Definitional problems in wife battering." Paper presented at the annual meeting of
            the Pacific Sociological Association, Anaheim.
    forthcoming "Processing battered women." Journal of Family Issues, December.
Field, Martha H. and Henry F. Field
    1973   "Marital violence and the criminal process: neither justice nor peace." Social Service
            Review 47(22):221-240.
Fields, Marjory D.
    1978   Excerpts from testimony before the House of Representatives Subcommittee on
            Select Education of the Committee on Education.
Fields, Marjory D. and Rioghan M. Kirchner
    1978   "Battered women are still in need: a reply to Steinmetz." Victimology 3(1-2):216-
            222.
Flynn, J., P. Anderson, B. Coleman, M. Finn, C. Moeller, H. Nodel, R. Novara, C. Turner,
    and H. Weiss
    1975   Spouse Assault: Its Dimensions and Characteristics in Kalamazoo County, Michi-
            gan. School of Social Work, Western Michigan University.
Fojtik, Kathleen
    1976   Wife Beating: How to Develop a Wife Assault Task Force and Project. Ann Arbor:
            Ann Arbor-Washtenaw County National Organization for Women.
Forer, Lucille
    1969   Birth Order and Life Roles. Springfield, IL: Charles C Thomas.
    1976   The Birth Order Factor. New York: David McKay.
Friedan, Betty
    1974   The Feminine Mystique. New York: Dell.
Frieze, Irene Hanson
    1978   "Self perceptions of the battered women." Paper presented at the annual meeting of
            the Association for Women in Psychology, Pittsburgh.
    1979   "Battered women's responses to battering." Paper presented at the annual meeting of
            the Association for Women in Psychology, Houston.
Ganley, Anne and Lance Harris
    1978   "Domestic violence: issues in designing and implementing programs for male bat-
            terers." Paper presented at the annual meeting of the American Psychological Asso-
            ciation, Toronto.

Gates, Margaret
  1977 "The battered woman: criminal and civil remedies." Paper presented at the annual meeting of the American Psychiatric Association, Toronto.

Gayford, J. J.
  1975a "Research on battered wives." Royal Society of Health Journal 95(6):288-290.
  1975b "Wife battering: a preliminary survey of 100 cases." British Medical Journal 1 (January):194-197.
  1975c "Research on battered wives." Royal Society of Health Journal 95(6):288-290.
  1976 "Ten types of battered wives." Welfare Officer 25(1):5-9.

Gelles, Richard J.
  1973 "Child abuse as psychopathology: a sociological critique and reformulation." American Journal of Orthopsychiatry 43(July):611-621.
  1974 The Violent Home: A Study of Physical Aggression Between Husbands and Wives. Beverly Hills, CA: Sage.
  1975 "Violence and pregnancy: a note on the extent of the problem and needed services." The Family Coordinator (January):81-86.
  1976 "Abused wives: why do they stay?" Journal of Marriage and the Family 38(4):659-668.

Gillespie, Dair L.
  1971 "Who has the power? The marital struggle." Journal of Marriage and the Family 33(August):445-458.

Gil, David G.
  1971 "Violence against children." Journal of Marriage and the Family 33(November):637-648.

Gingold, Judith
  1976 "One of these days—pow! right in the kisser: the truth about battered wives." Ms. 5(August):51-54, 94.

Glick, Paul C. and Graham B. Spanier
  1980 "Married and unmarried cohabitation in the United States." Journal of Marriage and the Family 42(1)February:19-30.

Goffman, Erving
  1963 Stigma: Notes on the Management of Spoiled Identity. Englewood Cliffs, NJ: Prentice-Hall.

Goode, William J.
  1969 "Violence between intimates." Pp. 941-977 in Donald J. Mulvihill and Melvin Tumin (eds.), Crimes of Violence. Washington, DC: Government Printing Office.
  1971 "Force and violence in the family." Journal of Marriage and the Family 33(November):624-635.

Grambs, Marya
  1977 "Memo to wife-beaters: Sacramento may break up your act." Los Angeles Times (March 27):vii-5.

Hafer, Barbara H.
  1976 "Rape is a four-letter word." Pp. 493-501 in Emelio Viano (ed.), Victims and Society. Washington, DC: Visage Press.

Hampton, Marilynne Brandon
  1979 Testimony submitted to the American Bar Association Hearings on Victim/Witness Intimidation, Washington, D.C.

Hanmer, Jalna
1977   "Violence and the social control of women." Paper presented at the annual meeting of the British Sociological Association in Sheffield.
Harrison, Cynthia
1979   Working Women Speak: Education, Training, Counseling Needs. Washington, DC: National Advisory Council on Women's Educational Programs.
Hartman, Heidi
1976   "Capitalism, patriarchy, and job segregation by sex." Pp. 137-169 in M. Blaxall and B. Reagan (eds.), Women and the Workplace. Chicago: University of Chicago Press.
Heer, David M.
1963   "The measurement and bases of family power: an overview." Marriage and Family Living 25:133-139.
Hilberman, Elaine and Kit Munson
1978   "Sixty battered women." Victimology 2(3-4):460-470.
Hilgard, Ernest and Gordon Bower
1966   Theories of Learning. Des Moines, IA: Meredith.
Hill, Winfred F.
1971   Learning: A Survey of Psychological Interpretations. New York: Chandler.
Jaco, E. Gartly
1977   Excerpts from class notes, May 26. University of California, Riverside.
Johnson, Allan G.
1977   Social Statistics Without Tears. New York: McGraw-Hill.
Johnson, John M.
1981   "Program enterprise and official cooptation in the battered women's shelter movement." American Behavioral Scientist (July).
Kelley, Robert K.
1974   Courtship, Marriage, and the Family. New York: Harcourt Brace Jovanovich.
Kempe, Henry, F. N. Silverman, B. F. Steele, W. Droegemuellers and H. K. Silver
1962   "The battered child syndrome." Journal of American Medical Association 181(July 7):17-24.
Kerlinger, Fred and Elazar Pedhazur
1973   Multiple Regression in Behaviorial Research. New York: Holt, Rinehart & Winston.
Kim, Jae-On
1975   "Multivariate analysis of ordinal variables." American Journal of Sociology 81:261-298.
Kim, Jae-On and Frank Kohout
1975   "Multiple regression analysis: subprogram regression." In Norman Nie, C. Hadlai Hull, J. Jenkins, K. Steinbrenner and Dale Bent (eds.), SPSS. New York: McGraw-Hill.
Kirchner, Rioghan M.
1977a   "Profile of a poor battered woman." Unpublished paper.
1977b   "Pregnancy and violence." Unpublished paper.
1978   "Relationships between early pregnancy, early marriage, education, and wife beating." Unpublished paper.
Komisar, Lucy
1976   "Violence and the masculine mystique." Pp. 201-214 in D. David and R. Brannon

(eds.), The Forty-Nine Percent Majority: The Male Sex Role. Reading, MA: Addison-Wesley.

Kremen, Eleanor
1976   "The 'discovery' of battered wives: consideration for the development of social service network." Paper presented at the annual meeting of the American Sociological Association, New York.

Labovitz, Sanford
1970   "The assignment of numbers to rank order categories." American Sociological Review 35:515-522.

Landers, Ann
1976a   "Beater egged on." Syndicated newspaper column, May 12.
1976b   "Beating hits close to home." Syndicated newspaper column, June 22.

Lemert, Edwin M.
1951   Social Pathology. New York: McGraw-Hill.
1972   Human Deviance, Social Problems, and Social Control. Englewood Cliffs, NJ: Prentice-Hall.

Leon, C. A.
1969   "Unusual patterns of crime during 'la Violencia' in Columbia." American Journal of Psychiatry 125(May):1564-1575.

Levinger, George
1974   "Physical abuse among applicants for divorce." pp. 85-88 in Suzanne Steinmetz and Murray Straus (eds.), Violence in the Family. New York: Harper & Row.

Liazos, Alexander
1975   "The poverty of the sociology of deviance: nuts, sluts, and perverts." pp. 250-271 in Stuart Traub and Craig Little (eds.), Theories of Deviance. Itasca, IL: F. E. Peacock.

Lion, John R.
1977   "Clinical aspects of wifebattering." pp. 126-136 in Maria Roy (ed.), Battered Women. New York: Van Nostrand Reinhold.

Lorenz, K.
1966   On Aggression. New York: Harcourt Brace Jovanovich.

Los Angeles Times
1979   "Reporter to be arraigned in stabbing death of wife." May 28:II(cc) 1, 6.

Lynch, Catherine G.
1977   "Women as victims—rape, battering, incest and muggings—victim advocacy and victims within the system." Paper presented at the annual meeting of the Sociologists for Women in Society section of the American Sociological Association, Chicago.

Lynn, Nancy
1977   "Middle class violence: spouse abuse in the suburbs." Paper presented at the annual meeting of the Sociologists for Women in Society section of the American Sociological Association, Chicago.

Mall, Janice
1979   "About women." Los Angeles Times, October 28: X-8.

Marsden, D. and D. Owens
1975   "Jekyll and Hyde Marriages." New Society 32(N-657):333-335.

Martin, Del
1976a   Battered Wives. San Francisco: Glide Publications.
1976b   "The economics of wife-beating." Paper presented at the annual meeting of the American Sociological Association, New York.

1979   Testimony for Hearings on AB546, April 23, State of California, Assembly Crimi-
       nal Justice Committee.
Martin, Ralph G.
1970   Jennie: The Life of Lady Randolph Churchill. New York: New American Library.
Marvin, Joyce and Arlene Gropper
1976   "Violence begins at home." Canadian (November 20):4-9.
Maynard, Mary
1979   "The response of social workers to domestic violence." Unpublished paper.
Mead, Margaret
1973   "Sex and temperament." pp. 658-671 in Alice Rossi (ed.), The Feminist Papers.
       New York: Bantam.
Melville, Keith
1976   Marriage and Family Today. New York: Random House.
Merton, Robert K.
1957   Social Theory and Social Structure. New York: Free Press.
Metzger, Mary
1976   "What did you do to provoke him?: an analysis of 'the battered wife syndrome.'"
       Unpublished paper.
Middleton, Audrey
1977   Excerpts from a speech at the International Sociological Association Seminar on Sex
       Roles, Deviance, and Agents of Social Control, Dublin, Ireland.
Mill, John Stuart
1971   On the Subjection of Women. Greenwich: Fawcett Premier.
Minnesota Department of Corrections
1979   Report to the Legislature: The Implementation of Minnesota Laws, Chapter 428,
       1977 and Minnesota Laws, Chapter 732, 1978 regarding Programs and Services for
       Battered Women. Lino Lakes: Minnesota Correctional Facility.
Montagu, Ashley
1973   Man and Aggression. New York: Oxford University Press.
1976   The Nature of Human Aggression. New York: Oxford University Press.
National Commission on Working Women
1978   An Overview of Women in the Workforce. Washington, DC: Government Printing
       Office.
Nichols, Beverly B.
1975   "The abused wife problem." Social Casework 57(1):27-33.
O'Brien, John E.
1971   "Violence in divorce prone families." Journal of Marriage and the Family 33
       (November):692-698.
Owens, David J. and Murray A. Straus
1975   "Social structure of violence in childhood and approval of violence as an adult."
       Aggressive Behavior 1:193-211.
Pagelow, Mildred Daley
1976   "Preliminary report on battered women." Paper presented at the Second Interna-
       tional Symposium on Victimology, Boston.
1977a "Secondary battering: breaking the cycle of domestic violence." Domestic Violence,
       1978: Hearings Before the Subcommittee of Child and Human Development, U.S.
       Senate, pp. 608-639. Washington, DC: Government Printing Office.
1977b "Blaming the victim: parallels in crimes against women—rape and battering." Do-
       mestic Violence, 1978: Hearings Before the Subcommittee of Child and Human

Development, U.S. Senate, pp. 521-554. Washington, DC: Government Printing Office.

1977c "Battered women: a new perspective." Domestic Violence, 1978: Hearings Before the Subcommittee of Child and Human Development, U.S. Senate, pp. 555-607. Washington, DC: Government Printing Office.

1978a "Research on domestic violence: what we have and what we need." Domestic Violence, 1978: Hearings Before the Subcommittee on Select Education of the Committee on Education and Labor, House of Representatives, pp. 272-290. Washington, DC: Government Printing Office.

1978b "Social learning theory and sex roles: violence begins in the home." Paper presented at the Ninth World Congress of Sociology, Uppsala, Sweden.

1979a "Kitchens, cultures, and the feminist movement." Aegis May/June:4-8.

1979b "Personal and material resources of battered women." Paper presented at the annual meeting of the Pacific Sociological Association, Anaheim, California.

1981a "Secondary battering: alternatives of female victims to domestic violence." pp. 277-300 in Lee H. Bowker (ed.), Women and Crime In America. New York: Macmillan.

1981b "Sex roles, power, and woman battering." pp. 239-277 in Lee H. Bowker (ed.), Women and Crime in America. New York: Macmillan.

Parcell, Stanley and Eugene Kanin
1976 "Male sex aggression: a survey of victimized college women." Paper presented at the Second International Symposium on Victimology, Boston.

Parnas, Raymond I.
1967 "The police response to the domestic disturbance." Wisconsin Law Review (Fall):914-960.

Parsons, Talcott and Robert Bales (eds.)
1955 Family, Socialization and Interaction Process. New York: Free Press.

Peterson, Nancy
1980 Beyond Battery: a Follow-up Study of Residents of a Woman's Shelter, Book One and Two. Santa Rosa, CA: YWCA Women's Emergency Shelter Program.

Pizzey, Erin
1977 Scream Quietly or the Neighbors Will Hear. Short Hills, NJ: Ridley Enslow Publishers.

Pleck, Elizabeth
1979 "Wife-beating in nineteenth century America." Victimology 4(1):60-74.

Pleck, Elizabeth, Joseph Pleck, Marlyn Grossman, and Pauline Bart
1978 "The battered data syndrome: a reply to Steinmetz." Victimology 2(3-4):680-683.

Pleck, Joseph and Jack Sawyer (eds.)
1974 Men and Masculinity. Englewood Cliffs, NJ: Prentice-Hall.

Pogrebin, Letty Cottin
1974 "Do women make men violent?" Ms. (November):49-50, 52, 55, 80.

Polit, Denise, R. L. Nuttall, and E. V. Nuttall
1980 "The only child grows up: a look at some characteristics of adult only children." Family Relations 29(1):99-106.

Rasko, Gabriella
1976 "The victim of the female killer." Paper presented at the Second International Symposium on Victimology, Boston.

Rawlings, Stephen
    1978 Perspectives on American Husbands and Wives. Current Population Reports, Bu-
          reau of the Census. Washington, DC: Government Printing Office.
Reiss, Ira L.
    1976 Family Systems in America. Hinsdale, IL: Dryden Press.
Richette, Lisa
    1978 Excerpts from testimony at the U.S. Commission on Civil Rights Consultation on
          Woman Battering, January 31.
Rose, Hilary
    1980 "In practice supported, in theory denied: an account of an invisible urban move-
          ment." International Journal of Urban and Regional Studies 3: 521-537.
Russell, Diana E. H.
    1976 "Introduction." In Del Martin, Battered Wives. San Francisco: Glide Publications.
    1980 "Rape in marriage: a case against legalized crime." Paper presented at the annual
          meeting of the American Society of Criminology, San Francisco.
Russell, Diana and Nicole Van de Ven
    1976 Crimes Against Women: Proceedings of the International Tribunal. Millbrae, CA:
          Les Femmes.
Safilios-Rothschild, Constantina
    1978 Excerpts from presentation at the session on family violence at the Ninth World
          Congress of Sociology, Uppsala, Sweden.
Saul, Leon J.
    1972 "Personal and social psychopathology and the primary prevention of violence."
          American Journal of Psychiatry 128(12):1578-1581.
Scheirell, Robert and Irwin Rinder
    1973 "Social networks and deviance: a study of lower class incest, wife beating, and
          nonsupport offenders." Wisconsin Sociologist 10: 56-73.
Schultz, Leroy G.
    1960 "The wife assaulter." Journal of Social Therapy 6:103-112.
Scott, P. D.
    1974 "Battered wives." British Journal of Psychiatry 125(November):433-441.
Selltiz, Claire, Lawrence S. Wrightsman, and Stuart W. Cook
    1976 Research Methods in Social Relations. New York: Holt, Reinhart & Winston.
Service Delivery Assessment for the Office of the Inspector General
    1980 Domestic Violence. Report for the Department of Health, Education and Welfare.
Shainess, Natalie
    1977 "Psychological aspects of wife-battering." pp. 111-119 in Maria Roy (ed.), Battered
          Women. New York: Van Nostrand Reinhold.
Smith, Eliot, Myra Marx Ferree, and Frederick Miller
    1975 "A short scale of attitudes toward feminism." Representative Research in Social
          Psychology 6:51-56.
Snell, John, Richard Rosenwald, and Ames Robey
    1964 "The wifebeaters wife." Archives of General Psychiatry 11(August):107-112.
Sourcebook of Criminal Justice Statistics—1976
    1977 U.S. Department of Justice. Washington, DC: Government Printing Office.
Star, Barbara
    1979 "Comparing battered and nonbattered women." Victimology 3(1-2):32-42.
Stark, Rodney
    1975 Social Problems. New York: Random House.

Stark, Rodney and James McEvoy III
　　1970　"Middle-class violence." Psychology Today (November):52-54, 110-112.
Steele, B. F.
　　1977　"Psychological dimensions of child abuse." Paper presented at the American Association for the Advancement of Science, Denver, Colorado.
Steinmetz, Suzanne K.
　　1977a The Cycle of Violence: Assertive, Aggressive, and Abusive Family Interaction. New York: Praeger.
　　1977b "Wifebeating, husbandbeating—a comparison of the use of physical violence between spouses to resolve marital fights." pp. 63-72 in Maria Roy (ed.), Battered Women. New York: Van Nostrand Reinhold.
　　1978a "The battered husband syndrome." Victimology 2(3-4):499-509.
　　1978b "Violence between family members." Marriage and Family Review 1(3):1-16.
Steinmetz, Suzanne and Murray Straus (eds.)
　　1974　Violence in the Family. New York: Harper & Row.
Straus, Murray A.
　　1973　"A general systems theory approach to a theory of violence between family members." Social Science Information 12(3):105-125.
　　1976　"Sexual inequality, cultural norms, and wifebeating." pp. 543-559 in Emilio Viano (ed.), Victims and Society. Washington, DC: Visage Press.
　　1977　"A sociological perspective on the prevention and treatment of wife-beating." pp. 194-239 in Maria Roy (ed.), Battered women. New York: Van Nostrand Reinhold.
　　1978　"Wife beating: how common and why?" Victimology 2(3-4):443-458.
Straus, Murray, Richard Gelles and Suzanne Steinmetz
　　1976　"Violence in the family: an assessment of knowledge and research needs." Paper presented at the annual meeting of the American Association for the Advancement of Science, Boston.
　　1980　Behind Closed Doors: Violence in the American Family. New York: Doubleday.
Strick, Anne
　　1978　Injustice for All. New York: Penguin Books.
Sutherland, Edwin H. and Donald R. Cressey
　　1974　Criminology. New York: J. B. Lippincott.
Sutton, Jo
　　1977　"The growth of the British movement for battered women." Victimology 2(3-4):576-584.
　　1978　"Dealing with the problem of the problem of battered women: nineteenth and twentieth century movement to help battered women and the responses to them." Unpublished paper.
Szasz, Thomas S.
　　1960　"The myth of mental illness." American Psychologist 15(2):113-118.
Tanay, E.
　　1969　"Psychiatric study of homicide." American Journal of Psychiatry 125(March):1252-1258.
Terry, Robert
　　1974　"The white male club: biology and power." Civil Rights Digest 6(3):66-77.
Time
　　1978　"The battered husbands." (March 20):69.
Truninger, Elizabeth
　　1971　"Marital violence." Hastings Law Journal 23:259-276.

Ulbrich, Patricia and Joan Huber
    1979   "The effects of observing parental hitting on gender-related attitudes." Paper presented at the annual meeting of the American Sociological Association, Boston.
U.S. Commission on Civil Rights
    1974   Women and Poverty. Washington, DC: Government Printing Office.
    1979   Women: Still in Poverty. Washington, DC: Government Printing Office.
van Crevel, Noor
    1978   Comments during an interview in Holland, August 29. van Crevel is a co-founder of Blijf m'n van Lijf, the Amsterdam shelter.
van den Berghe, Pierre L.
    1975   Man in Society. New York: Elsevier.
Vanfossen, Beth Ensminger
    1977   "Cultural myths about wife-beating." Unpublished paper.
Visser, Gwen L.
    1978   "Women's Center and Shelter of Greater Pittsburgh: a model for a sheltering community." Testimony presented at the Congressional hearings of the Select Education Subcommittee of the Education and Labor Committee.
Walker, Lenore E.
    1978   "Battered women and learned helplessness." Victimology 2(3-4):525-534.
    1979   The Battered Woman. New York: Harper & Row.
Ward, David, Maurice Jackson, and Renee Ward
    1969   "Crimes of violence by women." pp. 843-909 in Donald Mulvihill and Melvin Tumin (eds.), Crimes of Violence. Washington, DC: Government Printing Office.
Warrior, Betsy
    1977   Working on Wife Abuse. Cambridge: Warrior.
Waterbury, Mary Kathryn, A. R. Bisaccia, and J. T. Sheets
    1976   "Battered wives: must we draw the curtain and shut out the public gaze?" Fullerton: California State University, Nursing Department.
Weis, Kurt and Sandra Borges
    1976   "Rape as a crime without victims and offenders? A methodological critique." pp. 230-254 in Emilio Viano (ed.), Victims and Society. Washington, DC: Visage Press.
Wellins, Michael
    1980   Excerpts from an interview, March 31. Wellins heads the Crisis Intervention Unit of the Police Department of Orange, California.
Willer, David and Murray Webster, Jr.
    1970   "Theoretical concepts and observables." American Sociological Review 35 (August):748-757.
Wilson, Elizabeth
    1975   "Battered wives: a social worker's viewpoint." Royal Society of Health Journal 95(6):294-297.
    1976   The Existing Research into Battered Women. Camden Women's Aid: National Women's Aid Federation.
Wolfgang, Marvin E.
    1958   Patterns in Criminal Homicide. Philadelphia: University of Pennsylvania.
    1967   Studies in Homicide. New York: Harper & Row.
Wrightsman, Lawrence S.
    1972   Social Psychology in the Seventies. Monterey: CA: Brooks/Cole.

Young, Jim
    1976   "Wife-beating in Britain: a socio-historical analysis, 1850-1914." Paper presented at the annual meeting of the American Sociological Association, New York.

ABOUT THE AUTHOR

Mildred Daley Pagelow is an instructor of sociology at California State University, Fullerton and CSU Long Beach. After a number of years raising six sons and engaging in several careers, including portrait photography, she returned to academia. She graduated from CSU Long Beach in 1975; the following year she received her Master's degree and, in 1980, the Ph.D. in sociology, both from the University of California, Riverside. A number of her articles on violence against women and single mothers of various lifestyles have been published in professional journals, readers, and textbooks. She has also provided expert testimony on this topic for committees in both houses of Congress.